Leaving Home Before Marriage

Life Course Studies

David L. Featherman
David I. Kertzer
General Editors

Nancy W. Denney
Thomas J. Espenshade
Dennis P. Hogan
Jennie Keith
Maris A. Vinovskis
Associate General Editors

LEAVING HOME
BEFORE MARRIAGE

Ethnicity, Familism, and
Generational Relationships

Frances K. Goldscheider

&

Calvin Goldscheider

THE UNIVERSITY OF WISCONSIN PRESS

The University of Wisconsin Press
114 North Murray Street
Madison, Wisconsin 53715

3 Henrietta Street
London WC2E 8LU, England

Library of Congress Cataloging-in-Publication Data
Goldscheider, Frances K.
Leaving home before marriage: ethnicity, familism, and
generational relationships / Frances K. Goldscheider, Calvin Goldscheider.
260 p.   cm. — (Life course studies)
Includes bibliographical references and index.
ISBN 0-299-13800-3
1. Adulthood—United States.   2. Living alone—United States.
3. Single people—United States.   4. Intergenerational relations—
United States.   5. United States—Social conditions—1980–
I. Goldscheider, Calvin.   II. Title.   III. Series.
HQ799.97.U5G65   1993
305.24—dc20   92-56926

To the memory of
Ida and George Engeman

Contents

Figures

Tables

Preface

A revolution is in progress in the transition to adulthood. Whereas most young people once remained in the parental home until they married, in the last few decades a new pattern has emerged: young people leave home before marriage—and not just to dormitories or barracks, but to a separate home or apartment, either alone or with roommates. In this book, we explore this new phenomenon as it figures in the plans of young people and their parents and in the decisions they eventually make about their living arrangements.

What difference does it make whether young people leave home before · marriage? Does this shift reflect changes in their relationships with their parents and in their roles in the parental home? Does it change the role of marriage as a defining transition to adult status? Does it simply reflect their increase in resources—higher incomes among young adults and perhaps their parents—allowing both generations to "purchase" privacy? Or is it a response to changed ideas about the appropriateness of intergenerational coresidence? Has living independently from parents well before marriage become a new life course requirement, one that potentially competes with investments in education or with family responsibilities?

In this book we address these questions by looking at recent national data on the expectations and decisions of a large group of young people (60,000) and a sub-sample of their parents. The young adults were completing high school in the early 1980s and then beginning the process of moving out, weaving in living arrangement choices with the other decisions they were making in the crowded and rapidly changing years between 1980 and 1986.

We found that nonfamily living in young adulthood is a new and fragile life course stage. It is one that a substantial majority of young people expected to have (70%), even though they were not always realistic about what its costs might be. We also found that parents play an important role in determining whether their children finally achieve a spell of nonfamily living. Transferring resources to them, divorcing, and remarrying were all ways parents could influence their children's decisions, and parental expectations were often more important to the eventual outcome than were those of the children themselves. The results of our study demonstrate the variety of ways that living arrangements are really household-level rather than individual-level decisions.

Another surprise emerging from our analysis was that values pertaining to various dimensions of familism had far more impact on whether young adults expected and experienced nonfamily living in early adulthood than did measures of financial resources. Direct and indirect measures of values, such as attitudes about gender role traditionalism and parent-child relationships, or those indexed by ethnicity and religiosity, strongly influenced the routes these young people took to residential independence.

Most research on living arrangements changes has highlighted the importance of increases in resources—the general rise in affluence over time—far more than changes brought by decreased familism or secularization. To the extent that the cross-sectional differences we document mirror the shape of change over time, our results suggest that changes in values, more than increases in affluence, influence the decisions young adults make about living arrangements. We show that the relationships between resources and nonfamily living are fewer and weaker than are measures of values and preferences. It is clear that nonfamily living has simply not been as well accepted in more familistic ethnic groups and religious denominations as it has in the dominant, largely secular culture. This new life course stage is virtually taken for granted among highly educated Protestants and Jews—and hence, by most family scholars as well—but it figures much less clearly in other communities.

Our project evolved over a number of years. The idea to study young peoples' and their parents' expectations about nonfamily living in early adulthood first took shape on a boat taking us from Venice, Italy to Haifa, Israel. These ideas became the basis of a research proposal entitled "Premarital Residential Independence among American Ethnic Communities," funded by the National Institute of Child Health and Human Development (NICHD) as part of Center Grant No. P50 HD-12639 to the RAND Corporation, Santa Monica, California. As some portions of the analysis emerged and sparked ideas and hypotheses, we presented them as papers to colleagues in formal and informal settings, such as the meetings of the Population Association of America, the American Sociological Association, and NICHD/NIA-sponsored workshops on intergenerational relationships.

Some of these papers were revised and subsequently published as journal articles. Our new questions, focusing on the decisions themselves, on the role of parents, and on the strategies that we would follow to answer

xiv

them, led us to propose additional analyses, again with the support of NICHD, grant No. R-01-HD23339 ("New Patterns in the Transition to Adulthood"), awarded to RAND and Brown University. Thus, while parts of the analysis have appeared before as journal articles, their focus was on the plans of young adults rather than their behavior. The book format was chosen for the sake of presenting a more complete and systematic story than would have been possible otherwise.

Many have contributed to the whole that finally took shape. We particularly want to express our appreciation to Peter Morrison of RAND, who helped in assembling and encouraging the basic team in Santa Monica, and who supported our work throughout our decade-long series of peregrinations to the beaches of southern California. Our colleagues there listened patiently and provided numerous constructive suggestions as our work unfolded, most notably Julie DaVanzo, Arleen Leibowitz, Jim Smith, and Linda Waite. Most of all, these colleagues became friends and helped us make a home away from home. Ross Stolzenberg provided patient and thoughtful comments on the intergenerational flows portion of the research, and, most recently, Lee Lillard provided a welcome opportunity for us to expand on our ideas linking the expectations of parents and their children.

Most of the data analysis was carried out at RAND, and we are most grateful to Joan Keesey, who patiently constructed the files for the first analyses of expectations data, in the years when too little behavioral data were available to analyze. Patti Camp provided Herculean labors in constructing the files for the study of the actual leaving home process and for testing the wide range of statistical models that were at the heart of our argument. Final mop-ups were done by David Rumpel, helping us to turn over a few last stones. A portion of the analysis was also carried on in Providence, under a sub-contract from RAND to Brown University. Dr. Elizabeth Cooksey, then a graduate research assistant, thus had the opportunity to learn that the study of demography included considerations of intergenerational financial relationships (and that not all data are clean). We are grateful to all for their patient and thoughtful work and collegial suggestions. We are particularly indebted to the program in population at NICHD for supporting our research and facilitating its development.

We first began to piece together a whole from the various parts we had been seeing during a wonderfully productive month at the Rockefeller Study and Conference Center in the Villa Serbelloni, Bellagio (Como), Italy, under the sponsorship of the Rockefeller Foundation. Both as a retreat (in the Italian Alps!) and as a community of involved scholars, Bellagio provided a wondrous opportunity for two authors to write, sort, think, argue, and discuss, as well as to present evolving ideas to an inter-disciplinary group of researchers from around the world. We want to thank the Rockefeller Foundation for being supportive of the initial draft of this volume.

Important portions of this book (as well as plans for the analyses that went into it and the preface that we wrote when it was all over) were completed at the Engeman cottage, on Assembly Point, Lake George, New York. It is a concrete symbol of familism. Older generations have worked, played, loved, and passed traditions on to younger ones there. Children who had left home (or whose homes had left them) have re-turned over and over and found a home. We dedicate this book to the memory of Fran's parents, Ida and George Engeman, the founders of the cottage, and to all their children, children-in-law, grandchildren, grandchildren-in-law, and great-grandchildren. May our family traditions continue.

Lake George, New York
October, 1992

Leaving Home Before Marriage

1

Residential Independence and Adulthood

When do young people become adults, autonomous, independent, and socially recognized as grown-up? Does adulthood largely begin when children move out of the parental home? Or not until they marry and/or become parents? Has the end point of the "transition to adulthood" been changing, shifting toward an essentially individualistic event marking the "end of childhood" and away from a conception based on entry into adult family roles?

These questions are only the latest raised by the broader complex of changes that have reconfigured the life course in the twentieth century. For most of human history, survival pressures were such that people spent their lives and energies in production and reproduction, working to support not only themselves but others. But the growth in affluence and the extension of life expectancy have created new segments freed of one or both of these pressures, with the expansion of retirement from work into leisure and with the increased likelihood of surviving past the dependency of one's offspring into an "empty nest" marriage or into living alone. Hence, as ceasing to earn and/or to be actively parenting no longer signal the advent of "old age," so, perhaps, young people's attaining readiness for adult family roles is no longer the key to adulthood. The old symbols—puberty, the steady job, the filled hope chest—tied as they were to marriage and family, may have become less relevant to the "new" definition of adulthood, leaving separation from parents as the only key indicator of leaving childhood behind.

If so, then the family as a coresidential unit is being further narrowed. In the early stages of urban and industrial growth, maturing young people had if anything an *increased* likelihood of remaining home until marriage, allowing them to minimize expenses and save for marriage. More important, the growth in local economic opportunities no longer forced them to leave to become servants or apprentices in others' homes or to live in boarding houses in the city (Osterud 1980, Ruggles 1987). But even young adults who needed to leave home prior to marriage normally lived in

3

provisional or semiautonomous situations (Katz 1975), since their goal was less to *be* independent than to *become* independent—by acquiring the resources to establish their own families. Having their own place was rarely a goal in itself.

Contemporary marriage and parenthood have been redefined as optional elements of adult lives; most survey respondents affirm that "it is OK to never marry," even if the vast majority expect to do so themselves (Thornton 1989). Living separately from parents as early as possible, whether or not marriage follows later, may have become what indicates to young people that they are adults—and what reassures parents that they have succeeded in "raising" them. If so, the new signal that young people have become adults may now be moving out of the parental household before marriage, not just to attend school or serve in the military but to live independently of family. As a result, adulthood may be losing its family connotations, becoming focused increasingly on a much narrower economic consideration—the ability to support *oneself*. This independence probably needs to be shown symbolically by living separately from parents, even if one needs frequently to return, perhaps to make short stops to refuel financially and emotionally when changing jobs or completing a stint at school or the armed services, before moving out again (DaVanzo and Goldscheider 1990).

By moving out to live on their own before marriage, young people are contributing to the growth in nonfamily living, a phenomenon that has characterized a broad range of industrialized countries in the decades since World War II. Studies of living outside a family setting, often alone, have primarily focused on the elderly, among whom the increase in nonfamily living first occurred. Such growth has resulted to a great extent from the dramatic increase in the financial well-being of older persons, via the growth in size and coverage of old age pensions. Most have assumed that the increase in privacy for both generations that results when widows do not live with their children is a great benefit to all concerned, well worth the loss of efficiency that results from the need to maintain separate households. However, the increase in privacy and independence experienced by young adults and their parents brought about by nonfamily living may have greater costs than appear for the elderly.

THE STUDY OF NONFAMILY LIVING IN YOUNG ADULTHOOD

Why study residential autonomy among young people? A simple, if perhaps not fully satisfying, answer to this question is that this element of the transition to adulthood has never been the subject of full-scale study in the United States, although some of these issues have been studied for Australia (Young 1987). We know a great deal about recent changes and variations in the transition to marriage, to parenthood, and to full-time work (Modell 1989; Rindfuss, Morgan, and Swicegood 1988), and these at least are phenomena that have been part of young adulthood throughout recorded history. Most studies of early adulthood have assumed that residential independence was somehow tied to one or more of these other life course transitions—marriage, school, or economic independence—and, therefore, was not a separate transition, worthy of study in its own right. However, a recent analysis showed that this is not the case: neither leaving home nor attaining full residential independence (outside of dormitories and barracks) was closely linked with other transitions in young adulthood, since many attend college while living with parents, and others leave home despite not being in school or the military, married, or even employed full time (Goldscheider and DaVanzo 1985). Hence, residential autonomy in early adulthood has not received detailed study because it is new, particularly in its unraveling links to other dimensions of the life course.

Because it is new and unstudied, nonfamily living among young people is also mysterious, with public confusion over recent trends and theoretical confusion about what it means for young adulthood and for the institution of the family. The recurring hysteria in the press about finding any unmarried adults living with their parents seems to suggest that nonfamily autonomy is increasingly *required*—that much of the press's readership feels that to live with parents after reaching some "adult" age, such as 18 or 21, is a sign of dangerous immaturity (e.g., *U.S. News and World Report* 1981; Lindsey 1984; Cowan 1989; Gross 1991), even though few would want most young adults to marry at these young ages.

Further, such press reports typically argue that the phenomenon of young adults remaining "in the nest" is *increasing*, when, in fact, the likelihood that young unmarried adults would be living with their parents has declined sharply over the last forty or so years. Table 1.1 shows the living arrangements of young adults aged 18 to 24 in each of the census years 1940, 1950, 1960, 1970, and 1980. The categories are "family head" (the vast although decreasing majority of whom are married); "other family member" (who are overwhelmingly children living in their parental homes at these ages); "primary individuals" (persons living alone or as head of a group of roommates in a separate household); and "secondary individuals" (those living in group quarters or in households in which they are not the head).

In 1940, five out of six (82.4%) unmarried young males and females aged 18 to 24 lived with their parents (row 6), and less than 1 percent

Table 1.1.   Living arrangements of young adults, 1940–1980

Living arrangement	1940	1950	1960	1970	1980
1. Family head	23.8	33.7	39.6	36.0	28.2
2. Other family member	62.8	51.1	42.0	42.3	45.5
3. Primary individuals	0.9	1.0	2.3	4.5	9.2
4. Secondary individuals	12.5	14.2	16.1	17.2	17.1
5. Total	100.0	100.0	100.0	100.0	100.0
6. % "children" (2) among the "unmarried" (5 − 1)	82.4	77.1	69.9	66.1	63.4
7. % autonomous (3) among the nonfamily (3 + 4)	6.7	6.5	12.5	20.7	35.0

Source: Calculated from Kobrin 1976 (table 3); U.S. Bureau of the Census 1985 (table 4).

lived as heads of their own independent household. The proportion of unmarried young adults living with their parents declined continuously, if not dramatically, between 1940 and 1980 (from 82% to 63%), but full residential autonomy increased more than ninefold (row 3). The result was that the proportion autonomous among those living outside of families increased from 7 percent in 1940 to 35 percent in 1980.

Part of the confusion over the "return to the nest" may lie in the decline in the proportion forming new families, since the boom in family headship peaked in 1960, drawing large proportions of young adults into an independent residence via marriage, and then declined nearly to 1940 levels. Some of this increase in nonmarriage increased the proportion of the total living in the parental home (from 42% in 1960 to 45% in 1980). But the proportion of the *unmarried* living at home continued to decrease.

The popular press appears to identify more with the parents than with the young adults. It may be that part of the "problem" of young adults living in the parental home is that the responsibilities of children of all ages to their parental households appear to have dwindled greatly. When most people see a multigenerational household, they assume that the younger members are making little contribution to the parental household economy, either financially or via household labor, and they are often right (Goldscheider and Goldscheider 1991, Goldscheider and Waite 1991). As a result, young people (and many of their parents) probably feel that to live together after the end of school is a continuation of childhood (even if the young person is among the few making adult-level contributions to the domestic economy). They need to move out on their own to live independently, alone or with roommates in a nonfamily household, however distant their prospects for marriage. And their parents may be increasingly glad to see them go, welcoming the options of the empty nest, since in many cases, parents' lives have been changing as well.

6

Added to the confusion over trends in young people's patterns of living arrangements is considerable ambivalence about what their likely consequences might be. As with the increase in living alone among the elderly, powerful American values about independence make the growth in nonfamily living among young adults also seem highly desirable. But actually, little good research has been done on the consequences of living arrangements for adults of any age. This lack is particularly critical in young adulthood, since young people have many years for any consequences to have their effect, and the high density and rapidity of other life course changes during these ages could magnify any impact. There is clear evidence that living outside a family setting in young adulthood delays marriage (Goldscheider and Waite 1991) and alters young people's attitudes toward several dimensions of traditional family roles: young women who have lived independently prior to marriage increase their expectations to be working during their family-building ages and decrease their expected family size; and both young men and women increase their approval of young women combining work and parenthood (Waite, Goldscheider, and Witsberger 1986).

But there may be other costs as well. There is some suggestion that living with family is *healthier*, mentally and physically. Most of those living outside a family setting may be able to construct a supportive network of social ties, but some may not, risking loneliness, depression, and illness (Kobrin and Hendershot 1977; Kisker and Goldman 1987; Riessman and Gerstel 1985). More clearly, if living independently before marriage becomes a needed current symbol of adulthood for young people, its costs may be met by reduced investment in their own futures. The new challenge of attaining residential autonomy before marriage is likely to make it more difficult for young adults or their parents to use living in the parental home as a means to reduce costs. Hence, it may become more difficult for young adults to save to complete more years of schooling or to acquire a financial cushion for meeting the expenses of starting a family.

ANSWERING (SOME OF) THESE QUESTIONS

Together, these considerations suggest residential autonomy in nonfamily contexts among young adults is a new phenomenon that requires detailed study. It is an increasing pattern that is likely to have major consequences for other transitions in early adulthood—family, work, and educational decisions. It may also have important implications at later points in the life course. Indeed, nonfamily living in young adulthood may be the last in a series of nonfamily processes emerging in America, and in Western countries generally, which together emphasize autonomy and individualism, continuing to replace the family network and community with the "I" and the "me" of selfhood. And yet we know almost nothing about it to help us understand its pattern and possible consequences, how it emerges in the life course, and with what it is associated. This study is designed to tell us more about residential autonomy among young American adults. We ask four key questions:

1. Has living in nonfamily residences become normative? Do most young adults *expect to* live in nonfamily settings before they marry and thus presumably attempt to organize their transition to adulthood in such a way to include it, even if they expect to marry eventually? Or has residential autonomy emerged primarily because of recent delays in age at marriage, which simply allow more time for residential independence before marriage?

2. Who is more likely to expect and/or experience leaving home before marriage? What do differences by gender, race or ethnicity, social class, religion, or attitudes toward family roles tell us about the forces that have brought about an increase in nonfamily residential patterns and what the future might bring?

3. How does nonfamily living fit into the broader transition to adulthood? How does it relate to the other changes under way in that transition, in school, work, and family?

4. What is the role of parents in the decision to leave home before marriage? Is the residential autonomy of the younger generation simply the result of the decisions of young adults, or do parents have an input? What happens when parents and their children disagree over whether young people should remain home until marriage? Who is more likely to "win" when parents and children have different views about the timing of residential independence and marriage?

There are a variety of ways to study these questions. As social scientists, we have selected the best source of evidence available to analyze these patterns in detail—a large-scale study of young American adults completing high school in the early 1980s, who were reinterviewed biennially through 1986. This survey presents us with a rich body of important information that allows us to address these questions about the emerging pattern of leaving home in the transition to adulthood.

EXPECTATIONS, PLANS, AND NORMS
FOR RESIDENTIAL AUTONOMY

To understand whether residential autonomy separate from marriage is becoming normative—a goal young people feel they should plan successfully to attain in early adulthood—we focus a major portion of our analysis on expectations about residential autonomy, both those of the young adults themselves and those of their parents. We interpret the expectations of young adults as reflecting to a large extent their *plans* for the future. Although some may be expecting "the worst" to happen, in most cases (up to 80%), young people feel in control of these dimensions of their lives and are optimistic that they can realize their expectations (Hogan 1985). Hence, there is considerable basis for arguing that expectations should be reasonable predictors of actual patterns, assuming no major unpredictable changes. Having information on the expectations of young adults is likely to help us understand and predict what young adults will actually do in the critical young adult years as choices of marriage, education, and work are densely interrelated.

In addition, the expectations expressed by young adults also can be seen as indicators of *preferences* for particular life-styles and family relationships. Undoubtedly, many young adults' expectations are also based on a realization of the limitations of their situation, so that they expect less than they prefer. But by taking into account some of the social and economic constraints on their behavior, we can treat the remaining influence of their expectations on behavior as a reflection of their actual preferences, at least as measured at a given time.

Young adults' expectations about nonfamily living are of particular importance at this stage of the life course since these young adults are precisely in the position of emphasizing the past constraints (and benefits) of family living and the future possibilities of autonomy and independence. Further, to the extent that these young adults share their plans and expectations with each other, these individual expectations can be interpreted collectively as *norms*—the pressures they feel about living arrangements decisions for their generation. Hence, the examination of expectations is of value not only at the individual attitudinal level but also at the normative level; not only for individual young adults as the basis for their planning but as reflecting the preferences and norms of large segments of the youth cohort that we are examining.

We also interpret parental expectations as reflecting (1) their own plans and (2) what they see as the normative pressures on them and their children, although here the argument is necessarily more indirect. Certainly for many of the decisions their children are making, parents can have relatively little influence, such as about when their child finds a potential mate willing to marry him or her. But for many decisions, parents have control over key elements involved. This is particularly the case for the financing of higher education; parents also have control over their children's continued residence in the parental home.

9

We compare the level of residential independence expected by each generation with that achieved. This helps us understand whether leaving home is an expense likely to compete with other potential uses of young people's scarce resources or is simply an opportunity that comes along for those with extra time or money. We study in detail the determinants of these expectations and compare the factors that influence them and those affecting their actual residential behavior in the first six years after graduating from high school. This provides a fascinating dialectic in the results: although most of the forces operating to increase or decrease young people's expectations for residential autonomy also affect their later behavior, many differences between expectations and behavior appear.

These differences force us to disentangle why some factor or context that has a large effect on young people's expectations could have little impact on their later behavior, or vice versa. How do young adults construct their expectations about the next few years of their lives? What do they take into account, and what do they fail to? The answers to these questions help to identify the social structural contexts that support residential autonomy in young adulthood (or not), even for those whose expectations might be different from their opportunities. In turn, these contrasts show how normative change interacts with social structural change and the relative importance of each in the transition to adulthood.

We look first at young people's actual living arrangements decisions in the first six years after high school graduation and compare them with the trajectories they had expected as well as with those their parents had expected for them (chap. 2). Expectations in this area have a fairly strong impact on later behavior. Throughout the chapters that follow, the differences between factors influencing expectations and those shaping behavior begin to pile up, and we weave these threads together explicitly, including a consideration of who are the "poor planners," those who were least able to follow through on their expectations about experiencing residential autonomy before marriage and either "fell into it" when they did not expect it or found that the means for attaining it were not available (chap. 8).

RESIDENTIAL AUTONOMY FOR WHOM?

We focus in detail on the factors that influence residential autonomy before marriage in young adulthood. Although we cannot study this new phenomenon over time, we can examine many clues about how change is likely to have come about—and what the future might be—by examining whether there are group differences in residential autonomy and what

kind there are. Generally, finding that those with more financial resources are more likely to make a given choice, such as moving away from
home to independent living, implies that increases in economic levels
over time are likely to increase the numbers making that choice, in this
case, increasing residential autonomy before marriage. Similarly, finding
that resistance to premarital residential autonomy is more characteristic
of recent immigrant groups would also suggest that it is likely to increase
in the future, as these groups adapt to the dominant society and its orientation toward residential autonomy in young adulthood. We develop a
basic approach to variation in residential autonomy before marriage in
chapter 3.

Our assumption is that nonfamily living in young adulthood, like nonfamily living among the elderly, is an expense that requires more resources than familial coresidence and is a challenge to *familism*. "Familism" is a general term that implies that family roles and relationships are
at the core of people's lives and thus the axes around which society is
organized. In pursuing this approach, we will analyze a series of classic
indicators of variation in familism.

ETHNICITY AS FAMILISM

We examine a key indirect indicator of familistic behavior—having an
ethnic origin from a more familistic culture—in chapter 4. This allows us
to see whether young Asian- and Hispanic-Americans are as oriented
toward residential independence before marriage as members of the ethnic majority and provides a new look at the black family. We also analyze measures indexing ethnic change, such as geographic dispersion,
English-language use, and generation. This allows us to see whether
these groups are likely to blend into the dominant culture over time or
whether they will remain distinctive unless they integrate residentially
and linguistically.

RELIGIOSITY AS FAMILISM

Religion and religiosity are also key supports to familism generally and
are likely to help us understand who is more oriented toward residential
autonomy before marriage. The American religious mosaic is in many
ways as rich as its ethnic mosaic, and we probe its connections to premarital residential independence by comparing denominations, looking
at structural measures such as enrollment in religious schools and religious service attendance and examining the effects of personal religious
feelings (chap. 5). This also allows us to elaborate our analysis of ethnicity

by investigating whether religious differences operate in the same way among different ethnic and racial groups.

But how do ethnicity and religiosity influence premarital residential independence, and might not familism be an important influence even among nonminorities and the less religiously affiliated? We link residential autonomy to two dimensions of familism that are changing rapidly in the United States, reshaping the relationships between parents and children and between men and women (chap. 6). Parent-child relationships have been changing both during childhood, where parents are increasingly oriented toward training their children to be independent rather than obedient, and in adulthood, where parents and their children can expect to spend many years linked together. Residential separation seems to be part of this process.

Even though approval of traditional male-female relationships, as indicated by measures of gender roles, might not seem to have important connections to residential autonomy, we discover significant connections with the gender revolution. When linked with residential autonomy, we identify some aspects of the gender revolution that appear to be weakening familism, as young men and women affirm the greater importance of nonfamily over family roles. There are also clues that aspects of the gender revolution might not be weakening familism but instead may be *restructuring* family roles for men and women.

PREMARITAL RESIDENTIAL INDEPENDENCE IN THE TRANSITION TO ADULTHOOD

Among the elderly, nonfamily living normally emerges as the result of the loss of family ties, as children grow up and leave home and one's spouse dies or leaves. It is a relatively stable living arrangement, often lasting for several decades, that ends only when age and infirmity require residential support, either with family or in a nursing home. But young adulthood is not a stable time in people's lives. It is punctuated by many transitions—with probably more changes than any other time in the life course. There are transitions in schooling, work type, and intensity, as well as in social and family relationships (Rindfuss 1991). It is a period when young people work out their connections with their parental family and continue the courtship process on their way to eventually founding families of their own through marriage and/or parenthood.

What can we learn about residential autonomy when we study young adults, relative to the analysis of the living arrangements of persons at other stages of the life course? What can we learn about young adulthood from the analysis of their premarital residential autonomy? The answer to both questions should also help us understand the value of studying residential autonomy and its determinants.

The timing of marriage is central in planning for and experiencing residential autonomy. Those who marry early have relatively little time after completing school to make the investment in a separate home. We focus on the extent to which residential autonomy might simply be a reflection of change and variation in marriage age or has become a new life course requirement that might require postponing marriage to achieve (chap 7). From chapter 7 on, residential autonomy moves away from a one-dimensional concept—do those who expect and attain residential independence do so via premarital residential autonomy or via marriage?—by adding a second dimension that reflects the timing both of marriage and residential independence. This allows us to examine under what circumstances young adults are less oriented toward premarital residential independence because they expect to marry early, or despite the fact that they expect to marry late, as well as under what circumstances they are oriented toward premarital residential independence even more than their late marriages would imply, or despite their likelihood of early marriage.

Given the rapid changes in other roles, however, we also wanted to examine how residential independence relates to progress in school and parenthood. In particular, we investigate whether poor planning in these areas (as indicated by a poor fit between expectations and behavior about how long to remain in school and the timing of parenthood—as well as marriage) is likely to trigger premarital residential independence or preclude it (chap. 8). Here we investigate whether residential autonomy, despite its link to having enough resources to "afford" separate living, is also linked with prematurely ending education.

THE FAMILY AND THE FAMILY ECONOMY

Where do parents fit in? Leaving home changes not only the residential family lives of young adults but also those of their parents'. Parents are not likely to be merely passive actors in this process. Usually, parental feelings and actions matter. The decision to leave the parental home involves the complex of norms, preferences, and plans of young adults and of their parents. Residential autonomy is the decision of the household as a whole. As such, parents are likely to play a significant role in the deci-

13

sion of who continues to live in the household. They are more likely to be in control of resources, even as they are less likely to share the emergent values and attitudes of the new generation. Parents and their own generation are likely to view the residential autonomy of their children in ways that are different from the perspective of their children. Their view is not only from a different angle but takes into account their own interests in privacy and autonomy. So the process of nest leaving involves decisions and values, expectations and plans of two generations, each reflecting their own perspective even as they share some of the same values and attitudes.

WHOSE FAMILY?

We first consider whether some parents might need to have their children leave early, since they no longer have the support of a co-parent or have remarried, which frequently involves discord in the relationships between stepparents and stepchildren and between the spouses with asymmetrical relationships with the children. Leaving home can reduce both sorts of discord, but if the lessons young people have learned at their parents' knees sour them on marriage, this might delay leaving home. We analyze the effects of living in a mother-only or stepparent family on leaving home to residential independence or to marriage (chap. 9). We consider as well any differences in the effects of family structure by ethnic group, class, and gender to see whether the near-institutionalization of one-parent families, as seems to have occurred among African-Americans, reduces the impact of family structure for these young adults.

WHOSE RESOURCES?

Throughout these analyses of familism, the resources for separate living are indicated with a general measure of parental socioeconomic status. But the question needs to be raised about how parents make their resources available to their children and whether or not they do, since in some families even today, children are contributing to their parents' support rather than the reverse. We unpack our basic measure of familial socioeconomic status in two ways (chap. 10). First, we examine how much of the socioeconomic effect is really a consequence of parental income and how much reflects the often antifamilistic effects of attaining high education. Second, we analyze the consequences of intergenerational financial flows directly, to discover how much parents, even those in a weak financial position, subsidize their children's activities in young adulthood, and vice versa. In particular, we build on our insights about family structure

14

to see if part of the stepfamily effects operate through the reduced likelihood stepfamilies provide financially for their children.

WHOSE IDEA IS RESIDENTIAL INDEPENDENCE?

Finally, we return to our finding that young adults' expectations have an
effect on their later residential behavior and ask whether their parents'
expectations have an impact as well (chap. 11). Does having parental support (either to leave home before or remain home until marriage) increase
the likelihood that one or the other pathway out of the home will be
taken? And how does disagreement between the generations in expectations about residential independence before marriage play itself out?
Who "wins"? And does generational disagreement affect the timing of
leaving home?

By focusing our analysis of residential autonomy in the transition to
adulthood around these main themes—familism, ethnicity and religion,
and intergenerational relationships—we learn a great deal about this
emerging process in young adulthood. This is the primary purpose of our
study. In turn, by studying residential autonomy as it unfolds in young
adulthood, we also learn a great deal about the dynamics of familism,
ethnicity, and religion as well as of intergenerational relationships.

Ethnic and religious groups develop means to cope with change or to
defend against it, and premarital residential independence provides a lit-
mus test of the ways they find. The general concept of familism also appears to be under pressure, as a whole host of family changes are under
way, including the decline in fertility and proportions married, the rise in
divorce, the decline in gender role segregation (both in the workplace
and perhaps increasingly in the home), and the increase in residential
separation of family members. The process of moving from the parental
home toward residential autonomy is interesting in itself and should also
be viewed as part of a larger picture of family change. Intergenerational
relationships are the fulcrum of family change, the means whereby parental resources—and parental family structure—are transmitted to the next
generation and the future. Premarital residential independence—or remaining in the parental home until marriage—focuses our attention on
what the major definition of the transition to adulthood is becoming.

15

2

Routes to Residential Independence
Expectations and Behavior

Changes in the family, particularly the increasing independence of young adults, are well known. The creation of a period of time between living in the parental home and marriage among young adults, in the United States and in other Western countries, has resulted in what we have referred to as nonfamily living or premarital residential independence. We need to clarify this phenomenon in the transition to adulthood, as young people and their parents first begin to look ahead to the establishment of residential independence, and it then unfolds. Then, we can discover whether the determinants of the normative aspects of nonfamily living differ from those of the behavior itself.

This chapter presents information on the expectations of young adults and their parents about the type and timing of residential transitions as well as on what actually happened in the first six years after high school. We contrast the expectations of the parents with those of the young adults and compare the expectations of each with actual patterns. In this way, we document the extent to which the expectations of young adults and their parents are useful predictors of what young adults actually do. We are interested both in the *timing* of the residential transition (two, four, and six years after high school) and in the *route* taken to their new residence (before or at the time of marriage).

In particular, we ask:

1. Have societal level patterns of independence become part of the expectations of most young adults as they plan their transition to adulthood? Or is nonfamily living something that simply happens as young people defer marriage in the years after high school?

2. Are the plans young adults make about the timing of residential independence and marriage shared by their parents? Or are parents more likely to expect their children to remain at home until they marry?

3. How do the plans of parents and young adults about nonfamily living affect what eventually happens? Do parents or children predict the out-

come more accurately, and when they disagree, who is the more accurate predictor? Or, more simply, who "wins" when there is generational disagreement?

WHAT DOES LEAVING HOME MEAN?

The High School and Beyond (HSB) survey[1] provides direct information on expectations for the timing of marriage as well as for the timing of the transition to full residential independence. Both young adults and their parents were asked, "When do you expect (your child) to marry?" and "When do you expect (your child) to live in your (his/her) own home or apartment?" We use these questions to distinguish those planning to remain residentially dependent until marriage from those who plan to have an independent residence while still unmarried.

The question on the timing of an independent residence does not focus on leaving home per se, although it is directly equivalent to asking about the expected age of leaving home for the two-thirds of young adults who went directly from their parents' home to one of their own. But about one-third of young adults lived for a few years in college dormitories, military barracks, and other institutional settings before setting up an apartment, alone or with others.[2] How should we interpret these intermediate forms of residential independence?

On the one hand, young people living in dormitories and barracks are away from home a great deal and away from daily involvement with, and observation by, their families. On the other hand, they are not entirely on their own. They have little responsibility for managing the tasks associated with finding, establishing legal rights in, and maintaining themselves in an apartment or house (including shopping, cooking, and cleaning).

It is also the case that young adults in these sorts of living arrangements, particularly those attending college, are home a great deal. College semesters are typically little more than a quarter of a year. Taking together the fifteen-week summer vacations, the long break in the winter, and assorted other fall and spring holidays, it often seems both to young adults and to their parents and siblings that they are still living together much of the time.

Finally, these sojourns are for a special purpose, one that *requires* going away, at least for most military assignments and for many colleges as well. Hence, when these activities end, which happens in a relatively few years, young people must either move back or move on. Many move

17

back. Although those who went away to college are less likely to be living with their parents after finishing school than are comparable young people who lived at home while attending school, they are more likely to move home than those already living in an apartment (Goldscheider and DaVanzo 1986). Hence, although we will normally refer to this residential transition as one into "a home of one's own," we will sometimes refer to it as "leaving home," even if it is not precisely so for some cases.[3]

THE ROUTE TO RESIDENTIAL INDEPENDENCE

There were no direct questions in the survey on the expected route of residential independence—whether the respondents expected to leave home and establish an independent residence before marriage. However, respondents were asked when they expected to marry, and we used this information to establish the route young people expected to take. We matched information about expected marriage age with the expected age for setting up an independent home or apartment. If young people's answers to these two questions showed an age at independent residence a year or more younger than the age they expected to marry, we assumed that they were actually planning to establish some sort of a home of their own before marriage and included them in the category, nonfamily living. If they gave the same age for marriage as for establishing an independent residence, they were classified as expecting to leave home at marriage.

Nearly everyone expected both residential independence and marriage. More expected residential independence for some period before marriage than expected to remain residentially dependent until marriage. This was the case among both parents and young adults, with more young adults expecting nonfamily living than their parents (fig. 2.1). Among young adults, seven out of ten expected residential independence before marriage. In contrast, a bare majority of their parents expected such a route to residential independence, with 56 percent expecting their child to leave before marriage. These data document unambiguously that nonfamily living has been incorporated into the social definition of the transition to adulthood and is expected by most young adults and their parents.[4]

Where is nonfamily living located within the life course in early adulthood? It must be substituting either for time spent in residential dependence within the parental family or for time in a new family formed by marriage. This new segment of the life course replaces family living— either with parents or with a spouse, or some combination of both. Through the examination of the timing of residential independence and

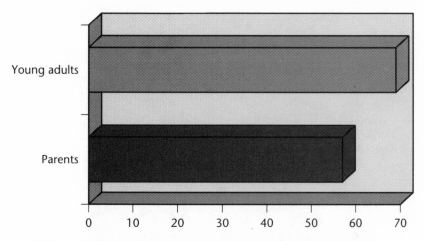

Fig. 2.1.   Proportions of young adults and parents expecting nonfamily living

the relationship between expected nonfamily living and marriage, we shall clarify where nonfamily living replaces living with the family of origin and delays new family formation through marriage.

THE TIMING OF RESIDENTIAL INDEPENDENCE

How close in time to high school graduation do young adults expect residential independence? Few young adults (11%) expected that such independence would be deferred more than six years after high school (fig. 2.2). Young adults expecting to leave home before marriage anticipate much earlier residential independence than those expecting to wait until marriage to establish a residence independent of their parents. Among young adults expecting premarital residential independence, nearly half (45%) expect to leave home within two years after high school; 96 percent expect to leave home within six years after high school. In contrast, among those who link leaving home with marriage, only 30 percent expect this joint outcome within two years and only 81 percent within six years. Marriage thus appears to be the slower route to residential independence. Those planning residential independence prior to marriage clearly expect to get an early start, reducing the period of time lived within the parental family.

Nonfamily living also impinges on the life course by reducing the formation of new families through delaying marriage. Less than 5 percent of young people expecting to leave home before marriage expected to marry within two years after high school, compared with fully 30 percent of

19

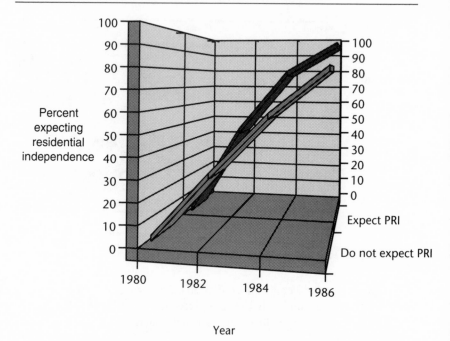

PRI = premarital residential independence (nonfamily living)

Fig. 2.2. Expected timing of residential independence by whether nonfamily living is expected: young adults

those expecting to leave home when they married (fig. 2.3). Even six years after high school, little more than half of those young adults who expect to leave home before marriage expected to have married, compared with nearly seven out of eight of those expecting to leave home at marriage.[5]

PARENT-CHILD DIFFERENCES

Young adults are expecting nonfamily living to reduce time spent both in the parental family and in the new family formed through marriage. While marriage timing primarily involves decisions by the young adult, leaving the parental household is a joint decision that directly involves the parents. What are the expectations of parents about the timing of their child's leaving home and the route taken?

Fewer parents expect nonfamily living for their children than their children do for themselves. Moreover, within the six-year window of young adulthood after high school, the older generation foresaw a more gradual move to independence than did the younger generation. The biggest difference between parents and their children was in the first two years after high school: only 26 percent of the parents but 41 percent of the young adults expected residential independence. Generational differences are reduced over time: after four years, 69 percent of young adults and 61 percent of parents expected the young adult to have achieved residential independence.

These data show that parents share young adults' expectation that leaving home before marriage will be the dominant route out of the home and that residential independence will occur within a few years after high school. However, young adults expect earlier residential independence than their parents, and more expect it before marriage. Further, the data suggest that parents are more reluctant than their children to view nonfamily living as reducing the time of residential dependence of children on the parental family.

Disagreements between parents and their children over the timing

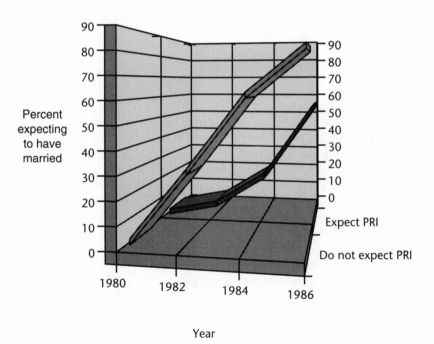

Year

PRI = premarital residential independence (nonfamily living)

Fig. 2.3. Expected timing of marriage by whether nonfamily living is expected: young adults

21

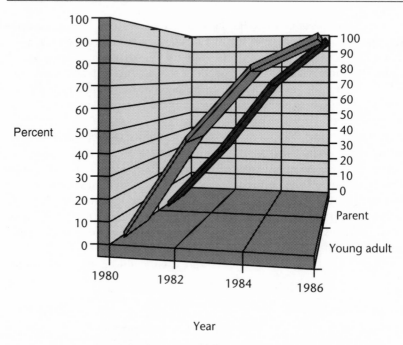

Percent

Year

Fig. 2.4.   Expected timing of residential independence: young adults and parents

of this residential transition result only in part because more young adults than parents expect premarital residential independence. But even among parents and young adults who both expect premarital residential independence, parents expect leaving home at older ages than projected in the expectations of their children (fig. 2.4). This difference also characterizes parents and young adults expecting residential independence at marriage: parents expect a later age at marriage and hence longer residential dependence than do young adults (data not presented). This combination of generational differences—parents who were expecting the route associated with earlier marriage but expecting later marriage for each route compared with young adults—leads to a striking generational similarity: the ages parents and young adults gave for their marriage expectations were nearly identical. About 60 percent of both students and parents expected marriage by the sixth year after the end of high school, with relatively little difference in earlier years. Young adults simply expect to spend more of their unmarried years living independently of their parents than do their parents and to find time for nonfamily living even given an early expected marriage age. Parents do not expect their children to leave home before marriage unless they expect that marriage will come relatively late.

22

WHAT ACTUALLY HAPPENED? THE TIMING
AND ROUTE OF LEAVING HOME

What were the actual patterns of residential independence of these young adults two, four, and six years after high school? How closely did their behavior resemble the patterns they and their parents expected? Whose expectations (the parents' or the young adults') were closer to what actually happened?

Two years after high school, 25 percent of these young adults had established an independent residence, 15 percent while unmarried and 10 percent at marriage (table 2.1).[6] About three-fourths were not yet residentially independent (50% were still living at home, and an additional 25% were in dorms or barracks, i.e., in semiautonomous living arrangements). More than half (57%) had experienced residential independence by four years after high school; within six years, 80 percent had lived in a

Table 2.1. Route to residential independence: expectations (young adults' and parents') and behavior (weighted)

Route to residential independence	By			
	Year 2	Year 4	Year 6	Ever
Actual behavior				
Residential independence via:				
PRI[a]	15.3	35.2	49.5	—
marriage	9.6	22.1	30.4	—
not independent	75.1	42.7	20.1	—
Total (%)	100.0	100.0	100.0	
PRI as percent of independence	61.4	61.4	61.9	—
Young adults' expectations				
Residential independence via:				
PRI[a]	32.8	54.4	66.2	—
marriage	9.5	18.2	25.6	—
not independent	57.7	26.8	8.2	—
Total (%)	100.0	100.0	100.0	
PRI as percent of independence	77.5	74.9	72.1	69.6
Parents' expectations				
Residential independence via:				
PRI[a]	16.7	38.5	52.4	—
marriage	11.1	22.5	35.5	—
not independent	72.2	39.0	12.1	—
Total (%)	100.0	100.0	100.0	
PRI as percent of independence	60.1	63.1	59.6	55.5

[a] PRI = premarital residential independence

23

"home of their own"; only 20 percent of the initial cohort were still living at home.[7] Overall, six out of ten who established a new home took the nonfamily living route; four out of ten left via marriage. But this timing was much slower than they expected; further, fewer enjoyed a period of residential independence prior to marriage than had been anticipated.

As a result, the proportion experiencing nonfamily living two years after high school was quite close to the expectations of parents but significantly less than the expectations of young adults: 33 percent of young adults had expected nonfamily living by then, and 17 percent of their parents had expected it for them; however, only 15 percent of the young adults had actually taken this route within two years after high school. Four years after high school, 34 percent of the young adults experienced nonfamily living, a pattern expected by 38 percent of the parents but 54 percent of the young adults. Six years after high school, 50 percent of the young adults had experienced nonfamily living, an outcome expected by 52 percent of their parents but by 66 percent of the young adults.

Young adults *underestimated* the likelihood they would delay leaving home until marriage; parents *overestimated* the extent of marriage as the route for leaving home during these years. Six years after high school, 30 percent of the young adults had left home via marriage, about midway between the 36 percent expected for them by their parents and the 26 percent expected by the young adults themselves. Since we know that parents and their children expected marriage at about the same time, it is clear that for many young people, the "extra" window before marriage in which they had attempted to schedule nonfamily living did not materialize.

In terms of eventual nonfamily living, it also looks as if the final tally will be somewhere between the amounts expected by young adults and by their parents. At the end of the six years, the proportion of young adults who had left home before they married (50%) was close to the total parents thought would *ever* leave via this route (56%). If few of the 20 percent still living with parents six years after high school leave home while still unmarried, the parents will have been right on target. However, if almost all leave home before they marry in the years after 1986, the eventual proportion experiencing nonfamily living (70%) will be identical to the level expected by young adults in their senior year of high school. But since a significant proportion of these young adults are likely to remain at home until they marry, it is most likely that for this cohort, the proportion of young adults experiencing nonfamily living will be less than they expected but more than their parents expected for them— about midway.

While the *routes* out of the parental home appear to be between the young adults' and their parents' expectations, both parents and young

24

adults erred in the same direction in terms of timing. Each overestimated the extent to which the young adults would have achieved residential independence by six years after high school. It is unclear what caused this result, although the difficult job and housing markets encountered by young adults in the early 1980s undoubtedly played an important role (Easterlin 1987).

It is also unclear what the consequences are of this lack of fit between expectations and experience. It is likely that parents were unhappy with the fact that more of their children were at home than they expected, and their children may have been unhappy about this as well. A lot of the concern over "the return to the nest" during the 1980s may reflect this disappointment, since young unmarried adults have continued to leave home at earlier ages throughout the post-World War II period (Heer, Hodge, and Felson 1985). It may be that in the 1960s, behavior was running ahead of expectations, particularly for parents. By the 1980s, when the young adults of the 1960s were themselves parents, expectations had caught up and even run ahead of what was possible for young adults in the very different economic conditions they were encountering.

It is also possible that some of the young adults who left home because they married may be distressed that they never experienced a period of nonfamily living, with possibly negative consequences for their marriages. Perhaps disappointed expectations also make their mark later in adulthood, in the relationships of parents and their children and perhaps in the relationships of married couples (the young adults' marriages and perhaps also their parents') as well.

EXPECTATIONS AS PREDICTIONS OF BEHAVIOR

Do expectations matter at all, even for the behavior in question? Are the expectations of young adults and their parents accurate predictors of actual behavior? There is considerable disagreement about the importance of expectations as predictors of demographic behavior, with many arguing that only conditions later on, at the time people are actually deciding about having children, or moving, are relevant to the decision they eventually make (Hendershot and Placek 1981, Speare 1990). Here we ask whether expectations about residential independence predict later behavior. We take the issue a step further, much like those who consider the expectations of both husbands and wives in the parenthood decision are beginning to do (Thomson 1983), asking whether parents or their children are more accurate in expecting the timing of leaving home or the route taken out of the home.

We have already shown that there are discrepancies in the aggregate between the average expectations of young adults and of their parents and also discrepancies between these expectations and actual behavior through six years after high school. Now we link specific parents' expectations with those of their own children as well as with their children's later behavior. Do parents and their children agree about the route expected out of the parental home—before or at marriage? Are the children of parents who expect nonfamily living more likely to expect it for themselves than average young adults are?

There is clearly a relationship between the expectations of parents and their children. While by chance, about 50 percent of parents and children would agree if there were no relationship between parents' and children's expectations, in fact, parents and children agree on the expected route out of the home in about two-thirds of these families (fig. 2.5). Of these harmonious families, two-thirds share an expectation for nonfamily living, and one-third agree on marriage as the expected route to residential independence. When parents and their children have different expectations about the route out of the home (35%), it is the child who expects to leave home before marriage in seven out of ten families, while the parent expects leaving home at marriage. In only three out of ten disagreeing families do parents expect their child to leave home before marriage, while their child expects to leave at marriage (about 10% of total families).[8]

Further, those who expected nonfamily living were considerably more likely to experience it than were those who expected leaving home at marriage. Six years after high school, 54 percent of those who expected nonfamily living actually achieved it compared with 35 percent of those who did not expect it (table 2.2). Similarly, those who linked leaving home with marriage were more likely to leave home at marriage when compared with those who expected to leave home before marriage: 44 percent of the young adults who expected to leave home at marriage did so six years after high school compared with 25 percent of those who expected to leave home before marriage. However, many who reported they would leave home only at marriage actually experienced nonfamily living, and many others who expected to leave home before they married either married from home or were still waiting to leave.

Interestingly, an equal proportion remained at home among both groups: 21 percent of those who expected nonfamily living were still residentially dependent in 1986, the same percentage as those who expected to remain home until marriage. Of course, since late marriage was more commonly expected than late nonfamily living, the latter group is less likely to feel that their plans have been frustrated than those expecting to leave home at marriage.

The timing of leaving home, especially early timing, is less predictable

26

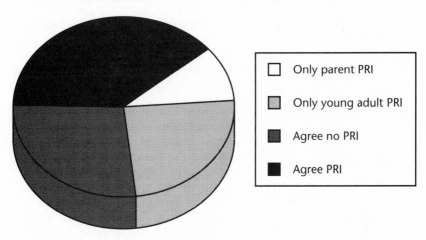

PRI = premarital residential independence

Fig. 2.5.   Parent-child expectations about routes to residential independence

from expectations than the route out of the parental home. Early marriage is an exception, since 52 percent of those who had expected to be married and living in their new home two years after high school actually were, suggesting that marriage plans in many cases were quite far along. In contrast, only 12 percent of those who expected to leave home at an early age before they married established their new home via marriage. More dramatically, those who expected nonfamily living two years after high school were almost wholly unrealistic, since only 20 percent actually did so. This was still a higher proportion of nonfamily living than was the case for those expecting to be living in married residential independence by that date (11%), but clearly, plans for early nonfamily living were rarely achieved.

Parents actually did rather better in their predictions about their children's residential behavior in early adulthood. Data in table 2.2 confirm at the family level the conclusions we reached after examining the aggregate data: the expectations of parents are more closely related to the behavior of their children than are the expectations of the children themselves. Thus, there is a higher level of actual nonfamily living if parents expected their children to leave home before marriage than if their children expected it.

The differences are most dramatic in the first two years after high school. While only a fifth of young adults experienced nonfamily living among those expecting it so early, this increased to one-third among those whose parents expected such early independence. Parents expecting

Table 2.2. Relationship between expectations and behavior: parents and young adults

| | Actual behavior | | | |
	PRI[a]	At home[b]	Married	Total
Young adults' expectations:				
		1986		
PRI	54	21	25	100
No PRI	35	21	44	100
		1982		
PRI by 1982	20	67	12	100
Marry by 1982	11	37	52	100
Parents' expectations:				
		1986		
PRI	61	16	23	100
No PRI	34	21	45	100
		1982		
PRI by 1982	34	52	14	100
Marry by 1982	6	25	69	100
Young adults' and parents' expectations:				
		1986		
Both PRI	64	14	22	100
Neither PRI	24	18	58	100
Child = PRI, parent = not	44	22	34	100
Parent = PRI, child = not	54	18	28	100

[a] PRI = premarital residential independence.
[b] "At home" includes those living in semiautonomous living arrangements such as dormitories and barracks.

early marital independence were also more prescient than were young adults. We documented above that 51 percent of young adults with such expectations realized them; fully 69 percent of parents expecting a child's early marriage were correct. Since many fewer parents expected such early departures, it is likely that their greater record of success reflects the fact that parents were involved in the process only when plans were pretty firm. It is also likely that parental agreement is necessary for success in realizing residential independence so soon after high school for most young adults, the majority of whom are still in their teens.

The differences are less sharp six years after high school, but the edge still goes to the parents. Among young adults whose parents expected their children to leave home before marriage, 61 percent experienced nonfamily living compared with 54 percent when they themselves expected it. For marriage, there is almost no difference between the generations.

When parents and young adults agree, their expectations are even better predictors of actual behavior than the expectations of either alone: taking into account both the expectations of parents and children enhances the prediction of actual behavior. Young adults who expected and their parents agreed that they would leave home before they married were the most likely to have already achieved nonfamily living by 1986 (63%); similarly, those sharing an expectation with their parents that residential independence would be delayed until marriage were the most likely to have taken that route by 1986 (56%). This suggests that although parents generally make better "predictions" of their children's life course path, young adults themselves have some influence on the outcome.

The parents' view is also more likely to prevail when there is disagreement. In cases where young adults expected to leave home before marriage but their parents did not, only 43 percent had established an independent residence, whereas 51 percent were no longer residing with their parents if it was the parents who expected nonfamily living *but not* the young adults. Apparently, young adults not only often need their parents' support to experience nonfamily living but they can be talked into it as well. Even more surprisingly, parents appear to have been better able than their children to predict residential independence at the time of marriage, although the difference here was somewhat smaller: when the young adult expected to remain dependent until marriage and the parent expected residential independence before marriage, only 29 percent had actually achieved independence via marriage by 1986; in the reverse case, 35 percent of the young adults had established a new household via marriage by 1986.

NEXT STEPS

Evidence on expectations has been treated in two distinct but complementary ways. Expectations about leaving home before marriage have been viewed as shared norms for a particular cohort about that which is desirable or preferable, all other things being equal. Since all other things are rarely equal, we anticipate that there will be gaps between these expressed norms and actual behavioral outcomes. It is therefore legitimate to investigate separately the determinants of nonfamily living norms and the determinants of actual nonfamily living. We can compare these sets of determinants and isolate the discrepancies between the factors that are more closely tied to normative expectations and those that are linked to actual behavior, as well as those factors that are related to both. And we can identify the factors associated with a narrower or a larger norm-behavior gap.

A second approach treats expectations as direct predictors of actual behavior. We can ask whether the expectations of children are better predictors of nonfamily living than the expectations of their parents. We can
also investigate the contexts where expectations are better predictors of
behavior: Which set of background factors enhances the predictions of
actual behavior? Are those with high levels of education, more economic
resources, or who are white Protestants more likely to carry out their
plans to leave home before marriage successfully than those with less
education and resources or those who are black? Which family contexts
more strongly link expectations to behavior? We also can isolate the importance of intervening events (e.g., marriage, job, education), over the
six-year period in bringing expectations closer toward behavior. How
much do unanticipated events in the life course of young adults upset
their ability to translate their expectations into behavior? When there is
conflict between the expectations of parents and children, which social
contexts enhance who wins (in terms of actual behavior)?

These orientations provide the guidelines for our subsequent analyses.
We build on the basic patterns we have described in this chapter by adding in a series of background variables and contexts to clarify the determinants of these processes and examine the role of marriage, life course
events, and parent-child conflict in understanding these new family
forms. Our objective throughout is to retain the twofold view of expectations as norms of young adults and as predictions of their actual behavior.

APPENDIX: EXPECTING FAMILY EXTENSION
AND LIFETIME NONMARRIAGE

Not all cases were easy to classify. In addition to a set of single ages as
possible answers to these questions, young people also had the option to
say that they never expected to marry or leave home as well as that they
had already done so. Very few in this final year before finishing high
school had married or left home (although the picture would be quite
different among those who were not still in school): only 1 percent said
they were already married, and 2.9 percent said they had left home.

We do not consider further those few (0.8%) who had already done
both, since we could neither tell when or in what sequence these events
occurred. But for those who had left home but were still unmarried, as
well as those already married but living with their parents at home, the
sequence between leaving home and marriage can be established, as can
at least some elements of timing. The data in table 2.3 show how often
young people and their parents gave these unusual responses (in lines 3,

Table 2.3. Expected marriage and residential independence sequences of young adults and parents

Expected residential independence sequence	Percentage of	
	Young adults	Parents
	(weighted)	
1. Marry after establishing residential independence[a]	64.4	55.6
2. Marry at the same time as residential independence	24.6	35.4
3. Never marry but expect residential independence	5.8	0.7
4. Marry before establishing residential independence[b]	4.3	7.5
5. Marry but never establish residential independence	0.3	0.7

[a] Includes those already in an independent residence but unmarried.
[b] Includes those already married but not yet in an independent residence.

4, and 5) relative to responses indicating expectation to have a home before marrying (line 1) or when marrying (line 2). Some answered the survey questions in a way that suggested that they expected to make these transitions in reverse order, with marriage *followed* by a period of continued residential dependence on parents; some expected never to make one or the other transition, that is, to never marry or to remain home forever. How did we decide how to treat these cases?

On the one hand, there was no explicit question, "Do you plan to live with your parents for a while after you marry?" and the two questions on age at which the respondent expected to marry and age at which he or she expected to set up an independent home were not even asked consecutively, since there were questions about the timing of having children, finishing school, and taking a job in between. Reflections on these issues after thinking about marriage might have led to a reevaluation of the age they expected to establish a new home, and some might not have gone back to change their answer to the earlier question to correspond with their revised thinking. And, as is the case with all such data, some people may have given ill-considered or even random responses to hypothetical questions such as these.

On the other hand, these answers could reflect a realistic assessment of possibilities. Some young people who expect to marry sooner or later might be living with a disabled parent and might be planning to build a new family together in their current home, at least for a while. If so, answers implying a transition to a new home after marriage might make

31

sense. Similarly, since it is not uncommon for young couples to double up for the first few years of marriage, some may expect this. Finally, in any group quite a few never marry, and in recent years, attitudes have changed, making it more likely that young people might assert that this is, in fact, their expectation (Thornton 1989). Let us consider these possibilities in turn.

We looked at those expecting to continue to live with their parents for a while after marriage in two ways. We thought it likely that in situations such as parental dependency, the parent would also expect such continued coresidence—maybe not all of them, but certainly many of them. And, in fact, about the name proportion of parents expect their children never to establish a new home, or to do so after marriage, as do the young adults themselves. However, when we examined whether these were the *same* parent-child pairs, we found that the young adults who seemed to be expecting to double up with their parents were no more likely to have parents who expected such an eventuality than were any other young adults.

Further, we examined the later behavior of young adults in families in which either they or their parents expected coresidence after marriage. We found that such living arrangements did happen—and not extremely rarely—at least among those marrying in the first few years after high school graduation. However, almost none were persons whose answers suggested that they were expecting it.

These tests suggest that although such coresidence occurs, it is almost never planned for. Rather, it is the unexpected outcome of decisions made after high school, such as what commitments to make in a loving relationship and how much money is available to spend for rent after decisions are made about continuing in school or perhaps continuing a pregnancy. These decisions evidently lead some young couples to live with one or the other set of parents. The parents, at least in some cases, accommodate the young couple even when they arrive unexpectedly. Hence, most of those giving answers implying expected coresidence must have answered inconsistently, whether because they changed their minds as they went from question to question or because their answers reflected little of what was in their minds. Other tests we did suggested that these cases closely resembled in other ways those expecting to marry when establishing a new home. Since moving them into that category would imply less change in their answers than would assigning them to the category "expecting to establish a new home before marriage," we chose not to ignore these cases but to classify them as expecting a traditional route out of the parental home.

Response error seems less plausible for those who expected never to leave home or never to marry, since these were explicit categories of response. They raise, instead, another problem: how seriously we should treat any of the answers young people and their parents give to hypothetical questions about events some time, possibly far, into the future. This is one of the most important questions for our analysis. In chapter 1, we discussed our reasons for taking these replies seriously, useful as indicators not only of young people's plans but also of their preferences and of the normative pressures on them. We shall continue to consider this issue in different ways in later chapters.

We examined those who expected either never to have their own homes or never to marry with some simple behavioral tests. Those who expected never to have an independent residence married early but were no more likely to still be living in the parental home by six years after high school than any other category in table 2.3. In fact, they closely resembled those who expected to marry and establish an independent residence at the same time. Similarly, those who expected never to marry were as likely to have married as most of those who had expected to marry eventually, including those who expected to marry late (more than six years after high school) and those who expected to marry between four and six years after high school. Only those who expected to marry very early were distinctively more likely to have married in the six years after high school than those who said they "never would marry." Hence, taking a conservative strategy and basing our decisions on early and late marriage patterns, we assigned those expecting to marry but never experience residential independence with those expecting a new home at or after marriage; those expecting never to marry were classified with those expecting to establish a separate home before marriage.

In brief, expecting to leave home before marriage, in contrast to expecting to establish a home only at marriage, indicates quite stable life plans that are tied most strongly to the age they expect to marry. As we demonstrated with data in figure 2.3, 50 percent of those who expect the more traditional path to residential independence also expect to be married within three years after the end of high school; in contrast, the median expected duration to marriage after high school graduation of those expecting to establish a home before marriage is nearly six years. These views of early adulthood are related to a complex matrix of other factors in their past lives and future plans, and they appear to attain them, far more so than those professing goals about such relatively rare behavior as lifetime nonmarriage or never having a home of their own.

3

Leaving Home Before Marriage
The Basic Patterns

By the 1980s, leaving home before marriage had evidently become institutionalized in the United States, as it was integrated into the normative
expectations of both generations and the dominant route out of the home
(chap. 2). A substantial majority of young adults expected to live away
from their parental home and its family-oriented life-style before they
married (70%), and at least a narrow majority of their parents also expected this of their children (56%). Further, more than 60 percent of the
young adults first observed to set up an independent residence within six
years of their senior year in high school did so in nonfamily households.

Premarital residential independence, both as something expected and
something achieved, is one of the most recent consequences of a broad
complex of changes that has been slowly decreasing the centrality of families in industrialized societies, increasingly limiting family life to the most
private and personal realms and removing family considerations from the
broad arena of individual activities and decisions tied to education, work,
politics, and religion (Thornton and Lin, forthcoming). The United States,
as a Western industrialized society, may never have been as familistic as
some Asian cultures and even among Western cultures, may be more
individualistic than most, holding values that tend to pair dependence
and autonomy as opposites, with little concern for the potential effects
maximizing independence might have on possibilities for developing and
maintaining *interdependence* and community (Bellah et al. 1985). Nevertheless, most evidence suggests that a reduction in familism characterized all industrializing societies.

The precise details of how the transformation from rural, subsistence
economies to complex industrial/information economies influences family
structure and relationships, how prior family and social structures shape
patterns of change, what alternative structures might be created to reinforce family ties, and *how long* the process takes are all unknown. Nevertheless, it seems clear that as new social and economic opportunities
have led to increased affluence, the importance of the family as an "in-

surance" mechanism against unemployment, poverty, and sickness has greatly declined, Affluence has also created far-reaching demographic changes that are still working to reshape the lives of men and women, extending them and reducing their focus on family tasks and relationships (Goldscheider 1992), a process by no means over.

While these transitions have begun in all industrial societies, changes in the family do not happen all at once or occur equally among all populations. Change is more likely to characterize those whose values and economic circumstances are undergoing the most rapid transformation. Some groups, for example, certain ethnic and religious communities, have resisted these family changes more than others. Not all groups have participated equally in the general increase in affluence; full educational and occupational opportunities have not been accessible to everyone. All of these socioeconomic differences may have implications for the emergence of nonfamily residential autonomy. It is likely that children of the native born are more likely than children of immigrants to embrace new patterns; urban residents and the more educated were often in the forefront of the family revolution (Schultz 1975, Haaga 1988). Reflecting the newness of these patterns, young adults coming out of high school in the 1980s were more likely to share these nonfamily values than their parents who were growing to adulthood in the mid-1950s.

Thus, while the family revolution appears ubiquitous, a more systematic and careful examination suggests that a range of family changes and a diversity of responses to them are typical in contemporary, industrial societies. By examining this variation and diversity at one point in time, we can make some inferences about the processes shaping the broader changes over time in the family revolution. If we compare who gets left out of family change to those who are in the forefront and contrast groups that are more and less receptive to change, we can clarify the contexts within which change occurs and begin to understand why the transformation has taken place. The examination of variation in family structure and values, even at one point in time, facilitates understanding family changes over time. Most important, by studying variation and generational attitudes, we can shed light on the emerging contexts of family relationships in contemporary American society.

Therefore, our analytic question shifts from identifying the general contours of leaving home and marriage characterizing contemporary American society to an analysis of particular contexts that lead to more or less nonfamily living. We then can specify those factors that reinforce more intensive family patterns and those that result in greater nonfamily autonomy. Hence, we turn from the general societal-level features associated with nonfamily residential autonomy (chap. 1) to an investigation of the determinants of leaving home before marriage among a group of young adults.

We begin with the basic question, What are the major sources of variation in the extent of leaving home before marriage? We focus on both expectations and actual behavior and examine whether the factors that determine expectations for residential independence before marriage are similar to those that influence actually doing so. This analysis allows us to test whether expecting nonfamily residential autonomy shapes the routes out of the home in young adulthood. We present an overview of the major factors we expect to influence nonfamily autonomy in the transition to adulthood and attempt a first test of our argument. In subsequent chapters, we expand our analysis to clarify how these factors work and what explanations are most consistent with the evidence.

THE NEW FAMILY ECONOMY

The changing relationship between the family and the economy is one of the master themes in the study of the transformations of Western societies (chap. 1). In preindustrial communities, family and economic spheres were tightly integrated, so that economic consumption and production took place in a family context; the family was the central institution around which other activities revolved. In the industrial era, family and economic activities have become increasingly differentiated, reducing the connections between these spheres of activity. The family has not become fully independent of economic activities, nor is the economy without important family connections. Rather, the connections between family and economic processes have been realigned and what has emerged is "a new family economy" (Goldscheider and Goldscheider 1989b).

Four major processes are associated with the development of this new family economy:

1. Increasing affluence, which alters the resources available to the family and changes its control over members of the younger generation, as they gain more independent access to resources

2. Increasing group integration and assimilation, which shifts people's commitments away from family loyalties reinforced by ethnic and local communities toward the broader national community, based on individual-based, achievement-oriented values

3. Increasing secularization, which leads away from religiously based culture and institutions toward secular values and institutions

4. Increasing egalitarianism, which reduces the power of men over women and parents over their children

Each of these four processes has been linked at the societal level to many family changes, including those that increase the autonomy of young adults (see the overview in Goldscheider and Goldscheider 1989*b*; also see Kuznets 1978, Levy 1965, Burch and Mathews 1987). Thus, for example, increasing affluence and universalistic values have fueled the shift from extended to nuclear family structure, with concomitant increases in the autonomy of young adults to marry, migrate, and head their own households.[1] Egalitarianism and the increasing similarity in gender roles have allowed young women more of the freedom in young adulthood previously experienced by young men. Secularization has led to the development of new values, altering the ways in which young persons make choices among the variety of options available in the transition to adulthood.

To study the contexts influencing whether young adults expect or experience nonfamily living, we translate these four processes into group- and individual-level indicators. We begin by considering the most general translations. We use a socioeconomic status scale as our first indicator of affluence. Our reasoning is that socioeconomic status is highly correlated with financial resources that allow young adults (and their parents) to plan for residential autonomy before marriage and to be able to carry out these plans. Attachment to a particular ethnic group will be used as one indicator of commitment either to familism or to American values of independence from family constraints. We include region with our analysis of ethnicity, to represent other key contexts likely to be shaping family patterns, given the more recent rural history of the South and the West's role in leading family change. Religious affiliation and denomination will be used to measure the extent of secularization; gender differences will index egalitarianism.

The broader processes associated with family change unfold over time, while the measures that we use were obtained for one period of time only and thus are imprecise reflections of these processes. Hence, we do not claim to test the specific relationships between processes and values associated with change, on the one hand, and the transformation of the family, on the other. Our goal is more modest: we use theoretically grounded societal-level processes to generate parallels at the individual and group levels to guide our analysis of the emergence of new residential forms in the transition to adulthood.

We therefore use these categories as a convenient heuristic device for organizing a vast array of complex processes. Many variables are encompassed within these categories, and, as we shall indicate in subsequent chapters, there are complex and detailed linkages within and between the indicators we include. At this point, however, we will treat these basic categories quite simply in our analysis, examining only one indicator among many within a category and suggesting only some of its multiple meanings.

Our analysis does take into account the *interrelationships* that exist among these indicators. For example, there is an overlap between racial group affiliation and social class membership. To establish and understand racial differences in nonfamily living, therefore, we need to disentangle the "racial" from the "social class" elements of racial group affiliation. In analyzing premarital residential independence for young African-Americans, for example, we will neutralize the overlap between race and social class to distinguish the effects of their lower average socioeconomic status or something else about their life-style, family structure, or values. Toward this goal, we take into account the effects of each variable when examining the other (i.e., controlling in the statistical sense using a multivariate format). When we identify differences in nonfamily residential autonomy by gender or by class, for example, we are more confident that there is a direct effect that does not reflect the influence of other factors.

In this chapter, then, we examine the factors linked to nonfamily residential autonomy in the least complex way, testing what we call our "basic model." That model focuses on socioeconomic status, region, gender, and categories of race, ethnicity, and religion to explore their influence on expectations and behavior. In subsequent analyses, we will refine each of these variables and examine their complex interactions.

EXPECTING PREMARITAL RESIDENTIAL INDEPENDENCE

We begin by examining the influence of the factors in our basic model on expectations for nonfamily residential autonomy. Expectations were first articulated by young adults when nearly all were still living in their parents' household, before experiencing any residential independence. Focusing first on a single outcome—expectations—allows us to concentrate on the effects of these basic factors, without introducing the complexities of the relationship between expectations and behavior. We will then highlight differences in these factors' influence on actual residential behavior in the six years after the completion of high school. In our analyses in later chapters, when the complex interrelationships between expectations and behavior have been examined more closely, we will see how these more detailed analyses illuminate the dialectic between them.

SOCIOECONOMIC STATUS AS AFFLUENCE

Socioeconomic status implies a broader, interrelated range of factors, including financial resources, education, and life-style as well as the extent

of intergenerational financial exchanges. Residential autonomy requires
financial resources to purchase privacy and autonomy and responds to the
values for independence relative to family-related commitments that often accompany higher education. Residential independence in young
adulthood implies a life-style of higher consumption that allows the daily
work and leisure activities of parents and their young adult children to be
more separated from each other. Hence, we expect that young adults
from families with higher socioeconomic status will be more likely to expect nonfamily residential autonomy. Our measure of socioeconomic
status is a scale constructed by the survey group based on a combination
of parental education, occupation, family income, and material posses-
sions in the household (Jones et al. 1986; also see chap. 10 and Appendix
A, below).

Consistent with our argument, there is a direct relationship between
our measure of the parents' socioeconomic status and their children's expectations for premarital residential independence, although the effect is
not dramatic (fig. 3.1 and table B3.1): the higher the score on the socioeconomic scale, the greater the probability of expecting nonfamily residential autonomy. Our equation predicts that only 64 percent of those in
the lowest decile of socioeconomic status expect nonfamily residential
autonomy, compared with 73 percent of those in the highest decile.[2]
Clearly, some or all of the dimensions of socioeconomic status simpli-
fied in this scale encourage young people to expect nonfamily residential
autonomy.

The general relationship between socioeconomic status and nonfamily

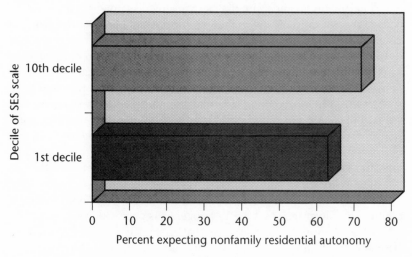

Fig. 3.1. Socioeconomic status and expecting nonfamily residential autonomy

residential autonomy expectations is weak in these data, suggesting that two refinements should be made before we conclude that young adults' expectations are really quite so unresponsive to parental resources. First, the combined index of socioeconomic status joins measures of education, occupation, and income and hence confuses resources and tastes. We need to separate these two elements so we can measure their relative importance. Second, socioeconomic status is measured as a parental trait and then related to the expectations of their children and assumes that young adults have access to the income and financial resources of their parents. The financial flows between the generations should be measured directly to refine our analysis of the affluence factor. Both these extensions will be addressed systematically when we expand our analysis to include parents (chap. 10).

FAMILISM AS REFLECTED IN
ETHNIC IDENTIFICATION AND REGION

Ethnicity

Ethnic group identification implies that local community loyalties and ascriptive criteria are likely to be used to reinforce particularistic family commitments and obligations. In concrete terms, this means, for example, that an Italian shopkeeper with close ties to his fellow Italian neighbors and his kin will prefer to hire his neighbor or cousin, since this, in turn, will encourage the new employee's kin to do the same for the shopkeeper's children. The transformation of employment leads to the establishment of modern corporations, which attempt to use their personnel departments to seek out the best-qualified people, establishing exchange relationships only with their employees and not with their kin and neighbors.

To the extent that nonfamily residential autonomy is an emerging feature in the contemporary United States, it follows that those who are more integrated into the American value system are more likely to be characterized by nonfamily residential autonomy. In contrast, those who are part of communities that emphasize traditional values of family cohesion and commitment are likely to remain in the parental home until they marry. Belonging to a minority ethnic community may thus be a good indicator of the lack of full integration into American society and the emphasis on traditional family values.

The richness of the ethnic and racial data in this survey allows us to examine ethnic groups that are heterogeneous on a wide variety of characteristics. We can distinguish those that are mostly first generation (e.g., Hispanics) from those that are primarily of earlier immigrant waves; those with distinctively low socioeconomic status (e.g., blacks) from the few (such as Asians) that have been particularly successful economically. Similarly, some groups have been characterized by the rapid relative upward mobility of women despite patriarchal cultural sources; this appears to be the case for Jews and many Asians and may be true for the black community as well. Other groups are thought to be considerably more patriarchal and controlling of women, particularly Hispanics.

We expect that young persons who are from ethnic groups with a high proportion of first-generation immigrants, such as Hispanics, will be less likely to expect nonfamily living. In contrast, the combination of high proportions of female-headed families, discrimination, and poverty may affect the routes young blacks take to residential independence. It is difficult to speculate about nonfamily residential autonomy among Asian-Americans since, on the one hand, they have a tradition of family solidarity and obligations, which should be associated with remaining home until marriage, while, on the other hand, they also have experienced rapid upward social mobility in recent decades, which should be associated with residential independence before marriage.

We start with a relatively simple classification of racial and ethnic categories, including in the basic model Asians, blacks, and Hispanics.[3] Figure 3.2 (and table B3.1) shows that, net of other factors (region, gender, and socioeconomic status), blacks are the most likely to expect nonfamily living and Asians and Hispanics the least likely; non-Hispanic whites are in the middle on a scale with about the same range as that by region.

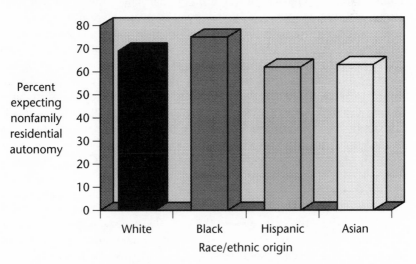

Fig. 3.2.   Race and ethnic origin and expecting nonfamily residential autonomy

41

Blacks are 6 percentage points more likely than non-Hispanic whites to expect nonfamily residential autonomy (74.5% compared with 68.7%).[4] In contrast, both Asian and Hispanic seniors in high school are about 6 percentage points less likely to expect nonfamily living than non-Hispanic whites (63.1% and 62.2%, respectively).

These racial and ethnic differences in expectations raise new questions: Do blacks in the South, where many blacks are still concentrated, have even more extreme levels of premarital residential independence expectations? Are Hispanics and Asians who use a foreign language even less likely to expect nonfamily living than those who do not? Moreover, the Hispanic classification contains a wide array of communities that differ both in the countries they come from and where they are residentially concentrated. Cubans have had a distinctive history of immigrant selectivity and residential density, as have Mexicans, that might influence their residential transition to adulthood. These and related questions will be investigated in chapter 4.

Region

Regional variation reflects both preferences and resources. Because of their very different histories, geographic regions vary in economic opportunities and markets as well as in educational opportunities; they may vary as well culturally and in the extent of familism and family-peer pressures. Thus, for example, research has shown that the western area of the United States is a region of greater individualism and of new forms of nonfamily-oriented behavior. In California, in particular, there is a relatively strong rejection of segregated family roles for women, resulting in earlier nest leaving among daughters and higher divorce rates among women. Californians are more likely than residents of other states to delay both marriage and remarriage. Marital roles in California also seem to be the most egalitarian, with relatively lower rates of fertility compared with other areas of the country and the highest household headship rates among married women (Castleton and Goldscheider 1989). In contrast, the South is a region characterized by greater differentiation in the lives of men and women (Mason, Czajka, and Arber 1976) and less involvement by children in the household domestic economy (Goldscheider and Waite 1991).

The areal classification used in our study is based on the region where the young adult lived in the senior year of high school. This measure most nearly identifies the place where these students grew up—better than, for example, region of birth—since parental migration rates are lowest when children reach school age (Speare 1970). Nevertheless, the regions we consider are very large geographic areas and are only crude approximations of the specific communities within which these young adults grew up.

There is a substantial regional effect on expectations about leaving home before marriage. Three peripheral regions stand out from the center of the United States—the Pacific region, New England, and the South. Young adults living in the southern region are significantly less likely to expect nonfamily residential autonomy than those living in the central and mountain regions: 63.4 percent compared with 68.4 percent, all other things being equal. In contrast, those living in the New England and Pacific regions are the most likely to expect nonfamily residential autonomy (74.5%). These results suggest that the country as a whole shares some common orientation on this issue, with the broad central and mountain regions resembling each other strongly. The results for the southern and Pacific regions were as expected; it is not clear at this point what factors account for New England's distinctiveness from the rest of the country.

There are several possible explanations for these regional differences. They may represent a genuine regional effect, in which the influence of growing up, say, in the South, characterizes all who do so, whatever their other characteristics. But these regions may also differ in other ways. For example, we do not currently take into account differences in religious fundamentalism. If members of more fundamentalist religious groups are very unlikely to expect premarital residential independence *and* are heavily concentrated in the South, this could account for part of the differences we observe here. We will explore this issue in greater detail in chapter 5, which analyzes religion and religious denominations in greater detail.[5]

SECULARIZATION AS RELIGIOUS AFFILIATION AND DENOMINATION

Secularization and the decline in religious group affiliation have been linked to changes in family norms and behavior. Affiliation with traditional religious groups implies both identification with and involvement in the institutions and values that characterize particular religious systems, together with a greater commitment to those values that stress the importance of family and of involvement in the religious community. These values and the institutions that reinforce them should help to maintain the linkage between residential independence and marriage. Those who are identified with a religious group that puts less stress on family-based values and those who are not affiliated at all with a religious group should be more likely to expect to leave home before marriage.

We begin with a simple categorization of the white population and show that there is relatively little difference in premarital residential independence expectations among Protestants, Catholics, and Jews (68%, 70%, and 71%, respectively).[6] It is possible that religion is simply not salient for this issue. However, both Christian groups are relatively heterogeneous: Protestants are made up of a wide range of denominations, and Catholics in the United States differ sharply in their countries of origin. This overall categorization may mask important variation within either or both of these broad religious groups. Further, belonging to a religious group may have much less meaning than feeling strongly about its precepts and being closely involved in them through frequent attendance at religious services. We will attempt to see whether religion continues to have little impact when we examine these facets in more detail in chapter 5.

The lack of Jewish distinctiveness in residential expectations is also somewhat surprising. Jews have been characterized as having strong family values and a cohesive family structure, which should make them less likely to expect nonfamily residential autonomy. However, they tend to marry later and to stress high levels of independence and autonomy for their children. If so, parents would facilitate the independence of their children (which, in turn, increases their own privacy), even while maintaining strong family ties (Goldscheider 1986; also see chap. 5). We may be observing a balance of these forces at this point.

GENDER AS EGALITARIANISM

Men and women experience different life course patterns, with women marrying and becoming parents at an earlier age than men and developing a firm commitment to the labor force later than men (Leibowitz, Klerman, and Waite 1992). This is because men and women face a different structure of roles in early adulthood. Men are still expected to be the primary wage earner, with greater responsibility for supporting the family. Women, in contrast, are still expected to take primary responsibility for children and household management. Hence, marriage is normally a more central role for women, since it defines their obligations and allows for their economic support. These traditional gender roles have given rise to and reflect different preferences and values associated with manhood and womanhood.

Gender differences may reflect how boys and girls are socialized about their adult roles and their gender role attitudes and the family and career expectations of parents about their sons and daughters. They may also

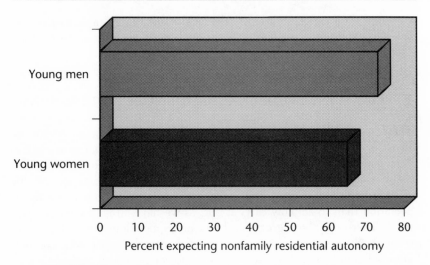

Fig. 3.3.   Gender differences in expecting nonfamily residential autonomy

reflect a greater willingness among parents to invest in the autonomy of their sons than in the autonomy of their daughters. In particular, they allow men more independence before marriage, which should facilitate nonfamily residential autonomy in young adulthood.

The data confirm this pattern and show that young adult males are more likely than females to expect premarital residential autonomy (72.9% compared with 64.8%), controlling for socioeconomic status, region, and ethnicity (fig. 3.3). These gender differences in expectations are less than those by ethnicity and region, about the same as differences by socioeconomic status, and more than those by religion. How much of these differences can be attributed directly to gender role attitudes or to different marriage trajectories of men and women will be examined in chapters 6 and 7.

Gender differences, along with ethnic, social class, and regional differences, show that there is considerable variation in the factors affecting expectations for premarital residential independence but that some factors seem to have a greater influence on expectations than others. However, differences in expectations are relatively small, which suggests that nonfamily residential autonomy is a normative requirement for most young adults (males and females, from all groups and regions, and from all family backgrounds), one that young people may try hard to realize as they continue to make decisions about work, school, family, and residence in their transition to adulthood. How many of these young adults actually carry out their expectations? Are the factors that determine whether they actually experience nonfamily residential autonomy the same as those that shape their expectations?

EXPERIENCING PREMARITAL RESIDENTIAL INDEPENDENCE

There are several bases for anticipating that the determinants of expectations for nonfamily living and actual nonfamily residential autonomy in young adulthood might be very different. Young peoples' expectations are likely not to take into account fully many of the constraints to realizing residential independence before marriage; it is easier to express an expectation than to actually carry it out, as we have already seen in chapter 2. There may be a great gap between expectations and behavior for students from poorer families, who while sharing the expectations of their more affluent classmates, have access to fewer resources to facilitate realizing them. If this is the case, socioeconomic status would be more strongly related to behavior than to expectations for nonfamily residential autonomy. Similarly, members of more recently arrived ethnic groups such as Hispanics might underestimate the disapproval that might be expressed by their ethnic kin and neighbors about taking the route to nonfamily living. This would also result in smaller differences in expectations than in behavior. In contrast, young men who do not share the nonfamily living expectations of other men might have underestimated the pressures from their peers—or their parents—to achieve independence and find it difficult to remain dependent until marriage.

We examine data that can clarify these possibilities, focusing on the *proportion* achieving residential autonomy without having married among those becoming residentially autonomous. This measure can be thought of as a "route ratio" in that it focuses our attention on the relative sizes of each route among those becoming independent. As such, it is potentially influenced by the timing of marriage and leaving home, since among groups marrying late, for example, even if only a few leave home early, they are likely to be choosing the route to nonfamily autonomy. However, it is closest to our measure of expectations (which is also a route ratio, except based on the full range of ages rather than truncated at six years after high school). We will postpone a consideration of the greater complexities introduced by taking into account the effects of the timing of marriage and leaving home, seeing that while some patterns change, most do not.

On average, over the four to six years after high school we could observe, about 65 percent of those who established an independent residence did so via nonfamily residential autonomy, not much below the level they expected (69%) eventually to attain.[7] Group differences that emerged in the basic model predicting the actual route to residential independence are also generally similar to the pattern already shown for expectations. Thus, young men who achieved residential independence were more likely to do so before marriage rather than at marriage, relative to young women; those living in the New England and Pacific regions were more likely, while those living in the South were less likely, than those living in the center of the country to have experienced nonfamily living. Higher socioeconomic status led to more residential independence before marriage; blacks had a higher probability of residential independence before marriage, while Hispanics normally waited until marriage to establish a separate household. Table 3.1 shows this comparison precisely for the categories of our basic model.

Asians present the only major inconsistency in direction between factors associated with expectations and factors associated with behavior. They were *less likely* to expect residential autonomy before marriage than the group as a whole but were *more likely* to actually experience it among

Table 3.1. Expecting and achieving residential autonomy

	PRI[a] percentage	
Category	Expected (ever)	Achieved[b] (by 1986)
Total	69	65
Highest decile of SES	73	81
Lowest decile of SES	64	50
South	63	58
Pacific and New England	74	72
Other regions	68	66
Hispanics	62	56
Asians	63	70
Blacks	75	76
Other (white)	69	65
Other religions[c]	68	59
Catholics[c]	70	70
Jews[c]	71	83
Males	73	73
Females	65	58

[a]PRI = premarital residential independence
[b]On average, for those becoming independent during the period of observation
[c]Non-Hispanic, non-Asian, nonblack
Source: Values predicted from regression coefficients in table B3.1.

those who established an independent residence. We shall attempt to unravel this anomaly when we analyze the values and the educational and marriage patterns of this group in more detail.

As we anticipated, there were also much *greater* differences among groups in behavior than in expectations. Differences in the experience of nonfamily living sometimes only exaggerated the differences we saw in expectations by relatively small amounts, but sometimes the differences in magnitude were very large. The most extreme example of this appears for religious affiliation. The differences in expectations among Catholics, Jews, and others (primarily Protestants) were very small, with a range of 3 percentage points. However, the gap between Protestants and Catholics in behavior was 11 percentage points (59% vs. 70%) and between Protestants and Jews was fully 24 percentage points (59% vs. 83%). Socioeconomic status also showed much greater impact on behavior than on expectations. Whereas the gap in expectations between those whose families were in the upper decile of socioeconomic status and those whose families were in the lowest decile was only 9 percentage points (64% and 73%, respectively), their lives actually diverged by 31 percentage points, since only 50 percent of the poor group who achieved residential independence did so in a nonfamily context, compared with 81 percent for those at a comparable extreme of wealth.

Ethnic and gender differences in expectations were only moderately exaggerated in eventual behavior: the 12-percentage-point range in expectations among blacks, Hispanics, and Asians increased to 20 percentage points for actual behavior, and the gender gap grew from 8 to 15 percentage points. Only the regional differences were essentially stable when comparing expectations and behavior.

EXPECTATIONS AND BEHAVIOR IN THE BASIC MODEL

Most of the factors that we have considered in the basic model affect both expectations and actual patterns, albeit in different ways. But do expectations have any direct influence on behavior once the factors in the basic model are taken into account? For example, does the similarity between the effect of socioeconomic status on expectations for nonfamily living and on actual residential independence result from the fact that people of higher socioeconomic status are more likely to both expect and experience nonfamily living but that expectations and behavior have no direct link? Or do the expectations themselves have a separate influence, even among those of low socioeconomic status and among members of other groups that are otherwise less involved in this new life course pattern? To answer these questions, we included expectations about nonfamily living in the basic model of factors affecting the actual patterns of nonfamily residential autonomy.

This analysis shows that expectations are significantly and positively related to actual nonfamily residential autonomy, net of the variables in the basic model (table B3.1). The difference between the two groups is substantial: among those who expected nonfamily living, fully 75 percent of first independent residences were nonmarital, while this was the case for 51 percent of those who expected to remain residentially dependent until marriage. Nevertheless, the relationship is far from total: knowing expectations is not sufficient for predicting nonfamily living, since many who expected nonfamily living did not experience it, and many who expected to wait for residential independence until marriage actually experienced a period of residential autonomy before they married.

These findings are prima facie evidence that expectations are valuable as predictors of actual nonfamily living in young adulthood, although it still helps to know other characteristics of young adults to explain their actual behavior. The effects of socioeconomic status, ethnicity, gender, and region remain strong, continuing to influence the residential decisions of young adults whatever their expectations. The strength of the contexts that shape young adulthood is reflected in the fact that half of those who did not expect nonfamily residential autonomy are predicted to experience it.

NEXT STEPS

We have examined the basic factors influencing nonfamily residential autonomy and have also shown that expectations influence behavior. The next several chapters are designed to build cumulatively on the basic model to sharpen our analysis, add depth to the interpretations, and test competing explanations as new variables are added and new dimensions investigated.

We have the first evidence of the importance of affluence, familism, secularism, and egalitarianism, as measured by socioeconomic status, ethnicity and region, religious affiliation, and gender, in shaping nonfamily living in the transition to adulthood. Our goal is to unpack these concepts to reveal the processes that underlie them. Chapters 4 and 5 focus on the contexts within which ethnic, racial, and religious differences are stronger or weaker, to clarify how ethnic differences in late-twentieth-century America can continue to influence nonfamily residential autonomy. Measures of religious values, community networks, and personal religious self-identity are examined, together with information on foreign language use, generation, and ethnic residential concentration, to uncover why these groups vary in their expectations and behavior.

Egalitarianism is treated in the context of male-female and parent-child relationships (chap. 6). We explore gender differences directly, testing connections between nonfamily residential autonomy and gender role attitudes among young men and women, and examine the effects of parent-child relationships on the route to residential independence. These family themes reinforce our understanding of the ways ethnic, racial, and religious communities support traditional family forms, including the association of autonomy with marriage.

We then focus on the life course changes in early adulthood, maximizing the power of the longitudinal data collected in the 1980s during the critical six years after high school graduation. In chapter 7, we examine the extent to which late marriage facilitates nonfamily residential autonomy and separate factors that influence it via delayed marriage from those whose effects operate directly on the decision to leave home to nonfamily living independent of marriage age. In the six years after high school, young people experience other changes in their plans, as unanticipated events involving schooling, parenthood, and even marriage occur. In chapter 8, we examine how robust nonfamily residential autonomy is to changes in these other domains of early adulthood.

In the final section, we turn to the broader question of the family context within which young adults form their expectations and attempt to act on them. We ask in chapter 9 whether the structure of the family (intact, one-parent, or blended) affects whether young adults expect and do in fact experience nonfamily living. Then, in chapter 10, we turn to disentangling the factors associated with socioeconomic status to see how parental resources get transferred to young adults—via tastes, as in parental education, or via monetary resources, that is, family income, particularly income that is transferred directly between parents and children. This sets the stage to focus directly on the attitudes of parents on the nonfamily living of their children and the role of parents in supporting this pattern of residential autonomy for their children. We then investigate what happens when parents and children disagree over the route to residential independence in young adulthood.

4

Racial and Ethnic Communities
The Structural and Cultural Bases
of Family Values

What are the factors that account for the persistence of racial and ethnic differences in routes to residential autonomy in the 1980s? Why should young people in American high schools, overwhelmingly native born and surrounded by the homogenizing effects of modern mass media, display family patterns that vary systematically by racial and ethnic origins? Having shown that these differing expectations and choices about residential independence persist even after taking social class into account, how do we account for the continuing distinctiveness of these groups? Under what conditions do assimilation and integration occur in family patterns in young adulthood?

We have linked the increase in residential independence before marriage among young adults to the emergence of individualism and universalism. As familistic values and obligations have been deemphasized and the importance of community is replaced by a focus on the individual, young adulthood has increasingly come to include nonfamily living. Many racial and ethnic communities are not fully integrated into American society; does this account for their greater residential dependence before marriage?

American society is heterogeneous in terms of ethnic and racial communities, with diverse national origins for its population, differences in length of stay and exposure to "American" culture and values, and variation in the access to the opportunities that facilitate economic success. How do these factors affect the transformation of family life implied by nonfamily living in young adulthood among the communities and subgroups that comprise the American racial and ethnic mosaic? Blacks have developed unique family patterns characterized by late marriage and nonmarriage that may reflect their particular history and current position (slavery and continued discrimination) in American communities. Does this imply that blacks are more likely to leave home before marriage than at marriage? In contrast, relatively recent immigrant groups exposed more narrowly to American society and contemporary family values and

51

life-styles tend to have higher levels of family cohesion. They have originated primarily from communities where the family has been a more central institution for economic activities and for defining the social roles of adults and children. Leaving home before marriage reduces parental influence over children and diminishes familistic orientation (Waite, Goldscheider, and Witsberger 1986). Are recent immigrants more likely to live at home until marriage in the transition to adulthood?

Research has documented that differences among racial and ethnic groups on other dimensions of family structure and family norms are often as great as those by income or education. Significant variation in extended family ties and in the prevalence of households headed by women characterize blacks, Hispanics, and whites (Tienda and Angel 1982; Angel and Tienda 1982; Cooney 1979; Bean and Tienda 1989). Moreover, the probability of nonfamily living has been shown to differ among many diverse ethnic groups (see Kobrin and Goldscheider 1982 and the series of studies in Goldscheider and Goldscheider 1989b). Asian-Americans, for example, tend to leave home later (Goldscheider and DaVanzo 1989, Kanjanapan 1989), and unmarried Hispanics and blacks are less likely than white non-Hispanics to live independently (Hernandez 1989).

What is less clear is why these family norms *persist* among racial and immigrant groups. To what extent are ethnic family values transmitted across generations, and what social structural conditions are conducive to that transmission? Racial discrimination is endemic in the United States, yet an increasing number of blacks have become middle class and attained high levels of education. What are the patterns of residential autonomy among the children of the new black middle class? Have educated and wealthier black families developed patterns that more closely resemble those of white middle-class families?

The assimilation of immigrant groups is a frequent outcome of increased exposure to American society, yet this is clearly not inevitable; its pace must vary. What mechanisms sustain and reinforce familistic values among young adults? Foreign-language use and ethnic regional concentration may be the bases for communal group cohesion as distance increases from foreign roots. In this chapter, we sort out the combinations of factors that maintain racial and ethnic communities and thereby continue to influence the living arrangements of young adults.

We will refer to these indicators of the intensity of interaction within ethnic and racial groups as "ethnicity." Ethnicity maximizes exposure to other members and their values, potentially muting the impact of broader American society and values. Thus, while some of the variation among racial and ethnic groups reflects values and preferences, these are transmitted in families, communities, and neighborhoods. To understand how

52

ethnicity operates, we have to examine the structures and the contexts that reinforce and sustain these values through interaction within the community. The central questions we pose in this chapter are, What are the contexts leading to racial and ethnic differences in the expectations and behavior about routes to residential independence among young adults? What are the sources of differentiation among the heterogeneous array of these communities in American society?

To address these questions, we shall explore the relationships between nonfamily living and the contexts that differentiate racial and ethnic communities. Ethnicity (or ethnic intensity) is indicated by residence in the region of greatest ethnic concentration, where ethnic associations should be most intense; exposure to the general culture is reflected in distance from the immigrant generation; using a language other than English serves as a measure both of exposure to ethnic culture and as a mechanism of interaction among ethnic group members.

CULTURE, STRUCTURE, AND PLURALISM

Our perspective blends several research and theoretical traditions, integrating those that emphasize the centrality of cultural values as the basis for ethnic continuity with those that focus on the structures of communities and the networks of interaction among groups. The first research tradition is explicitly cultural, examining ethnic intensity primarily in the context of immigration and the cultural "baggage" that accompanied immigrant groups to America (Gordon 1964, Glazer and Moynihan 1970). Since the origin culture ordinarily differs from the receiving one, the immigrant generation is closer to the sources of ethnic values. Within this orientation, foreign-born status and ethnic-language use are indicators of closeness to the community of origin and its culture. Individuals lose their foreignness over time by learning and using English and, hence, increased exposure to the receiving society. This framework predicts that those whose generation is closer to the foreign born as well as users of a foreign language will be less likely to expect and experience nonfamily independence, all other things being equal.

With its emphasis on the cultural dimension of ethnicity, this framework views ethnicity as a transitional influence operating during the process of ethnic acculturation and assimilation in American society. If other things were indeed equal, this would probably be the case: the influence of foreign roots should diminish as generation in America increases and as foreign-language use declines. However, language use need not decline automatically, unlike generation. Foreign-language use is both a remnant of the origin culture and a continuing mechanism of communication among community members.

Hence, foreign-language use can reinforce ethnic social networks and facilitate the extension of the origin culture to children who are American born, signaling an ethnic community's cohesiveness, not just the cultural legacy of the immigrant generation. Use of an ethnic language at home, in the neighborhood, and in school strengthens ethnic networks and current values. Therefore, using a foreign language extensively is a powerful link to the origin culture. Even as the language itself changes over time in the United States, borrowing more and more words from the surrounding culture, embedded within it are assumptions, images, and information about the society from which immigrants have come. Those who use foreign languages extensively in their daily relationships are likely to be much more in tune with the mores associated with the origin society. Applying this viewpoint, with its emphasis on the structural influences maintaining ethnic and generational continuity, we expect that users of a foreign language, even those with native-born parents, will be less likely to expect to or to actually leave home unmarried.

Language use and the linkages that support it are not the only structures that can impede cultural assimilation. There is another research tradition that has been sharply focused on the structural and ecological dimensions of ethnicity. Noting that an exclusive focus on immigrant culture and foreign-language use fails to account for the continuing salience or even reemergence of ethnic communities in later generations, this structural approach stresses the importance of ethnic neighborhoods and regional concentration as a major continuing basis for linking individuals to the community. This research tradition shifts our focus from forces leading to change—acculturation—to the forces reinforcing continuity; racial or ethnic residential concentration can provide a basis for group or community cohesion, even when its members are no longer foreign born and no longer use an ethnic language (Yancey, Ericksen, and Juliani 1976; Goldscheider 1986; Lieberson 1980; Portes and Bach 1985; Massey 1989; Alba 1990).

Geographic concentration implies a relatively large ethnic community and, hence, the possibility of developing more extensive ethnic networks based on regional and neighborhood interaction. For individuals to melt away their ethnic distinctiveness, then, would require geographic mobility, that is, moving to communities of less intense ethnic group concentration. For those remaining within the ethnic community, generational succession and even learning and using English might not lead to acculturation. Hence, we argue that those who remain in areas of racial and ethnic residential concentration will be less likely to expect or experience nonmarital residential independence, notwithstanding their generation in America or their use of a foreign language.

Our framework assumes that ethnic/racial groups have the potential to be fully integrated into American society of the late twentieth century. It applies to all immigrant groups, whether from Europe, Asia, or Latin America. However, given the history of American black-white relations, the potential for the integration of blacks into the dominant white society is extraordinarily circumscribed.

Discrimination against them has resulted in continued concentration residentially and in social class categories (education, income, and occupation). As a result, distinctive black life-styles and values, communities and normative orientations, have been reinforced. Hence, while disadvantage and social class continue to be critical social dimensions accounting for black/white differences, the values and norms that have come to distinguish blacks from whites may also influence their life course decisions. Marriage and family structure have become particularly distinctive, with high levels of expected nonmarriage. The ubiquity of race and racism in American society is likely to result in national patterns of residential autonomy among blacks that vary mainly by social class. However, it is possible that blacks in the South will be characterized by more distinctive black family patterns than blacks in other regions. As with immigrant groups, time in and of itself does not compel integration; social structures reinforce distinctiveness, however these structures are maintained.

In our approach, then, we view ethnic and racial factors as having both structural and cultural components. Geographic concentration and speaking a foreign language imply both community interaction and the transmission of culture; all contribute to the maintenance of distinctive communities, racial and ethnic. Therefore, we need to focus on the structure of social networks (the multiple ways members of racial and ethnic communities are involved and interact formally and informally with each other) and on the values transmitted within these networks to discover how they are linked to the expectations and behavior associated with young adults' pathways to residential autonomy in the transition to adulthood. This chapter focuses on the structures that maintain ethnic and racial distinctiveness. (The specific family values that may characterize these communities are analyzed in chap. 6.)

Our approach treats ethnic "assimilation" as a variable process in pluralist societies. Immigrant groups invariably appear somewhat "different" for a while, since it is difficult to assimilate instantaneously. As some groups experience greater exposure to the broader society through generational succession, they vanish entirely. High levels of interethnic marriages demonstrate the erosion of ethnic distinctiveness for many national origin populations in the United States (Alba 1976, 1983). Other ethnic groups, however, can maintain cohesion over a somewhat longer period through continued language use and geographic concentration. However, for ethnicity to be maintained in place over many generations, only those who maintain a distinctive set of values, whether through the development of their own institutions or through continued out-group discrimination, should be able to preserve their familistic orientations.

We apply this reasoning by focusing on variation in expectations and behavior about nonfamily living among (1) blacks, (2) Asian-Americans, (3) four subpopulations of Hispanics, and (4) non-Hispanic whites. Together, these diverse groups span a broad racial and ethnic spectrum, ranging from groups resident in the United States for centuries to those for whom a majority have foreign-born parents.

The Asian-American community in the United States is increasingly heterogeneous, reflecting selective immigration patterns over the last century. Some have experienced high levels of educational attainment, resulting in a range of foreign-language usage patterns that facilitate greater acculturation to American family values (see Martinez-Luz and Goldscheider 1988). Most remain concentrated in the Pacific region, with strong family ties and norms that emphasize family obligations. Given the small number of Asians in the HSB survey sample, we are only able to tap into this heterogeneity with measures of foreign-language use, generation, and regional concentration, rather than by distinguishing specific national origin groups.

The Hispanic classification also contains a heterogeneous array of groups that differ both in the countries they come from and where they are concentrated residentially in the United States. Cubans, for example, have had a distinctive history of immigration and residential settlement, as have Mexicans. There is some evidence that younger persons from different Hispanic origins are converging with each other to form a single Hispanic-American group (Hernandez 1989, Bean and Tienda 1989). In chapter 3, we treated Hispanics as a single group; in this chapter, because of their large numbers in the sample, we are able to test the validity of that approach by examining nest-leaving patterns for four Hispanic groups: Cubans, Puerto Ricans, Mexicans, and a residual category of "other" Hispanics.

Hispanics overall are about six percentage points less likely to expect nonfamily residential autonomy than non-Hispanic whites (68% vs. 62%), and about 11 percent fewer leave home via this route than non-Hispanic whites. Figure 4.1 (and table B4.1) shows that this is largely a Mexican pattern; young adults from Puerto Rico and from other Hispanic origins are no different from non-Hispanic whites.[1] In contrast, Cubans have a

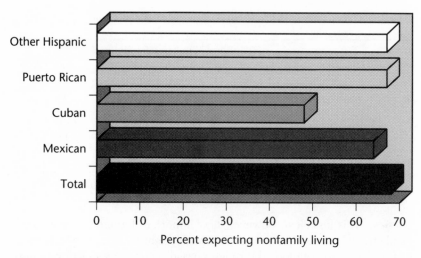

Fig. 4.1.   Percent expecting nonfamily living among Hispanic groups

strikingly lower likelihood of expecting the nonfamily route to residential autonomy (48%). Internal Hispanic differences appear less for behavior, with only Cubans having a significantly greater likelihood of favoring leaving home to marry.

How much of these differences among Hispanics and between Hispanics and others are due to their closeness to the foreign-born generation and to foreign-language use? Are the children of the foreign born and users of a foreign language less likely to expect or achieve nonfamily living? Does the effect of using a foreign language persist into later generations? To answer these questions, we begin our focus on indicators of ethnic and racial intensity, starting with generation and language.

GENERATION AND LANGUAGE

Comparing early generations with later generations allows us to estimate the rate of generational change. How much change occurs from the immigrant generation to later generations? Does the velocity of generational change vary from one group to another, and do differences between groups in the speed of generational change tell us something about their communities? To answer these questions, we use an indicator variable that distinguishes young adults with at least one foreign-born parent from those with both parents born in the United States.[2]

Using a foreign language extensively is also an indicator of closeness to the origin culture and a powerful means for maintaining ethnic distinc-

Table 4.1.   Group differences in generation status and foreign-language
            usage (unweighted)

Group	Foreign-born parent	Language use index[a]
Total	24.7	1.00
Asians	70.3	3.20
Blacks	14.0	0.15
Mexicans	34.2	3.86
Cubans	92.0	6.13
Puerto Ricans	59.8	4.41
Other Hispanics	38.7	2.33

[a] For this table, the average value on the language use scale of 0.38 was indexed at 1.00.

tiveness. It is less clear, however, how important foreign language use is in all circumstances. In more densely settled ethnic areas, in which ethnic distinctiveness is reinforced through myriad social processes (e.g., ethnic schools, businesses, and other formal and informal networks), language may be less important. Families can speak English (perhaps maintaining certain key phrases or intonations) and still create strong ties to their origin culture in their children. Hence, we ask, What are the circumstances in which language use relates strongly to ethnic distinctiveness, and what are the circumstances in which it does not?

Much detail was available to measure foreign-language use. We drew on ten separate questions that tapped its frequency in specific contexts, including family, school, peer groups, and stores, thereby capturing major structural contexts of the ethnic community. From these details, we constructed a scale indicating average level of foreign-language use across these ten contexts.[3]

There is substantial variation among these central groups. Overall, 25 percent of these young adults had a foreign-born parent (table 4.1).[4] The vast majority of young Cuban-Americans reaching the high school senior year in the early 1980s had foreign-born parents (92%), and Asian-Americans showed a level nearly as high (70%); in contrast, only 14 percent of blacks did not have two native-born parents.

All of these young adults reached their senior year in an American high school. Nevertheless, there is substantial variation in language use, although this is clearly a different dimension from generation. The same groups are at the extremes: blacks are least likely to have a foreign-born parent and make the least use of a foreign language; Cubans have the reverse pattern. Although Asian-American young adults are, by a considerable margin, more likely to be children of foreign-born parents than are Mexicans (70% vs. 34%), they use a foreign language less than Mexican young adults. This shows that declining language use and distance from the foreign-born generation do not always go hand in hand and should be treated separately in an analysis of ethnicity.

Using a foreign language strongly influences both expectations and behavior, with somewhat greater effects on expectations than on behavior (fig. 4.2, table B4.2). Among those who use a foreign language maximally, only 52 percent expect nonfamily residential autonomy, compared with 70 percent among those who never use a foreign language, a range of 18 percentage points. The range is only 11 percentage points between these two groups for actual behavior, with 66 percent of those attaining residential autonomy taking the nonfamily route among wholly English users compared with 55 percent among these who use a non-English language maximally.

Using a foreign language decreases the nonfamily route among nearly all groups, Hispanic, Asian, and non-Hispanic whites. The only exceptions are Puerto Rican Hispanics and the few black students who report the extensive use of a foreign language, each of whom resembles those who only use English (table B4.3). Thus, ethnic intensity measured by the use of a foreign language increases the probability of remaining—and particularly of expecting to remain—in the parental home until marriage for most but not all groups.

It is also the case that using a foreign language continues to influence

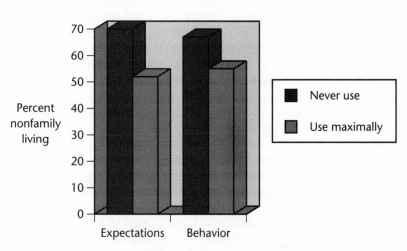

Fig. 4.2.   Non-English language use and nonfamily living

59

routes to residential independence in later generations, although its influence declines substantially after the early generation.[5] Those who are both children of the foreign born and extensive users of a non-English language are 26 percentage points less likely to expect the nonfamily route than others of their generation who only speak English; in later generations, the comparable range in foreign language use leads only to a 12-percentage-point difference. Hence, while the effect of using a foreign language remains a potent force in the lives of the later born, its effect is greatly enhanced when it is supported by other unmeasured aspects of first generation communities.

However, use of a non-English language serves to protect immigrant groups from some of the assimilatory forces that impinge on them. Increased socioeconomic status normally increases the likelihood of expecting and experiencing the nonfamily route to residential independence (chap. 3), but this is much less the case among users of a non-English language, at least behaviorally. Parental resources among non-English-language users do not get translated into increased nonfamily autonomy, evidently, unlike among those who only use English.

GENERATIONAL SUCCESSION

The simple fact of generational change has much less consistent effect. Among some groups, those with foreign-born parents are less likely to expect the nonfamily route, but this is not the case for all (table B4.3). The early generation is more familistic than later generations on this dimension among Mexicans, Cubans, and other Hispanics, even controlling for their higher level of non-English-language use; and generational differences are particularly marked for Cubans. However, generation appears to have no effect for Asians or Puerto Ricans (once their use of a foreign language is taken into account), and among non-Hispanic whites, those with a foreign-born parent are actually more likely to expect to and actually leave home before marriage.

There are two interrelated interpretations for the higher level of nonfamily autonomy among the early generation of white non-Hispanics. First, some are likely to have come from places of origin where the new norms about leaving home before marriage may have emerged as they have in the United States. Most come from England, Germany, and Ireland. If so, such immigrants should not be treated as coming from societies where leaving home is delayed until marriage.

Some recent immigrants may also be more likely to expect and experience later age at marriage. Evidence we shall discuss later (chap. 7) shows that marriage age is a critical variable influencing routes to residential independence. Children of foreign-born parents expect significantly later ages at marriage than young adults of later generations. Hence, even in this case, the linkage holds between having a foreign-born parent and the maintenance of origin values, but the values brought from some places of origins are later marriage age rather than a preference for intergenerational coresidence among young adults.

The only group for which the nonfamily route increases with generation in the United States is Hispanics and among Hispanics, only non–Puerto Ricans. Puerto Ricans, even of the first generation, resemble the dominant groups in American society, showing little sign of their Hispanic origin. Asians, in contrast, are quite familistic in their expectations (if not their behavior), and the lack of a generational shift paralleling Hispanics seems unusual. What these results seem to indicate is that generation per se is not a very meaningful indicator of the velocity of assimilation: where foreign-language use is sustained, ethnic distinctiveness can be maintained even into later generations; but the high level of English acquisition among Asians allows assimilation on this dimension in less than a generation.

Further evidence of the rapidity of assimilation that can occur very early in the immigration process is the strong effect that our measure of socioeconomic status has in the first generation, at least for residential expectations (table B4.3). Young adults from first-generation families that are struggling economically are very unlikely to expect nonfamily autonomy; among immigrant families that have achieved a high level of socioeconomic status, expectations are the same as for those in second-generation American families. This pattern is also characteristic of Asians in general: increases in socioeconomic status have a greater effect on expectations, reinforcing the portrait of Asians' rapid integration with other groups in the United States.

We have focused so far in the chapter on groups defined by race and national origin. Although we will analyze the impact of religion and religiosity later (chap. 5), one group bridges the ethnic and religious—the Jews. We examined the impact of generation and non-English-language use on differences between Jews and other non-Catholics. These data show that once generation and the use of a non-English language are included in the analysis, Jews become significantly more likely than others to expect nonfamily autonomy; before these factors were taken into account, Jews were only distinctive in their residential behavior. This suggests that unlike most other non-Asian, non-Hispanic groups, Jews, while likely to be members of a later generation, report some use of a non-English language. Evidently, ethnicity is operating in a different way among members of this group.

STRUCTURE AND ETHNIC INTERACTION

Culture, in terms of closeness to foreign origins, is one dimension of ethnic intensity; the other key dimension is structural, being close to one another and interacting in ethnic communities. The data are less well suited for measuring the extent to which people are embedded in, or distant from, relationships with others in their ethnic community (beyond the measure of frequency of non-English-language use). There are no measures indicating how many close friends or neighbors share one's ethnic background. However, we developed one measure that indicates whether the young adult lived in the census division in which most members of the group live, affording a crude measure of geographic concentration. This residential indicator was measured at the time of the senior year in high school. On this measure, 51 percent of Asians were living in the Pacific census division; 42 percent of Mexicans in the West-South-Central division; 68 percent of Cubans in the South Atlantic division; and 71 percent of Puerto Ricans in the Middle Atlantic division. About 40 percent of blacks were living in the South. Other Hispanics were too widely scattered regionally to measure clustering at this level.

Living in the region of one's ethnic group concentration substantially reduces the likelihood that young adults will expect or experience non-family residential autonomy (table B4.2). And unlike the effect of using a foreign language, region has stronger, not weaker, effects on behavior than on expectations. Thus, residing in communities where many co-ethnics live has an independent effect beyond the use of a foreign language and generation in America.

It is also the case that the effect of using a foreign language is much weaker among those not living in their ethnic region, compared with its effect within the region (table B4.3). Among those living in their ethnic region, those who use a foreign language maximally (with their family and friends and in the community) are nearly 30 percentage points less likely to expect the nonfamily route than those who use only English. Such foreign-language use only reduces this outcome by 12 percentage points relative to those speaking only English among those living outside their region of concentration. Hence, the effect of using a foreign language is powerful even outside the region of ethnic concentration. The effects of foreign-language use are strongly enhanced when it is supported by the greater intensity of interaction that characterizes ethnically concentrated communities. This pattern parallels the relationship between language use and generation, suggesting that indicators of ethnic intensity are mutually reinforcing.

Blacks, unlike immigrant groups, are not distinctive from non-Hispanic

62

whites generationally or in terms of foreign-language use, possibly because residential segregation is the dominant structural feature of black communities (Massey and Denton 1989). However, they have had a long history of regional concentration in the South, and we can measure the effects of living in their region of concentration.[6]

In general, residing in the South reduces nonfamily autonomy as a route out of the home, both in terms of expectations and behavior (chap. 3). Are black patterns distinctive in the South? The data show that there are no specific regional effects for blacks: the route to residential independence among blacks does not differ between southern and nonsouthern regions, either for expectations or behavior (table B4.3). Only whites living in the South are significantly different from those living in nonsouthern areas. Thus, the gap between blacks and whites is much greater in the South than outside the South. The effect of being black transcends regional differences, as it did among the small number of blacks who use a foreign language.

CONCLUSION

Foreign-language use, ethnic residential concentration, and generation in the United States are key aspects shaping the speed of the assimilation process, at least insofar as it relates to variation in the routes young people take or expect to take to residential autonomy. Where immigrant groups can maintain daily proficiency in their ethnic language, particularly when they have a spatial area within the United States that provides them with high ethnic residential densities, they remain distinctive in their family patterns. Ethnic-language use continues to matter at least somewhat, even beyond the early generation, and serves to reinforce ethnicity at a low level, even outside the ethnic region. But where these supports are lacking—if an ethnic language is not maintained and where there is no ethnic residential clustering—assimilation can occur in less than a generation.

Rapid assimilation is particularly characteristic of Asians. For them, generation in the United States makes no difference; the processes that normally take generations to accomplish are evidently often accomplished in less than one. Not only are they economically successful and increase nonfamily living for this reason but they also adjust their expectations strongly to increases in socioeconomic status; the same pattern characterizes their dynamics of language use.

Hispanics are also subject to strong assimilatory pressures, as their generation in the United States increases and they increase their daily use of the English language. But the establishment of large Hispanic residential areas evidently can shield them from these pressures to a great extent. Outside these areas, however, distinctions *among* Hispanic groups are weakening, and they are all moving in the direction of the general non-black pattern.

The importance of ethnic region reinforces the view of ethnicity that links its continuity to the development of structural processes that continue to bind fellow ethnics together, even in later generations and in the face of using only the English language. Jews provide an important, if tantalizing, example of this phenomenon, since their powerful communal institutions (religious and secular) have the potential to reinforce ethnicity for them more than for most other immigrant groups. Yet our results suggest that their distinctive pattern, which emerges when their "foreignness" in terms of generation and non-English-language use is taken into account, is one *supportive* of nonfamily living. Part of the key to their distinctiveness may lay in the religious basis of their group identity and the values and institutions associated with religion. We turn to the broader issues of religiosity and its impact on residential independence in the next chapter.

5

Religion and Religiosity

An emphasis on familism is widespread in American society, reaching beyond minority ethnic and racial communities. This is because religious institutions (to which a large proportion of Americans belong) and religious values (to which even more subscribe) powerfully reinforce family obligations (Thornton and Fricke 1989, Greeley 1989). Such values strengthen familism on a wide variety of dimensions, stressing closeness and respect for parents, the centrality of the marriage bond, the importance of parenthood, and family-centered roles for women (see chap. 6). In a sense, then, religious values constitute a "religious culture" that reinforces family orientations, much as ethnic cultures do for those coming from more family-centered places of origin.

While religion is a source of family-reinforcing values, American society has become increasingly secular. Secularization usually means (1) that religious groups come to emphasize less literal interpretations of doctrine, (2) that individuals affiliate with less religiously intensive groups, and (3) that individuals come to identify less with religion and with the institutions and values that characterize particular religious systems, distancing themselves from the religious culture. Although most Americans consider themselves religious, together, these dimensions of secularization have led to a decline in the centrality of religion for critical decisions throughout the life course.[1] Hence, there are parallels between secularization and the integration and assimilation of immigrant-ethnic groups.

Residential independence prior to marriage among young adults is therefore consistent with the increasingly secular nature of society, with the weakening of other ties with parents, with a decrease in the importance of marriage in adulthood, and with the general emphasis on individual rather than on family obligations. Secularization results in the increasing independence of young adults both from religion and from the family values and obligations associated with religious commitments. Thus, religious values and the institutions that reinforce them should also strengthen the linkage between residential independence and marriage

65

in the transition to adulthood. Those who consider religion important in their lives, who are affiliated with religious groups (and, in particular, who are identified with a religious group that puts more stress on family-based values), should be less likely both to expect and to experience nonfamily residential autonomy in the transition to adulthood.

While secularization can erode religious values, not all persons become secular, and new forms of religious expression can emerge. The spread of religious fundamentalism is one conspicuous form of religious revival and is clear evidence of the importance of continuing religious activities and religious expressions. The continuous value placed on religion and the proliferation of religious institutions in contemporary American society are among the reminders that religiosity remains important in the lives of individuals.

By "religiosity," we mean both the expression of religious values and identification with religious institutions. Religiosity can be thus thought of as "religious intensity," paralleling our use of "ethnic intensity" (chap. 4). As interaction within ethnic and racial groups forms the basis for maintaining ethnic and racial intensity, interactions within religious institutions can strengthen religion and serve as a mechanism for the transmission of values that reinforce family centrality. In this sense, religiosity implies both cultural and structural dimensions. Religious values, as Will Herberg (1955) argued, can be expressed in personal religious feelings and in the decision to affiliate with a given religious denomination. But they can also be reinforced by involvement in religious institutional structures through church attendance and enrollment in religious schools. Religion and religiosity therefore focus on areas in which individuals and families voluntarily connect themselves to communities that uphold and strengthen familistic values.

When members of a community are linked to each other through religious institutions, such as churches or schools, they may be better able to maintain family-oriented norms. Although less tangible than ethnic geographic concentration and less conspicuous than foreign-born status, religious values may be as powerful in their effect on family processes. Family norms and life-styles may be maintained and transmitted through interaction among those who share similar religious affiliations and through exposure to religious family ideals in school and church.

A substantial body of research has developed documenting strong links between family values, on the one hand, and religious affiliation and religiosity, on the other. Large differences in expectations and attitudes about the timing of marriage and family size as well as average marriage age, proportions marrying, and the incidence of divorce have been documented among white religious groups (Protestants, Catholics, and Jews) and among Catholic ethnic subpopulations such as the Irish, Italians, Portuguese, and French Canadians (Goldscheider and Goldscheider 1985a, Kobrin and Goldscheider 1978). Religiosity influences attitudes toward sex roles (Scanzoni 1975; D'Antonio 1983; Thornton and Camburn 1989; Greeley 1989) as well as adolescent sexual behavior and attitudes (Thornton and Camburn 1987, 1989; Abrahamse, Morrison, and Waite 1988). There is also a substantial literature on the impact of religion on contraceptive use and family size among teenagers and adults, suggesting that religious values, despite changes in the recent period in the United States, retain a powerful influence in the critical decisions that many young adults make about family formation and family values (see, e.g., Goldscheider and Mosher 1988, 1991; Thornton 1989; Castleton and Goldscheider 1989; Abrahamse, Morrison, and Waite 1988).

However, some research has suggested that secularization has led to a homogenization of religious denominations, reducing differences in a wide variety of family-related behaviors. For example, Catholics and Protestants have become increasingly similar in their family size and contraceptive use patterns since the 1960s (Goldscheider and Mosher 1988, 1991). Consistent with these results, we found relatively small overall differences in both expectations for nonfamily living and actual residential autonomy among Jews, Catholics, and others in the non-Hispanic, non-Asian, and nonblack population (chap. 3).

Since significant variation has developed in the United States *within* these large religious categories, the broad designations "Catholics" and "Protestants" may obscure the importance of religious affiliation for family values. Religious denominations within the Protestant group reflect a range of values about familism. Catholicism has also evolved somewhat differently among different subcommunities, as evidenced by the divisions between Italian and Irish Catholics in many American cities. There is also increasing evidence of polarization in the religious observance of American Jews (Goldscheider 1986, Cohen 1983). Those who are not affiliated with either Protestant, Catholic, or Jewish religions are themselves a diverse category. Some of these "others" belong to smaller religious groups, including Buddhists, Moslems, and many other long-established religions, while some claim no religious affiliation.

In addition, the overlap of race or ethnic origin with religious denomination in contemporary America may lead to even more complex differences. Catholics from northern and western Europe differ from Catholics from southern Europe (as suggested by the Irish-Italian distinction), thus forming one type of ethnic cleavage. Hispanic-Americans are also largely Catholic, but their multigeneration residence in Latin America has produced a new element in the American Catholic mosaic. (We examined

Hispanics in detail in chap. 4, emphasizing their ethnic origins rather than their religious distinctiveness.) Race and religion are also tangled, since black Baptists are often quite different religiously from other Baptists. Some research has shown that black Catholics differ both from other blacks and from Catholics of other races (Abrahamse, Morrison, and Waite 1988; Goldscheider and Mosher 1988).

To clarify some of these complexities, we focus in this chapter on the effects of religious variation and religiosity on residential autonomy among black and non-Hispanic white young adults. We move beyond the simple classification of Protestant, Catholic, and Jew to extend religious affiliation in four directions. Among whites, we subdivide Protestants to distinguish more fundamentalist or conservative Protestant denominations from the more "liberal" denominations.[2]

Second, we separate white, non-Hispanic Catholics into two groups—those whose families came from southern Europe where family values are more likely to be emphasized and those whose families came from other regions. Third, we examine the influence of religion on blacks by examining the residential autonomy of black Protestants, black Catholics, and blacks of other religions. Finally, we expand the categories of affiliation for all racial groups to directly examine those who define themselves as "other" (i.e., Buddhists, Mormons, and a small number of "other Christians" who are not Catholic, not Protestant, and not Jewish) and those who respond that they were "none" (i.e., of no religious affiliation).[3] These extensions more closely approximate communities in the sociological sense than the broader categorization of religious groups that we examined in chapter 3.

We also consider three measures of religiosity, tapping the intensity of religious expression personally and institutionally: personal religious self-identification, the frequency of church attendance, and attendance at Catholic schools. In general, our argument is that these reflections of religious intensity should be inversely linked to premarital residential independence expectations and behavior. Residential autonomy should be less likely among those more exposed to religious values by being affiliated with some denomination, in particular, with fundamentalist Protestant denominations and Catholic groups; those who identify themselves as more committed religiously; and those who are more linked to religious institutions by their regular attendance at religious services and by their exposure to a religious education. These considerations lead us to hypothesize that those who are "more religious" on any of these dimensions should be more likely to expect to remain in their parental home until they marry and less likely to experience residential autonomy in the period immediately after high school.

These indicators reflect the multidimensionality of the religiosity/secularization spectrum. We use denomination to capture those Protestant groups that interpret doctrine more and less literally; those who consider that religion is important in their lives are expressing the centrality of religion for them. Those who do not identify with any religious group are distancing themselves from any religious culture and also from the institutions that express it. Similarly, those who never or rarely attend religious services have reduced their exposure to religious institutions, in contrast to those who attend regularly and particularly compared with those who attend religious schools. By distinguishing Catholics by origin and examining denominational affiliation among blacks, we directly link aspects of religiosity to ethnicity and race, illuminating the overlap between two sources of familistic values. These measures were designed to tap the personal expression of religious values and their linkages—their structural connections—to religious institutions. Consistent with our general argument, it is likely that personal and subjective assessments of religiosity will have greater effects on expectations for autonomy than on eventual behavior; structural and institutional indicators of religiosity are likely to have greater effects on actual patterns of premarital residential independence than on expectations.

The institutional structure of religious groups that provide links to members of the community in childhood (e.g., via schools and classes or youth groups) and in adulthood (via community centers, burial societies, missionary teas, or service organizations) is an important mechanism for the translation of expectations into actual behavior. Where there are more institutional supports for individual attitudes, the translation of attitudes to behavior will be stronger; where there is no institutional structure, the translation from norms to behavior will be more difficult. Those with no religious affiliation are therefore likely to have a weaker basis for translating their individualistic norms into actual behavior.

RELIGIOUS AFFILIATION

The data show that the two groups of Protestants—liberal and fundamentalist denominations—have very different family patterns in young adulthood (net of socioeconomic status, gender, ethnicity, and region), although they are distinguished much more by their behavior than by their attitudes (fig. 5.1, table B5.1). The gap between them in the proportions expecting autonomy is small, although it is greater than the overall differences among Protestants, Catholics, and Jews shown earlier (chap. 3); the gap expands dramatically in terms of behavior.[4] A difference of five per-

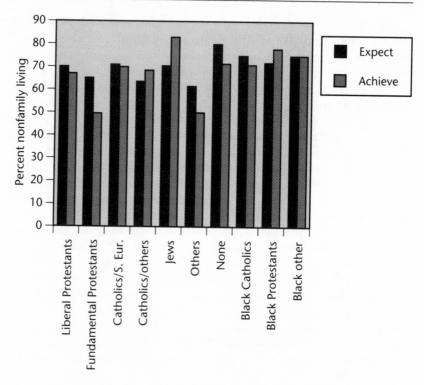

Fig. 5.1. Denominational differences in nonfamily living

centage points (70% of liberal Protestants expect to establish a separate residence before marriage, while only 65% of fundamentalist Protestants expect that pattern) increases to eighteen percentage points in young adulthood. Less than half of the more fundamentalist Protestants actually left home before marriage compared with two-thirds of the more liberal Protestants.

The data also show substantial heterogeneity within the Catholic group when they are distinguished by national origin. We separated Catholics from southern Europe (Italy, Spain, Portugal, and Greece) from other Catholics and examined the probability that they expected or experienced residential autonomy. There is a somewhat greater difference than that between the two Protestant groups in the proportions expecting nonfamily living: 64 percent of southern European Catholics expect autonomy compared with 71 percent of other Catholics. Unlike Protestants, however, there is much less difference among Catholics in actual behavior: 68.5 percent of Catholics from southern European origins actually left home before marriage compared to 70.4 percent of the Catholics from countries of origin less rooted in the extended family.

This pattern, in which Catholic differences are greater in expectations than in behavior, is similar to that which we documented earlier for Hispanics, most of whom are also Catholic (chap. 4), suggesting that this difference between expectations and behavior is a Catholic pattern for both white non-Hispanics and Hispanics. However, all of the Hispanic groups are considerably less likely to experience nonfamily living than are either of the non-Hispanic Catholic groups, a difference due in large part to very different marriage patterns among Hispanic and other Catholics, as we will discuss later (chap. 7).

Jews remain about average in their patterns of expecting nonfamily living (resembling liberal Protestants and other Catholics, with 71% expecting premarital residential independence), but they are far more likely to experience residential independence as unmarried persons in young adulthood than any of the Catholic or Protestant groups (83% compared with 70% or less). The results also confirm the importance of distinguishing between those of "other" religions and those of no religious affiliation. Only 62 percent of "other" religions expect nonfamily living compared with 80 percent of those with no religious affiliation; similarly, only half of those we included as "other" religions actually experienced residential autonomy compared with 72 percent of those who expressed no religious affiliation. Differences between the unaffiliated and liberal Protestants are much greater for expectations than later behavior. Since the parents of these young adults are less likely to be unaffiliated, the expression of nonaffiliation may reflect a temporary disaffection from religion in young adulthood. If so, the rejection of religious affiliation may have weakened by the time residential decisions are actually being made.

Blacks, as we have noted earlier (chap. 3), have relatively higher levels of expectations for nonfamily living and actual behavior. But blacks are increasingly heterogeneous religiously, with a growing proportion affiliating with the Catholic church. Is there internal heterogeneity among blacks distinguished by religion as there is among Protestants (distinguished by religious fundamentalism) and among Catholics (distinguished by ethnic origin)?

The data show that religion is a much weaker axis of differentiation for the black community in terms of premarital residential independence than for non-Hispanic whites. The Protestant-Catholic differences that characterize white young adults are much less among blacks, and there are no systematic patterns linking expectations and behavior among these young black Protestants, black Catholics, and blacks of other religions. The black status of young adults appears largely to override in importance

71

the religious characteristics of blacks (see Goldscheider and Mosher 1988). The overwhelming salience of race among American young adults vitiates the differentiating effects of religion.

Religious affiliation, then, has different meaning, depending on the context. It can contain sharp internal differences, as among Protestants, the various non-Christian groups, or Catholic origin groups, or it can be of relatively little consequence, as among blacks. When there are differences by religious affiliation, they suggest that more "liberal" religious groups are linked to greater individualism in the choice of living arrangements in young adulthood. This is the case for Protestants; those of "other" religions are also relatively familistic in both their expectations and behavior.

This analysis of religious affiliation also indicates that for all groups except for Catholics, the differences that appeared were greater for the experience of nonfamily living than for expectations. It appears that these differences arise less from the specific norms associated with these religious cultures than from differences in the structure of young people's lives among these groups during early adulthood. If so, we should consider indicators of religiosity—religious self-identity and structure—directly.

RELIGIOSITY

We have been using religious affiliation and denominational differences as indicators of various levels of commitment to familistic values, but clearly affiliation is a crude and not fully satisfactory measure of the intensities of religious expression. A response to a question about religious denominational identity by a high school student (e.g., "I am a Methodist") may mean little more than the acknowledgment of a nominal or even former family membership. It may not reveal much about the actual connections of young adults to that denomination, in terms of personal attendance at religious services and involvement in church activities, or about the extent to which the values associated with that religious group actually inform decisions about living arrangements.

Religious institutional involvement together with the intensity of religious feelings young adults express may be the important pathways by which religion influences young people's family relationships and as a result, residential autonomy in young adulthood. If so, the differences we have observed so far by religious denomination may simply reflect the fact that these denominations vary in the intensity of commitment they command and the fervor of religious feelings they evoke. It is also possible that young people who rarely attend church services and do not think of themselves as religious are less influenced by their denominational affiliation compared with the average for their denomination.

RELIGIOUS SELF-IDENTITY

To measure the sense of involvement and agreement with the teachings of religion, we used information on the extent to which a young person agrees with the statement, "I think of myself as a religious person."[5] Those with a stronger religious self-identity are less likely to expect non-family living than those whose religious self-identity is weaker (fig. 5.2, table B5.2). However, the impact of religious self-identity on actual behavior was much weaker. The average young adult characterized himself or herself as "somewhat" religious; but those who felt that they were "not at all" religious were nearly 10 percentage points more likely to expect premarital residential independence than those who consider themselves to be "very much a religious person" (72.5% vs. 62.9%). The comparable difference in actually experiencing residential autonomy, however, was only 2 percentage points (66.3% vs. 64.0%).

The effects of religious self-identity vary, however, by religious denomination. For some religious groups, religious self-identity had little impact on expectations about nonfamily living (table B5.3). This was the case both for the white non-Hispanic Catholic groups and for those with no religious affiliation. In contrast, greater religiosity substantially decreased expectations for premarital residential independence among the

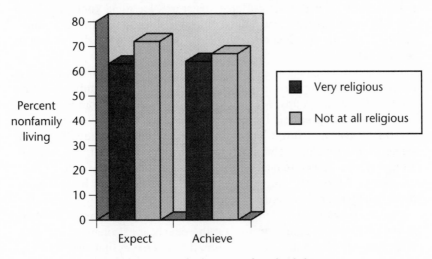

Fig. 5.2. Personal religiosity and nonfamily living

73

two Protestant groups, Jews, those of other religions, blacks, and Hispanics. It may be that family values are reinforced among Catholics in many ways that are less connected to religious feelings, so that even Catholics who do not consider themselves very religious share in the overall Catholic pattern. In a similar way, those few who express strong religious feelings despite having no religious affiliation may be abstracting religion almost completely from the rest of their lives. Their religious feelings perhaps are expressed more as poetry or mysticism and do not connect to family values and premarital residential independence.

There is also considerable variation among groups in the effect of religious self-identity on actually experiencing nonfamily living. As with expectations, the two white Catholic groups and those with no religious affiliation do not differ in their routes to residential independence by levels of religious self-identity, and they are joined by black Catholics and more fundamentalist Protestants (table B5.3). This suggests that the strong religious institutional structures associated with Catholicism dominate over personal self-identity in producing as well as expecting nonfamily living in early adulthood. These structures evidently influence black Catholics, whose levels of nonfamily living are far below those of all other blacks.

Fundamentalist Protestants show the same pattern as Catholics in that religious self-identity has little or no effect on the experience of nonfamily living. This finding suggests that the growing strength of fundamentalist groups among young adults, on college campuses (e.g., the Campus Crusade for Christ) and in community organizations (e.g., Operation Rescue), is generating powerful institutional structures for some young adults in the late twentieth century, influencing decisions about living arrangements among those affiliated with them, no matter what their religious self-identity.

In contrast, religious self-identity has a strong impact on experiencing residential autonomy among liberal as well as black Protestants, Jews, and the two Hispanic groups, Mexicans and Cubans, all of whom experience significantly less premarital residential autonomy among those who identify themselves as more religious than among those who identify themselves as less religious. The institutional structures associated with these groups are less linked to familistic values, so that only those with a strong religious self-identity express their commitment to family by remaining residentially dependent until marriage.

Hence, religious self-identity influences expectations for, and actual, nonfamily living in similar ways, but the effects are stronger on expectations than on behavior. This pattern is the reverse of that shown by denomination, in which there were greater behavioral than attitudinal differences. Each may reflect the same process. If religious denominations are more distinctive in terms of the structures influencing behavior than they are in terms of doctrine, at least as regards the family, then the strength of feelings about religion, not religious doctrine, matters for *expectations* about nonfamily living. But the social and institutional dimensions that are such an important part of the religious life may be more powerful in reinforcing *behavior* that is consistent with familistic values. Hence, denominations are more important than religious self-identity when young adults are making decisions about their new living arrangements. We attempt to clarify this institutional dimension of religion by examining the effects of frequency of attendance at religious services;[6] for Catholics, we examined as well whether they attended a Catholic high school.

CHURCH ATTENDANCE

The regularity of attendance at religious services has a strong impact on expectations for nonfamily living, even controlling for the effects of religious self-identity. (See fig. 5.3 and table B5.2.) On average, young people attend religious services a little more than twice a month. Holding religious self-identity constant, the analysis suggests that those who attend religious services regularly (as often as twice a week) are 14 percentage points less likely to expect to set up an independent residence before they marry than are those who essentially never attend. So whatever their religious self-identity, young adults who are exposed regularly to familis-

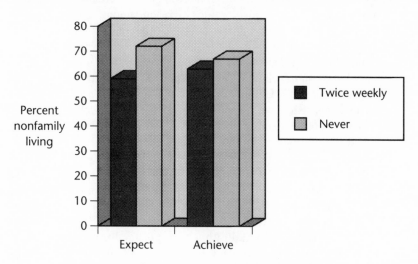

Fig. 5.3.   Attendance at religious services and nonfamily living

tic values through religious service attendance are more likely to expect a more familistic sequence of marriage and residential independence. However, as with religious self-identity, the effects of church attendance on actual nonfamily living are weak (although in the same direction) and not statistically significant. Those attending religious services twice a week are only 3 percentage points less likely to experience living in a nonfamily residence than those who never attend (63.4% vs. 66.2%).

Church attendance is not uniform in its effects on expecting residential autonomy before marriage, however, differing by religious affiliation much in the same way that religious self-identity did (table B5.3). Again, higher levels of religiosity as expressed by attendance at religious services decrease the expectation of nonfamily living among Protestants, Jews, those of other affiliations, Hispanics, and blacks. Catholics who are not from southern Europe also follow this pattern, unlike the case for religious self-identity. Only Catholics from southern Europe and those with no religious affiliation are not influenced in their thinking about routes to residential independence by regular attendance at religious services. Attendance appears to have less salience for these Catholics since high levels of attendance do not actually reflect greater commitments to the group, given the religious requirement at least to attend mass, a requirement not felt so strongly among some Catholics. The lack of effect among those who report no religious affiliation is consistent with the pattern linking religious self-identity to both expecting and experiencing nonfamily living.

The weak overall effect of church attendance on actually experiencing nonfamily living masks considerable variation among groups as well. Among liberal Protestants, Jews, those of other affiliations, and black Catholics, attendance at religious services at the end of high school reduces the later likelihood of experiencing residential autonomy before marriage. Variation in religious service attendance has little effect on Hispanic groups and other Catholics or on fundamentalist and black Protestants. This is consistent with the patterns found for expecting nonfamily residential independence, except that the two Catholic groups are reversed and the effects are generally weaker.

The weaker impact of religious service attendance on behavior than on expectations is not consistent with the hypothesis we presented, since religious institutions should have more power over behavior than over attitudes; regular exposure should reflect this fact. We do not know, however, how stable these patterns of religious attendance are over time and how much they reflect parental rather than personal preferences. Young adulthood is a volatile stage, and many patterns change when young adults leave home for dormitories or barracks prior to establishing an in-

dependent residence. Most religious institutions provide less program-
ming and fellowship for young single adults than for married couples and
younger children. By the time young adults are actually making decisions
about residential independence, the patterns of religious service attendance measured while they were in high school may be irrelevant, with
no lingering effects. Data on changes in religious service attendance over
time are needed to test this interpretation.

CATHOLIC SCHOOLS

Attendance at Catholic schools is often taken as a major formative experience, a structure that has the daily opportunity to influence those within
its walls. The effect of attending a Catholic school is strong for both expectations and behavior, but the direction is the opposite of other measures of religiosity for Catholics, since it *increases* the probability of expecting and actually leaving home before marriage. Subsequent analysis
shows that this result for expectations is solely a reflection of the extraordinarily late age at marriage expected among those attending Catholic
schools (chap. 7).

The effect of attending Catholic schools is distinctive among blacks,
making them more like whites than is the case among those who do not
attend Catholic school. Attendance at Catholic schools reduces nonfamily
living among blacks rather than increasing it (fig. 5.4, table B5.3). The
very high level of premarital residential independence among blacks is
reduced among those with a Catholic school background because it in-

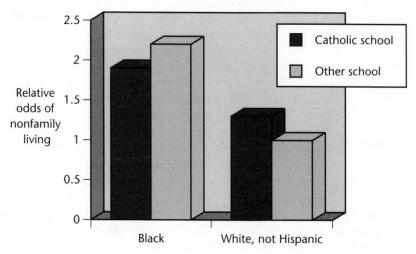

Fig. 5.4.   Racial differences in the effect of Catholic school attendance on nonfamily living

77

creases their likelihood of marriage. Paradoxically, then, by increasing the likelihood of marriage among blacks and decreasing it among nonblacks, blacks and whites who attend Catholic schools are more similar to each other than those who do not attend.

DOES RELIGIOSITY EXPLAIN DENOMINATIONAL DIFFERENCES?

Given the varied influence of religious self-identity and regularity of service attendance on nonfamily living among young adults, we can now ask, How much of the religious group differences in nonfamily living reflect differences between the groups on these dimensions of religiosity, and how much of the group differences remain after we take into account these differences?

When we take into account the strength of religious self-identification, the frequency of church attendance, and Catholic school attendance, there is little change in the influence of religious affiliation on expecting and experiencing nonfamily living. The patterns of differences in residential independence among religious groups described above were not influenced in any major way by differences among the denominations on these measures of religiosity. (Compare tables B5.1 and B5.2.) Only in two cases, among the nonaffiliated and among fundamentalist Protestants, did taking into account these processes alter *the size* of the differences. The distinctively higher probability of expectations for nonfamily living among the religiously nonaffiliated is reduced (but not eliminated) when these measures of religiosity are included. This suggests that part of their very high level of expectations is accounted for by their considerable distance from religious organizations and weak religious self-identity. The same process operates (but in the opposite direction) among fundamentalist Protestants, suggesting that their distinctiveness is largely a reflection of their high levels of religious intensity. However, the religiosity variables do not similarly reduce the likelihood of nonfamily living among Catholics. The effect of being Catholic on residential autonomy may reflect more than specific religious doctrines and include ethnic-cultural elements as additional sources of Catholic values about family obligations.

RELIGION, FAMILISM, AND AUTONOMY

We have shown that religious self-identification and participation in religious institutions reduce the likelihood of expecting and experiencing residential independence before marriage. Evidently, religious intensity serves to reinforce family values that maintain the residential linkage between the generations until marriage. However, religiosity and attendance at religious services have much stronger effects on reducing expectations than actually achieving it; and their effects are much more evident in some religious groups than in others.

The link between religion and familism early in adulthood is clearly a variable one, conditioned not only by the denominations in which young people grow up but also their ties to their churches and synagogues, the extent to which religious feelings have become a part of their life orientations, and how much of this changes during the rapid series of life course transitions in early adulthood. Religion and religiosity should connect to nonfamily living through family values, which, in turn, are shaped by the structural contexts of institutions and community networks that reinforce family socialization. Evidently, not all religious affiliations link to family values, and religious intensities are not necessarily reflections of familism; religion does not help us understand nonfamily living nearly as well as ethnic origins. Our analysis suggests some factors that may have shaped the growth of nonfamily living over time and perhaps some of the broader connections between religion and familism. Nevertheless, the keys to understanding nonfamily living among young adults may be in a more direct examination of familism per se.

6

Familism
Parental and Gender Relationships

Familism is the central theme in our interpretation of differences among ethnic and religious groups in the pathways young adults take to residential autonomy. We argue that the growth of nonfamily institutions and activities has reduced the centrality of family roles in many people's lives. Although the personal bonds of family may still be important for people's emotional well-being in the modern world, they have lost the political, social, and economic connections they had in the societies from which most ethnic communities originated and in which religious ideals took shape. Hence, those who are less closely linked to familistic ethnic or religious communities should experience higher levels of nonfamily living than members of other communities. The patterns we analyzed in the two preceding chapters strongly reinforce these interpretations.

Are there ways to examine the relationship between familism and residential pathways more directly, rather than by using ethnicity and religiosity as proxies for familistic values? Our measures of ethnicity and religiosity are relatively blunt, based on language use, generation, and regional residence for ethnicity and church attendance and self-identification as "a religious person" for religiosity. There may be many who have strong commitments to family centrality who fall outside these groups. If familism is accounting for the effects of ethnicity and religiosity on the choice of nonfamily living, then direct measures of familism should be related even more strongly than ethnic and religious measures to expecting and experiencing it. In turn, introducing measures of familism should help clarify its relative importance for understanding the distinctive residential patterns among ethnic and religious communities.

Familism itself is a difficult concept to pin down, since it is multifaceted, including relationships to extended kin as well as to nuclear family members. The "decline of the family" is often conceptualized in terms of the weakening of extended family relationships, including the decline in residential family complexity as well as in the power and prestige of elders relative to younger adults.[1] But another important dimension of familism

80

that appears to have been changing in the recent past involves nuclear family relationships, so that parental roles have become less important in people's lives, the definition of adulthood has increasingly become separated from marriage for women as for men, and even the universality of marital roles has come into question. It is on these latter dimensions of familism that we will concentrate.

TWO FAMILY REVOLUTIONS

Our approach to familism focuses on two revolutions in the norms underlying family life currently under way in Western societies. One revolution focuses on the relationships between parents and children; the second is reshaping those between men and women. Both of these revolutions have been viewed as part of the decline in familism, that is, in the decreasing importance of family relationships in adult life. They both also increase egalitarianism between family members (chap. 3). Young adults with less traditional attitudes about these two revolutions should be more likely to separate the establishment of an independent residence from beginning a new family via marriage. Further, ethnicity and religiosity may have been indexing variations in participation in these family revolutions, so that members of some ethnic and religious groups support more traditional relationships between parents and children and between men and women, relationships that emphasize hierarchy, dominance, and control. Hence, the differences that we documented among ethnic and religious groups might be reduced considerably or even eliminated when these underlying differences in familism are taken into account.

THE PARENT-CHILD REVOLUTION

The enormous growth of nonfamily living among young adults, by decreasing their joint residence with their parents, may reflect an important change in parent-child relationships—from an emphasis on children's obedience toward a greater stress on independence (Alwin 1988). As parents have lost power over their children's decisions about marriage partners and occupational choice in young adulthood, there is less need for parents to monitor their children's behavior closely to ensure compliance. Some argue that the new form familism has taken in modern societies should be characterized as "intimacy at a distance" (Rosenmayr and Kocheis 1963), emphasizing the importance of *choice* in such interactions as visits and telephone calls compared to the ubiquity of interaction among coresidents. Further, in families with substantial intergenerational conflict about life-styles and values, increased residential separation, by increasing privacy and geographic distance, becomes a mechanism for defusing parent-child conflict.

In more hierarchical families, however, coresidence is likely to be important. Parents need to supervise their children's activities more thoroughly, since they are likely to expect to exercise parental authority more extensively and longer, often until their children's marriage and beyond. While their children probably are unlikely to view residential closeness as positively as their parents do (since it is their own autonomy that is being sacrificed), many children raised in such families view intergenerational closeness as appropriate, even desirable. Being close to parents early in adulthood often provides young men increased access to economic opportunities through family networks and brings young women the promise of ongoing support in their future family roles.

THE GENDER REVOLUTION

Another central element of family change in the process of modernization is the growth of gender egalitarianism, in which the roles of men and women have become increasingly similar outside and even inside the home. Families have begun to move away from gender roles that emphasize differences between the sexes toward more egalitarian definitions of work and family roles for both men and women (Thornton 1989). These changes appear to result in an overall decline in familism, since they have increased women's involvement in nonfamily activities without commensurate increase in men's involvement in family roles (Goldscheider and Waite 1991).

Clearly, egalitarianism is an incomplete, if ongoing, process, even in the most modern societies. Women have become increasingly independent economically, with unmarried women supporting themselves much like men and married women sharing the provider role with their husbands. Nevertheless, female roles still revolve around activities and responsibilities within the home and the broader family network, while male roles concentrate on occupational and other activities outside the home. Even in childhood, the roles of sons and daughters are generally different within most families. Sons are given more independence than daughters, and daughters assume more family-centered roles, with more household tasks and baby-sitting expected of them than of their brothers (White and Brinkerhoff 1981, Goldscheider and Waite 1991). These differing orientations affect the timing that young men and women follow as they assume work and family roles in adulthood, so that young men marry at later ages than young women. Hence, traditional gender-based role differentiation allows young men more time for residential independence before marriage and often gives them greater access to the resources that could support it.

Increasingly, young women are emerging from more modern families who are less likely to expect to marry, who marry at older ages when they do, and who treat their careers as seriously as they do family formation and family obligations (Thornton 1989). Similarly, young men from such families are less likely to expect family- and children-oriented lives for their wives and perhaps even envision a more extensive role for themselves in shaping their children and their homes. The more egalitarian the roles of young women and men, the more similar their life course trajectories are likely to be. Gender egalitarianism should lead to greater equality in routes to residential independence, as in other dimensions of work and family life.

THE REVOLUTIONS AND RESIDENTIAL AUTONOMY

Young adults are more likely to expect nonfamily living for themselves than their parents are for them, and young men are more likely to expect and experience it than young women (chaps. 2 and 3). Here we go beyond these general differences to examine how leaving home before marriage is influenced by differences in familism resulting from the egalitarian revolutions in parent-child and male-female relationships. Specifically, we address three questions: (1) How do attitudes toward the importance of intergenerational family closeness affect pathways to residential autonomy? (2) What are the contexts that accentuate differences in routes to residential independence for young men and women? (3) How does holding egalitarian gender role attitudes influence expectations and actual patterns of residential independence?

PARENT-CHILD RESIDENTIAL CLOSENESS

The information we have available to indicate preferences for intergenerational residential closeness is based on a section of the HSB survey questionnaire that asked young adults about a range of issues that might be important in their future lives (such as becoming successful or contributing to their communities). One of these questions was, "How important is it to you to live close to parents and relatives?" The possible responses were "not at all important," "somewhat important," and "very important," which we have scaled to indicate increasing importance of closeness to parents (0, 1, 2). These young adults view living near their families as "somewhat important"; the overall average on this scale is 0.85. Young women consider this issue to be somewhat more important than do young

83

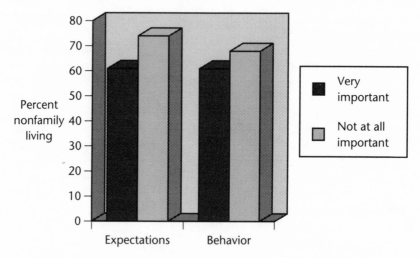

Fig. 6.1.   Influence of importance of parent-child closeness on nonfamily living

men, suggesting that parents and relatives can offer more support for the family roles of young women (homemaking, baby-sitting) than for the occupational roles of young men. Ethnic and religious differences are sharper: young Hispanics and Asian-Americans rate the importance of this dimension most highly (0.97 and 1.01); white Catholics are intermediate (0.88); and Jews and white Protestants consider this aspect of familism less important than any of the other groups (0.81 and 0.80) except blacks (0.76).[2]

Do these attitudes toward living close to parents and relatives as of the senior year in high school influence young people's pathways to residential independence, either in terms of expectations or later behavior? Young adults who felt that living close to parents and relatives was very important were considerably less likely to expect nonfamily living for themselves than those who responded that such residential closeness was not at all important—61 percent versus 74 percent (fig. 6.1; see also table B9.1).[3] The difference was not as great in terms of actual behavior over the next six years but was still fairly large: among those who became residentially independent, 61 percent of those who rated living near parents and family as very important took the nonfamily route to residential independence, compared with 68 percent of those who felt such residential closeness was not at all important.

This dimension of familism, in which young adults consider closeness to parents to be an important part of their adult residential arrangements, has a dampening effect on experiencing nonfamily independence, and particularly on expecting it. Since such closeness is more important for

Asians and Hispanics, is their distinctively lower level of nonfamily living a reflection of this dimension of familism? Assuming that the impact of rating parent-child closeness is the same for each group, nearly half of the difference between Hispanics and white non-Hispanics results from the differences they attach to the importance of living near parents; however, differences in behavior are relatively unaffected.[4] Almost all the difference between Asian-Americans and other young adults in residential expectations can be attributed to this factor. However, data on attitudes toward parental closeness do not provide any solution to the puzzle Asians pose vis-à-vis residential behavior (chaps. 3 and 4). Taking these attitudes into account has little effect on other patterns we have examined, except for blacks; nearly one-third of the greater likelihood that young blacks expect and experience nonfamily residential autonomy is linked with the *lower* importance they attach to being close to family members.

The importance young adults attach to living near parents and relatives has a much stronger effect on expectations among Hispanics and Asian-Americans than it does among others. Whereas rating such closeness as "very important" decreases the likelihood of expecting nonfamily living by 12.5 percentage points compared with those rating it "not at all important" among the group as a whole, the difference among Asians and Hispanics is more than 20 percentage points (fig. 6.2). Among blacks, in contrast, such closeness makes significantly less difference than among non-Hispanic whites.

Thus, for blacks and non-Hispanic whites, the connection between be-

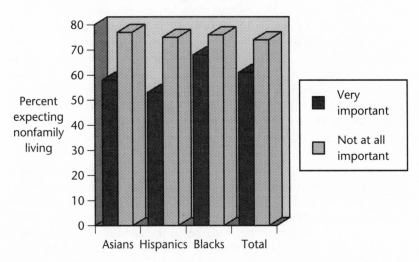

Fig. 6.2. Group differences in the influence of parent-child closeness on expecting nonfamily living

85

ing "close" and being in the same house is weak, consistent with the idea of "intimacy at a distance," while for Hispanics and Asian-Americans, "living close" seems to mean living with parents. However, these effects on expectations do not carry over to explaining actual residential independence. Like personal religiosity and even attendance at religious services, the feelings Asians and Hispanics express during their senior year about living close to family do not have any more impact on what they actually do than such feelings have for any other group. Actual choices appear to respond more to other, structural factors. Asians and Hispanics who expected early residential independence and rated family closeness as not important ended up taking routes to residential independence very much like others in their group who had wanted to live close to, and with, their parents. Their lives appear much more similar than their ideas.

GENDER DIFFERENCES IN CONTEXT

A second aspect of the family revolution relates to gender differences and ways in which men's and women's roles are becoming more similar. Gender differences in nonfamily living, like ethnic differences, pose the question of the relative importance of attitudes and contexts for understanding differences in the expectations and decisions of young men and women. Our general argument has been that gender differences reflect the ways that young people are differentially socialized with regard to residential independence, with greater independence encouraged for sons than for daughters. Moreover, parents may make differential investments in their sons and daughters, with consequences for the decisions young adults make about their careers and their families. Even among young men and women whose ideals are similar, considerations of their parents' responses and how their future lives might differ will affect what they can realistically expect in young adulthood. Young women whose ideals would lean toward nonfamily independence might not expect it, since they may anticipate that it will be more difficult to leave home as early as their male classmates, given that their parents have more traditional attitudes and may be willing to subsidize their daughters' early steps to independence less than they would their sons.

Young women might also have practical concerns about the timing of marriage, since it is important for women to enter the marriage market earlier than the men in their high school class. Both men and women expect husbands to be several years older than their wives. Hence young women must enter the marriage market at the age that young men who are ready to marry prefer. By the time their male agemates are ready to marry, they will be looking for women several years younger than themselves. As a result, part of the difference in the extent to which young men and women expect and achieve nonfamily independence should be related to the very different timing of their marriage markets, no matter what their ideals.[5] Hence these considerations should not lead even the most egalitarian young men and women to expect exactly the same life course pattern, requiring them to be sensitive as well to the contexts—of class, family, and marriage markets—that influence their choices.

Together, these considerations of parental attitudes, resource availability, and marriage markets suggest the need to analyze the effects of context on gender differences in residential autonomy. Specifically, we ask: (1) Do the children of parents with more resources show less gender differentiation than those whose parents are at lower levels of socioeconomic status, perhaps because higher-status parents provide more equally for their sons' and their daughters' independence before marriage? (2) Are familistic ethnic groups more likely to reinforce separate gender roles? Do the strong family orientations among Hispanics, for example, result in greater gender differences in their expected and actual routes to residential independence; and do the strong traditions of family cohesion among Asians contrast with black Americans to produce different gender patterns? (3) How do gender differences in living arrangements vary among religious groups and among those with different levels of religiosity? Traditional indicators of religiosity should lead women to place higher priorities on family obligations than on careers, translating into greater dependence of young women than of young men on their families before they marry.

We begin our examination of gender differences in residential autonomy by considering the effect of socioeconomic context. The data show that gender differences in expectations are much greater at low levels of parental socioeconomic status than at high levels (table B6.1). Among young people from families at the lowest decile of socioeconomic status, 70 percent of sons compared with 59 percent of daughters expected nonfamily living—an 11-percentage-point difference. But among families in the top decile of socioeconomic status, the gender difference is only 5 percentage points (76% vs. 71%).[6]

There is also considerable evidence for ethnic, racial, and religious group variation in gender differentiation but often in ways not fully consistent with a traditional-modern break (table B6.1). Data in table 6.1 show the percent of nonfamily living expected and experienced by young men and women in these groups (assuming that they have the same level of socioeconomic status and the same regional distributions).

Gender differentiation on this issue is large in two groups: Hispanics and white Protestants. Gender differences among Asians are particularly

Table 6.1. Predicted ethnic and religious differences in the effect of gender on residential independence

	Expectations			Behavior		
Group	Males	Females	Difference (M−F)	Males	Females	Difference (M−F)
Hispanics	71	55	16	65	50	15
Protestants[a]	73	64	9	69	53	16
Catholics[b]	73	67	6	72	65	7
Blacks	77	73	4	73	72	1
Asians	64	64	0	72	65	7
Jews[b]	70	76	−6	79	79	0

[a] Non-Hispanic, non-Asian, nonblack, non-Catholic, non-Jewish
[b] Non-Hispanic, non-Asian, nonblack

small for expectations and among young black adults are quite small on both measures. The male-female difference is actually *reversed* among Jews for expectations. As a result, there is far more variation in routes to residential independence for young women than for young men. The young men are clustered between 64 percent and 79 percent nonfamily, while the young women range from 50 percent to 79 percent. It is difficult to ascribe these ethnic differences to differences among groups in "traditional values," given that the largest gender differences are for white Protestants. The large gender differences among Hispanics are consistent with the common observation of greater gender inequality among Hispanics and fit our earlier findings about their favorable attitude toward children living close to parents and relatives. A general picture of high levels of familism characterize these young Hispanics. However, no simple interpretation of the small gender differences among blacks, Jews, and Asians is readily apparent from these data.

Ethnicity and religiosity may also serve to reinforce gender differences in routes out of the home, since traditional communities provide greater independence for men than for women. The data show that using a foreign language and living in one's ethnic region, which strongly reduce nonfamily living (chap. 4), have much larger effects on the expectations of young women than on those of young men. (However, each has the same effect on later behavior for women as for men. See table B6.1.) Thus, with increased English-language use and residential integration, women become more like men in their expectations for nonfamily living, but these measures of ethnicity have no effect on the gender gap in actually leaving home. Greater access to the majority culture's language and community may lead to attitude change, but these forms of access have little effect on the actual forces leading the lives of ethnic young men and women in different directions. There are no gender differences in the effects of generation status on either expected or actual routes to residential independence (table B6.1). The gender gap is thus not a function of length of exposure to life in America, at least on this issue.

Unlike ethnicity, measures of religiosity have their strongest gender effects on residential behavior, not expectations (table B6.1). Only religious self-identity reduces expectations for nonfamily living more for women than for men. Attendance at religious services and exposure to Catholic schools reduce the nonfamily expectations of both young men and young women. In contrast, all three measures of religiosity have a significantly stronger effect on the behavior of young women than of young men. In our overall analysis (chap. 5), neither personal religiosity nor overall church attendance had a significant effect on residential behavior. However, that result was masking the fact that both have a small but significant impact on women but not men. Attending Catholic school reduced actual nonfamily living overall, in large part because the effect for young women was so strong.

GENDER ROLES AND NONFAMILY LIVING: THE CONTENT OF GENDER DIFFERENTIATION

The different ways that gender interacts with context have allowed us to specify how the gender factor works for different socioeconomic, ethnic, and religious groups and in the context of ethnicity and religiosity. But beyond the *context* of gender is the *content* or substance of *gender* differentiation. What is it about gender differences in general that might shape residential choices?

The questions asked on surveys on tap gender role-related attitudes normally focus on women's roles and the revolution that is occurring with regard to them. Women, even mothers of young children, are increasingly working outside the home. Hence the critical issues have become, How does this phenomenon relate to women's family roles and responsibilities? Can women maintain their family roles as they take on these new obligations outside of the home (i.e., work and still be good wives and mothers)? Will they do so without upsetting the traditional male-female relationship further (i.e., by not drawing their husbands into household tasks)? Will women keep their family roles as the central, primary source of their identity now that they are also working?

Those who feel strongly that women should keep the family as the center of their lives and not let work (if they must do it) conflict with their total responsibilities for their children and for household tasks are espousing what we are calling a "traditional" view of family life.[7] They are concerned about the changes that are occurring in women's work roles and reject those that "feminize" men's household roles. In contrast, those who do not see the home as the central and exclusive task of women and prefer more egalitarian roles for men and women at work and in the home are welcoming these changes, espousing a more modern (or even "avant-garde") approach to gender roles.

The phenomenon of nonfamily living in early adulthood would appear to be more closely tied to the relationships between parents and their adult children than to male-female relationships. However, orientations toward nonfamily autonomy and toward egalitarian gender roles are similar in that they both require restructuring family roles and can both be understood as deemphasizing family roles and relationships in favor of independence from family, that is, independence and individualism.[8] We expect, then, that those with more modern attitudes toward gender roles, young men as well as young women, should be more likely to expect nonfamily living and to choose it as part of their life course strategies.

However, it is unlikely that differences in gender roles attitudes will explain all the differences between young men and women in expecting and experiencing nonfamily living. This is because residential expectations do not represent "ideals" in the same sense that sex role attitudes do. It is a real decision that young people plan for and perhaps achieve. As such, it is much more likely to be informed by realistic assessments of what is possible. (See our discussion of the relationships among expectations, plans, and preferences in chap. 1.)

The questions on gender role attitudes, after all, do not ask what sort of marriage young people actually *expect* to have. Young women who espouse the ideal of a perfectly egalitarian marriage might nevertheless expect to compromise, given the range of likely spouses, the likelihood that their spouses will be able to earn more income than they themselves will, and the ambivalent chauvinism of their otherwise very attractive current boyfriends. Young men with modern egalitarian ideals are also likely to expect to compromise them, given that they may have to compete on their chosen career ladders with men who marry domestically oriented wives and are thus freer to earn money with no additional responsibilities. Practical considerations are likely to be weighed along with ideals when young people consider whether they expect an interval of nonfamily living when they make decisions about setting up an independent household.

However, modern gender role attitudes should lead men and women to resemble each other more closely, even if not completely. The life courses of traditional men and women are very different, allowing more time for men to experience nonfamily living than for women, given the earlier marriage for women than for men. In contrast, young men and women holding more modern ideas about gender roles might each be planning a transition to adulthood featuring more education, extensive career development, and later marriage—a sequence for women that resembles men's. This life course pattern would provide more time for an interval of nonfamily living for both sexes. Hence gender role attitudes should have more influence on the routes to residential independence planned and taken by women than the gender role attitudes of men should have on their expectations and behavior.[9]

GENDER ROLE ATTITUDES AND RESIDENTIAL INDEPENDENCE

We use two questions to examine the relationship between gender role attitudes and the pathways to residential independence that young adults expect and experience. Each is based on a statement describing an aspect of family roles for which the student was asked whether she or he "agreed strongly," "agreed somewhat," "disagreed somewhat," or "disagreed strongly." Those who "disagreed strongly" were given the highest, or most modern, score.[10]

The first statement was, "Most women are happiest when they are making a home and caring for children." As we reverse the scoring, we call this measure NONFAM, since those with the highest scores disagree most strongly with it. Although this question focuses only on women and reflects a one-gendered view of the division of male and female roles, it is also a question about familism since it poses the "family vs. rest-of-life" trade-off very strongly. Both men and women are likely to disagree with this question if they see family roles and relationships as less important than achievement in the occupational sphere (or than politics, religion, or leisure).

The second statement was, "It is usually better for everyone involved if the man is the achiever outside of the home and the woman takes care of the home and the family." We call this measure EGALFAM. While this question taps gender relationships in terms of the division of roles within the family, it does so without challenging the importance of family per se. Both work and family are assumed to be the central adult roles. Thus, the first statement is a stronger rejection of familism, in that it approaches gender equality by removing women, like men, from the family to the workplace; the second statement raises the more familistic—but also more radical—question of gender equality in the home.

These are clearly rather separate dimensions of the general question of gender role change. For example, although young women are more modern in that they are more likely to disagree with both questions than young men, men are more likely to be egalitarian on the first question than the second (averaging 2.52 and 2.36, respectively); women are reversed (averaging 2.70 and 2.94, respectively). Hence, young men and young women in their senior year in high school were in quite close agreement about the possibility of women feeling happy and fulfilled through activities outside the home (with a difference of only 0.18); there is much sharper gender disagreement about shared roles within the home (with a difference of 0.58). This pattern suggests that even women who are concerned about male-female equity in terms of responsibilities at work and at home resist affirming that making a home and caring for children should be an unimportant part of their lives. Many men are evidently more willing for women to have lives outside the home than they are to alter traditional gender arrangements within the family.[11]

Our analyses of these measures of gender role egalitarianism explore their effects on residential expectations and behavior. We ask: Are those who have more modern gender role attitudes more likely to expect and experience the nonfamily route to residential independence? Which of the two aspects of gender roles is more closely related to the nonfamily pathway? Do these attitudes influence the expectations and behavior of women more than of men? We then examine whether the introduction of these gender role attitudes clarifies other gender differences in the relationships that we have documented to determine whether gender differences by socioeconomic status, ethnicity, and religion are consistent with attitude differences for these groups.

The results indicate that those opposing segregated marital roles and those denying the centrality of family for women differ in the ways we anticipated. The more modern the attitude toward the sexual division of labor in the workplace and at home, and the more modern the attitude toward female "happiness" outside the family, the greater the likelihood that young adults expected residential independence before marriage and had actually done so within four years after high school (fig. 6.3, table B6.2). Attitudes on modern female roles (NONFAM) have a stronger impact on residential pathways than attitudes measuring the division of labor within the household (EGALFAM), reinforcing our interpretation that those with modern attitudes toward the division of family tasks are somewhat more family oriented (at least on this dimension) than those who do not expect women to find happiness in family roles.

The NONFAM measure has a stronger impact on actual residential behavior in the first four years after high school than it does on expectations. This pattern is unlike other attitudinal measures we have examined— living close to parents and relatives, religious self-identity, and egalitarian gender role attitudes—that have greater effects on expectations than on behavior. We infer from this result that, in general, attitudes toward family and parents, and those that reflect fundamentalist religious values, are linked to residential choices through the formation of expected behav-

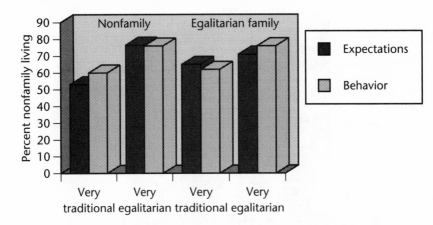

Fig. 6.3. Effects of gender role attitudes on nonfamily living

ior, that is, norms. In contrast, attitudes that deemphasize the family seem to have more powerful effects on the decision to live outside a family context.

When gender role attitudes are taken into account, differences between young men and women in residential expectations and behaviors increase.[12] This occurs because, on average, young men hold more segregated views on gender roles than do young women. Before their differing attitudes on these issues were taken into account, more egalitarian women were being compared with less egalitarian men. When men and women with the *same* orientation toward gender roles are compared, the difference between them in nonfamily expectations and behavior increases.

Further, the effect of holding more egalitarian gender role attitudes is much greater for women than for men, particularly for EGALFAM (fig. 6.4, table B6.3). Differences in expectations between men and women with a strong orientation toward a segregated division of labor in the home are much greater than between those with the most egalitarian attitudes. Traditional young men are more than 20 percentage points more likely to expect the nonfamily route than are traditional young women (69% for men and only 48% for women). In contrast, the gender difference was reduced by three quarters, to 5 percentage points, among young men and women who support an egalitarian division of male and female roles at home: 77 percent of very egalitarian young men and 72 percent of otherwise similar young women expected residential independence before marriage. Hence the effect of holding extreme attitudes about the division of labor only makes an 8-percentage-point differ-

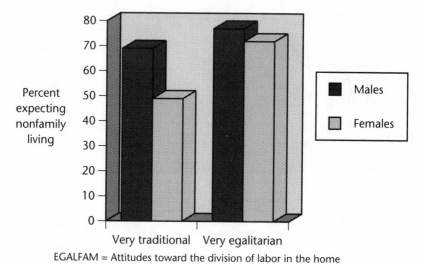

EGALFAM = Attitudes toward the division of labor in the home

Fig. 6.4.   Gender differences in effects of EGALFAM on nonfamily living

ence among young men but increases young women's expectations for residential independence prior to marriage by half, from 48 percent to 72 percent. (This difference is much less pronounced for actual behavior.)

GENDER ROLE ATTITUDES IN CONTEXT

What happens to the effects of the other variables in our "basic model" on nonfamily residential autonomy when these gender role attitude items are introduced? Part of the explanation of the other variables in our basic model may relate to differences in gender role attitudes. If so, including gender role attitudes in the analysis should further reduce group differences. It is also possible that differences in gender role attitudes suppress "true" differences between groups. This is what we documented in the analysis of gender: introducing gender role attitudes actually exaggerated the difference between men and women. Some differences between groups might be unaffected by including gender role attitudes, indicating that whatever is causing these basic differences between them is unrelated to gender role attitudes.

The effects of several of the variables in our basic model remain the same after introducing the gender role attitudes.[13] This is the case for differences by socioeconomic status and between blacks, Jews, and Catholics relative to Protestants. For example, the impact of socioeconomic status on nonfamily living remains virtually the same whether or not we take gender role attitudes into account. This finding indicates that there is no relationship between parental socioeconomic status and orientations toward gender role segregation, and therefore the effects of social class on nonfamily living are not being mediated through gender role attitudes. Similarly, the significantly higher likelihood of expecting and experiencing nonfamily living among blacks does not reflect differences in the attitudes between blacks and others toward traditional female roles.

Two groups show distinctive patterns when we take into account their gender role attitudes—Hispanics and Asians. We have documented that Hispanics are consistently less likely to expect or experience nonfamily living. When their gender role attitudes are taken into account, however, these differences are considerably reduced. About half of the lower Hispanic probability of expecting nonfamily living is accounted for by their segregated gender role attitudes, and the fairly small difference in behavior between Hispanics and others is entirely eliminated with the introduction of gender role attitudes. These findings are consistent with earlier results on closeness to parents among Hispanics and together suggest a more general conclusion: differences in both dimensions of familism account for the distinctive residential patterns of Hispanics.

A more complex pattern emerges for Asians. In general, Asians have a lower likelihood of expecting nonfamily living than others, and this appears to reflect in large part their very segregated gender role attitudes, despite their *lack* of gender difference in behavior. Indeed, when gender role attitudes between Asians and others are the same, Asians are somewhat *more* likely to expect a segment of nonfamily residential autonomy than others. But Asians are also more likely than others to experience nonfamily living, despite their traditional gender role attitudes. When their attitudes are similar to others, that is, when they are more modern, Asians are even more distinctive in their high levels of actual nonfamily living. So again, we need to look elsewhere for an explanation of the unusually high proportion of Asians choosing nonfamily living among those who become residentially independent, both relative to non-Asians and relative to their own expectations.

Hence these data show that the low level of nonfamily living among Hispanics is connected to their attitudes toward gender roles within the family. Their emphasis on residential dependence until marriage fits in with these attitudes. But differential gender role attitudes do not help account for the social class, religious, or race (black-white) differences that we have documented. Among Asian-Americans, the inclusion of gender role attitudes reverses their pattern but does not provide clues to their unique situation.

7

Exiting from the Home
The Timing of Marriage
and Residential Autonomy

The emergence of residential autonomy before marriage has coincided with a trend toward later marriage in the United States. These phenomena are interrelated. An older age at marriage has allowed young adults more time for residential independence prior to marriage. If premarital residential independence is simply substituting for marriage as a route out of the parental home, then there may have been no change in *when* young adults move out of the parental household. The critical difference is in *how* parental dependence ends, that is, whether young adults move out of the parental household to nonfamily residential independence rather than to marriage.

The first clue that nonfamily residential independence and marriage are not simply substitute routes out of the parental home is the evidence showing that those who leave home to nonfamily living do so at younger ages than those who leave home to marry. Moreover, those expecting nonfamily living expect later marriage (chap. 2). By inference, time for nonfamily living is being carved from both forms of family living, from the parental family and from marriage. This inference needs to be tested directly, taking into account the other factors linked to nonfamily living that might also be linked to later marriage. In this chapter, we investigate the relationship between these two routes out of the parental home and address the question, Is nonfamily living simply a reflection of the different ages that young adults plan to and actually marry? Or are some other factors leading to nonfamily living even among those planning to marry or actually marrying at the same age?

Viewed historically and broadly, it seems unlikely that the emergence of nonfamily residential independence was a direct or a simple reflection of the trajectories of marriage in the United States and in western European countries, since marriage ages have fluctuated dramatically, showing no simple trend and no similar level comparatively. Even when young adults married at a relatively late age, as in western Europe from the sixteenth century to well into the twentieth century, marriage was the normal pathway out of the parental home, so that children remained in their parents' homes for a decade or more after completing schooling to contribute to the family economy. Even those leaving before marriage rarely formed an independent household, going instead to institutional housing such as dormitories or barracks or living in some other family's home as a boarder, servant, or apprentice. Living in nonfamily households, alone or with housemates, was therefore rare even among those who left the parental home before they married. In the past, late marriage normally did not result in an interval of nonfamily residential autonomy.

The overall trends in marriage and household formation in the United States since World War II also do not reveal any obvious linkage between changes in marriage patterns and nonfamily living. Premarital household headship was increasing during the 1940s and 1950s despite declining ages at marriage (Rodgers and Thornton 1985). The percentage of unmarried young men age 18 to 24 in the United States who were "primary individuals," that is, household heads living alone or with nonrelatives, increased from 1 percent in 1940 and 1950 to 3 percent in 1960 and 13.3 percent in 1980 (Kobrin 1976, Goldscheider and DaVanzo 1989).[1]

PREMARITAL RESIDENTIAL INDEPENDENCE AND THE TIMING OF MARRIAGE

There are two mechanisms linking later marriage age and nonfamily living among young adults. First, delayed marriage allows more *time* for nonfamily living, and young adults are likely to need an alternative form of adult autonomy during their prolonged single state. This mechanism is straightforward, since those who marry soon after finishing high school have much less time for residential independence before marriage than those who marry later. So the simplest link between the timing of marriage and nonfamily living is the effect of marriage age on young adults' "exposure" to leaving home before marriage. The longer that time span, the greater the potential for nonfamily living as young adults are exposed for a longer period of time to the probability of moving out and living independently before marriage. The exposure factor should apply both to expectations and to actual nonfamily living. The later that marriage is expected, the more it makes sense to plan for an interim address that is away from the parental home. The later marriage actually occurs, the more likely that something will have "come up"—jobs, education, resources, or conflict with parents or siblings at home—that leads to residential independence.

The second link between marriage timing and nonfamily living is more complex. Both are routes to independence from the parental home and as such, indicators of individual autonomy. Marriage and nonfamily living can be viewed as alternative paths in the transition to adulthood and hence as competing choices. In the past, marriage was the key element in the definition of adulthood and for the social construction of new adult relationships, particularly for women. Childhood was only ended with the assumption of adult family roles; the increased control over one's life that comes with having an independent household was postponed until marriage. While some young adults in the past may have married in haste simply to escape the parental household, for most, setting up an independent household was simply the result of getting married.

Currently, establishing an independent household, without necessarily getting married, is the new symbol of adulthood (Riche 1990). As such, residential independence before marriage focuses attention on new forms of the parent-child relationship, since independence from parents results not from the achievement of some other status (i.e., marriage) but is itself the primary goal. Factors that encourage independence and autonomy from parents, then, should affect nonfamily living regardless of when young adults expect to marry.

The experience of nonfamily living may also have an effect on the timing of marriage and perhaps the nature of marriage and family life as well. Young adults who lived independently prior to marriage plan fewer children and have more egalitarian sex role attitudes than those who do not experience nonfamily living (Goldscheider and Waite 1991). So the two routes out of the home are likely to be connected, both because they are *alternative* responses to the issue of leaving the parental home and because they may have some causal relationship to each other. Marrying late may allow nonfamily living as a result; living independently may lead to delayed marriage. We therefore can view the determinants of nonfamily residential autonomy in two contexts: (1) factors that indirectly influence residential independence through the effects on the expected and actual timing of marriage, and (2) factors that shape the residential separation of parents and children in early adulthood, independent of the timing of marriage.

The difference between these two contexts can be clarified with a concrete example. Young men are more likely to establish an independent household before marriage than young women (chap. 6). This gender difference in nonfamily living could result from two quite different processes. First, women marry earlier than men. As a result, women would be less likely than men to leave home prior to marriage, or to expect to do so, because they have less time than men in early adulthood for residential independence. If this exposure factor is the primary reason that men are more likely than women to expect and experience nonfamily living, the relationship between gender and nonfamily living would be the direct consequence of marriage timing. Controlling statistically for the timing of marriage would eliminate the relationship between gender and premarital residential independence.

The higher level of nonfamily living among men could also reflect a second process: parents allow their sons greater autonomy than their daughters, so that gender differences in marriage timing may be accounting only in part for differences in nonfamily living. Parents might encourage family-centeredness for their daughters by maintaining the centrality of the male-female relationship as the definition of adulthood for women, rejecting nonfamily living in the process. In this case, the relationship between gender and nonfamily living would reflect parents' desire to supervise their daughters; sons would be more able to escape parental authority because conventional sex role definitions allow more independence for men. If so, controlling for the different timing of marriage of men and women would not account for all the gender differences in premarital residential independence.

Through introducing marriage timing into our analysis, we shall be able to disentangle these alternative connections to nonfamily living. Our objectives in this chapter are (1) to test systematically the links between expected age at marriage and expected premarital residential independence, and (2) to analyze the relationship between actual nonfamily living and the timing of marriage. These analyses will allow us to take a fresh look at our major findings and identify conditions where the timing of marriage has been the primary influence on nonfamily living—and where it has not.

EXITING FROM THE PARENTAL HOME

What factors influence the decisions of young adults to be residentially independent from parents? Of these, which are likely to have their primary impact on the timing of nonfamily living rather than on the timing of marriage? Some factors should increase residential independence per se. Since separate housing is expensive, resources should influence both marriage and premarital residential independence. Other factors should have opposing effects on nonfamily living and the timing of marriage. For example, tastes for privacy and independence may increase premarital residential independence but deter marriage. Let us consider more closely how resources and tastes influence the decisions to leave home and to marry in different ways.

Resources

Shared quarters allow many economies compared with living separately, from needing only one refrigerator or couch to savings on heating rooms in common use; there are many potential economies of scale when people eat together. So living at home is cheaper in most cases than any alternative arrangement for young adults. Further, there is evidence that parents rarely ask their children for an equal share of the collective living expenses (Goldscheider and Thornton 1992). Since parents have already worked out a division of household labor when their children were young, the low level of involvement of the children often continues into adulthood (Goldscheider and Waite 1991). When young people establish their own homes, they experience a marked increase in the time needed for shopping, cooking, and cleaning.

However, it is not clear whether marriage or nonfamily living is the more expensive living arrangement. Many assume that marriage is cheaper, at least compared with living entirely alone and supporting a separate household on one salary. At least until children are born, two incomes are normally available, and costs can be shared. But young adulthood is the most common age for group housing, in which several young people live together sharing common space. The married have less flexibility to add on an extra roommate by taking in a boarder, since there are much stronger expectations about privacy for married couples than for single individuals. Further, young singles may be less likely to treat their apartment as a home, in the sense of having a full set of appliances, new furniture, rugs, and so on, and may be more willing to furnish their place with castoffs and other used items or to do without a sofa or a lamp than young married couples. This interpretation is consistent with research showing that financial constraints in young adulthood inhibit marriage more than residential autonomy before marriage (Goldscheider and DaVanzo 1989; Christian 1989; Avery, Goldscheider, and Speare 1992).

Parents may also use resources to subsidize their children's independent living arrangements, encouraging their children to leave home either before or at marriage. Many parents are willing to help unmarried children with basic expenses even when they are not living at home (Goldscheider and Thornton 1992) but consider that marriage should mean financial independence (particularly for daughters, who have been "given away" into someone else's responsibility). Other parents may wish to facilitate their children's marriage and provide a married child with large sums such as a down payment on a home and other contributions that they would not provide for their unmarried children. Hence it is unclear how parental resources would affect gaining residential independence via nonfamily living or via marriage. Resources per se, however, should increase leaving home. How resources are used depends on what we have referred to as "tastes" or values.

100

Family Values

How do values relate to the timing of marriage? Recent trends toward later marriage have been interpreted as indicating a more egalitarian approach to marriage, particularly for women. Later marriage for women allows more time for acquiring the education and training necessary for assuming a full-time career. For both men and women, marriage delay can imply a decrease in the centrality of adult family roles in the home in favor of alternative sites for work and leisure.

However, there are large differences in marriage age, even among ethnic and religious groups with quite familistic values (Kobrin and Goldscheider 1978, Greeley 1989). Catholics, particularly those from northern and Western Europe, have a very late age at marriage. This pattern is thought to have emerged from past Catholic opposition both to reliable means of birth control and to divorce (Jones and Westoff 1979). In this context, late marriage serves as a control on total family size and as insurance against hasty, high-risk marriages. Further, even though Catholic contraceptive use now parallels that of Protestants, their later marriage age remains. In our sample of high school graduates, Catholic non-Hispanics expected to marry at about age 24, nearly a full year later than Protestants. Late marriage also characterizes Asians, who do not expect to marry until about age 25, perhaps as a result of their emphasis on educational attainment as a mechanism of social mobility. Jews and blacks also expect much later marriage; only Hispanics expect to marry nearly as young as do Protestants. Perhaps it is Protestant marriage patterns that are unusual, with early marriage and high levels of divorce. Ironically, then, for many, the conventional pattern of late marriage allows the emergence of a new route out of the home—nonfamily residential independence.

TAKING INTO ACCOUNT MARRIAGE TIMING

The key concept that we introduce into our analysis at this point is timing—of both marriage and residential independence. For expectations of nonfamily living, which assume eventual residential independence, we incorporate information on *expected* marriage age constructed from the question about the age young adults expected to marry.[2] In the analysis of actual nonfamily living, we introduce timing somewhat differently. We compare the odds of becoming residentially independent by marrying and the odds of residential independence before marriage for each time interval, in each case relative to remaining residentially dependent, which usually means remaining in the parental home. In this way, we are looking at the two routes to residential independence as *exit rates,* which are sensitive to their timing (from shortly after high school graduation to four to six years later). Up to this point, we have been examining what we will now begin to call a *"route ratio,"* measured by the extent of non-family living relative to the total who established residential indepen-dence either before or when they married. The route ratio was indepen-dent of timing.

Introducing marriage timing, that is, focusing on expected or actual exit rates, has a major effect on the proportion expecting or experiencing pre-marital residential independence. The later the expected age at marriage, the more likely it is that young adults expect to leave home before mar-riage.[3] Only 36 percent of young adults expecting to marry by age 20 expect to establish a separate residence before marriage, compared with 82 percent among those not expecting to marry until age 26.[4] Given the structure of our data, the few who may have experienced nonfamily living could not be observed among those who married within two years after finishing high school, while 62 percent of those still unmarried six years later had established an independent residence. (See chap. 2, table 2.1.) Clearly, then, as we expected, marriage timing strongly influences the likelihood of nonfamily living. Our key question, however, is, How does taking marriage timing into account by looking at exit rates affect our understanding of the differences in nonfamily living that we have ob-served to this point?

The results are very clear for gender. Almost the entire difference in expectations for nonfamily living and *all* of the gender difference in ex-periencing nonfamily living are due to the later age of marriage for men than for women. The 8-percentage-point difference between men and women in our basic model of expectations (73% vs. 65%: chap. 3) is re-duced to less than 2 percentage points when their different marriage ages are taken into account (compare tables B3.1 and B7.1).[5] The larger gender difference in the proportion experiencing nonfamily living based on the route ratio (73% for men vs. 58% for women) simply results from the large difference in when they actually marry. Nearly all of the gender difference in the proportions establishing residential independence before marriage must be linked to the gender difference in age at marriage. Young men simply have *more time* than young women for nonfamily living. Once marriage timing is taken into account, the likelihood of remaining with parents or leaving to set up an independent residence is essentially the same for unmarried men and women.

A more complex pattern emerges for many of our other findings when exit rates are examined, reflecting the additional analytic dimension that is involved. In all our earlier analyses of who actually experiences nonfamily living, we focused on the factors that lead young adults to choose one route to residential independence or the other, *given that they are leaving home*—the route ratio. When the question is posed in this way, some groups could be more likely than others to leave home before marriage from many combinations of routes and timing of residential independence. Some might be leaving more rapidly to marriage but even more rapidly to nonfamily living, so that nearly everyone is leaving home early, one way or another. Alternatively, some may be leaving comparatively rapidly to nonfamily living and slowly to marriage. A third possibility involves those who are marrying quite late and leaving late to nonfamily living but not quite as late as their marriage timing. If so, the few who established an independent residence would have done so disproportionately via nonfamily living. In this case, late marriage may be a traditional pattern, but it is one that nevertheless allows nonfamily living more easily than an early marriage schedule.[6] Finally, there may be those, the least familistic, who achieve nonfamily living relatively early but marry late, if at all.

Adding variation in timing moves our question from a single dimension (does some factor increase the likelihood of nonfamily living relative to marriage) to a multidimensional one—from the route ratio question to an analysis of exit rates. Being "early" or "late" on both the marriage track and the independence-from-parents track in early adulthood has to be taken into consideration. We analyze these by way of exit rates.[7] These possibilities are sketched in figure 7.1, which shows how the factors we have been considering affect the timing of marriage and nonfamily living both for expectations and behavior.[8]

The column headings distinguish exit rates to marriage. Groups that married significantly more slowly during the first six years after high school graduation than their respective comparison group (e.g., in the case of religion, the comparison group is nonfundamentalist Protestants such as Presbyterians) are placed to the right, under the heading "Late" timing of marriage. Groups that married significantly more rapidly are on the left, under the heading "Early" marriage timing. Factors that had no significant impact on the likelihood of marriage are placed under the moderate heading. The rows similarly define differences in the likelihood of leaving home to nonfamily living, independent of marriage timing, that is, exit rates. Where a result differs for expectations and behavior, this is indicated by a qualifying B (behavior) or E (expectations).

Starting in the upper left corner and considering the two dimensions together, we find those groups who expect and experience both early marriage and a low level of nonfamily living, independent of the age they marry. Young adults living in the southern region of the United States,

103

Timing of marriage

		Early	Moderate	Late
Odds of PRI	Low	South Fundamentalist Protestants Other religion (E) Ethnic region Religiosity* (B)	Church attendance* Foreign language Religiosity (E) Family close (E)	Blacks Asians Catholics Hispanics Foreign born Catholic school Family close (B)

	Average	Other religion (B)	(Prot 2, female,
			  white, central
			  region, etc.)
			None (B)
				Males (B)
				Northeast
				  & Pacific (B)
				Jews (E)
				EGALFAM (B)

	High	- - - - - - -	- - - - - - -	Males (E)
				Socioeconomic
				  status
				Northeast
				  & Pacific (E)
				Jews (B)
				None (E)
				NONFAM
				EGALFAM (E)

E = Expectations
B = Behavior
* = females only
PRI = Premarital residential independence (nonfamily living)

Fig. 7.1. Factors affecting exit rates to residential independence: married and unmarried

for example, leave home early to marriage but late, if at all, to nonfamily living, relative to those in the central regions of the United States. In contrast, those in the lower right corner marry late, but their level of nonfamily living is high, even taking into account their late marriage age. Those with families with higher socioeconomic status, for example, marry late but achieve early residential independence primarily while unmarried, relative to those of lower socioeconomic status.

A different but very common pattern combines low residential independence among the unmarried and late marriage—the upper right corner. Those in this category, such as blacks and Asian-Americans, marry late but nevertheless have low levels of nonfamily living, indicating low exit rates to residential independence by any route. There is no counterpart to this group: there are no groups or situations we have observed so far with high exit rates to both nonfamily living and marriage, that is, that connect both early marriage and high probabilities of premarital residential independence.[9]

This figure provides the basis for understanding the complex pathways to residential independence in young adulthood, one that alters several of the patterns we described earlier, when we did not take marriage age into account. Notably, these data clarify the persistent Asian anomaly that first emerged in our basic description of ethnic differences (chap. 3) and continued in the detailed examination of ethnicity (chap. 4). Asian-Americans were less likely than others to expect nonfamily living, but nonfamily living dominated among those who actually achieved residential independence during the first six years after high school. When we consider nonfamily living separately from marriage, however, it becomes clear that premarital residential independence is, indeed, very rare among Asian-Americans at these ages, just not so rare as marriage. This anomaly emerges because our measure of expectations for nonfamily living uses the full range of responses young people gave about the ages they expect to marry and have an independent residence—up to age 30 and beyond—while the measures of actual behavior only go up to about age 24. Most Asian-Americans had not yet left home and may not until they marry.

While some patterns are clarified by examining the different routes to residential independence, introducing exit rates generates new complexities. For example, the gender pattern reveals an inconsistency between expectations and behavior. While males clearly both expect to and do marry later than females, there are two entries for them, not one. Young men expected to achieve a higher level of nonfamily living than young women, even taking into account their later expected marriage age. However, there was no significant difference in their likelihood of establishing an independent residence before marriage. *All* of their greater likelihood of experiencing nonfamily living results from their later age at marriage. Hence we show males in the lower right corner on the basis of their expectations—Males (E)—indicating that they expect high levels of nonfamily living relative to females, even after taking into account their later expected marriage age. Males are also placed in the center of the right column on the basis of their behavior—Males (B)—indicating that they achieved their later expected marriage age but not their higher level of expected nonfamily living.[10]

This outcome for the gender difference—greater consistency between marriage expectations and behavior than between premarital residential independence expectations and behavior—is characteristic of the overall set of results. Although most tests comparing expectations for nonfamily living with the actual pattern of residential independence were consistent, a substantial minority showed mixed results, either with expectations for nonfamily living that were not carried out or with a segment of nonfamily living that was not anticipated. These group comparisons indicate that marriage and marriage timing are much more firmly institutionalized than nonfamily living, so that the factors that lead to differences in marriage timing between groups can be clearly anticipated. In contrast, some forces are apparently influencing young adults' expectations about nonfamily living in ways they cannot carry through, while other young adults are finding themselves in nonfamily living arrangements despite themselves. We consider these inconsistent results below and examine as well the ways in which taking into account marriage patterns sharpens our understanding of nonfamily living. In chapter 8, we will analyze factors that are likely to lead to a systematic mismatch between expectations and behavior.

MARRIAGE AND THE BASIC MODEL OF NONFAMILY LIVING

These new results give us the opportunity to consider again the findings we documented in previous chapters and to ask whether the differences in premarital residential independence that appeared in the analysis of our basic model, as well as in our detailed analyses of ethnicity, religion, and male-female and parent-child relationships, should be reinterpreted when we take into account marriage timing through the examination of exit rates. Clearly, the picture changed somewhat when we considered differences between males and females, since what had been a simple pattern, with males more likely to expect and experience nonfamily living, became more complex. We now understand that much of the young men's greater likelihood of expecting nonfamily living—and all of their greater likelihood of experiencing it—reflects differences between young men and women in the timing of marriage. How do exit rates reshape our understanding of the effects of socioeconomic status, ethnicity, region of residence, and the other variables we have considered?

CHANGES IN THE BASIC MODEL

As with gender, the results for socioeconomic status also reveal differences between expectations and behavior once exit rates are taken into account. The pattern that we observed earlier, in which those whose families have higher socioeconomic status are more likely to expect and experience nonfamily living, turns out to be primarily a result of the much stronger relationship between socioeconomic status and marriage timing than between socioeconomic status and nonfamily living. Those from families with higher socioeconomic status marry later than those from families with less. This is particularly the case for expectations. Controlling for expected marriage timing reduced the effect of socioeconomic status on expectations for nonfamily living dramatically. Thus, parental socioeconomic resources affect the expectations young adults have for premarital residential independence, but their influence operates primarily through delaying marriage, probably because of the relationship between education and age at marriage.

Parental resources have a much stronger effect on the likelihood of experiencing nonfamily living than on expecting it. The effects of socioeconomic status on actually delaying marriage and hastening nonfamily living were of nearly equal magnitude, and the larger impact was for nonfamily living, not for marriage. Clearly, young adults in families with high socioeconomic status are more likely to achieve nonfamily living, even though these resources are not linked to their expectations for it. The resources that young people did not take into account in forming their expectations about nonfamily living were used to realize them.

We will document in a subsequent analysis (chap. 11) that parental resources have a much stronger effect on whether parents expect nonfamily living than they do on the expectations of the young adults. This result, then, provides a clue that parental expectations might have a strong effect on young adults' behavior. Parents with higher socioeconomic status may use their resources to purchase privacy for themselves by subsidizing an independent residence for their children, even though their children had expected to remain at home until marriage.[11]

In contrast to socioeconomic status and gender, which have an impact on expectations for nonfamily living largely through a pattern of late marriage, controlling marriage age changes dramatically our understanding of racial differences in nonfamily living. We noted above that when we take into account the very late marriage age of Asian-Americans, their greater likelihood of experiencing premarital residential independence was reversed, so that both expectations and behavior were acting in concert. Such a reversal also occurred among young black adults, although in this case, *both* expectations and behavior are reversed when exit rates via marriage and via nonfamily living are considered. Blacks shift from being more likely to being less likely than non-Hispanic whites to expect or experience nonfamily living, once their extremely late marriage age is taken into account. Of all these groups, blacks are among the least likely to marry, so that most of the few who achieved residential independence during these years did so via nonfamily living. Taking their late marriage into account reveals that nonfamily living is actually not common among young blacks, just not quite as rare as marriage at these ages. This pattern characterizes all blacks—Protestants, Catholics, and others.

Hispanics also have somewhat later ages at marriage than non-Hispanic whites, so that the lower likelihood of premarital residential independence that Hispanics expect and experience is strengthened when we take into account their low exit rate to marriage. This pattern characterizes all Hispanic groups—Mexicans, Cubans, Puerto Ricans, and others. Hence, controlling for expected marriage age sharpens the differences we already observed for Mexicans and Cubans and reveals that both Puerto Ricans and other Hispanics, who were not distinctive before their later marriage was taken into account, are also less likely to expect or experience nonfamily living, relative to other groups. Clearly, racial and ethnic differences in the United States persist, both in marriage behavior (in most cases reflecting long-term differences among these groups) and also in the adoption of a relatively new family behavior, nonfamily living. Non-Hispanic whites have embraced nonfamily living as a life course pattern to a much greater extent than any other racial or ethnic group.

The regions of the country remain distinctive on most comparisons, once marriage age is taken into account. In each case, however, differences become less sharp, since marriage timing had been reinforcing differences in nonfamily living. In the South, young people both expect and experience low levels of nonfamily living and are characterized *as well* by early marriage. Those living elsewhere on the two coasts (the New England and Pacific regions) expect high levels of premarital residential independence, in part because of later marriage, and are more likely to experience it wholly because of late marriage. Hence, the low level of nonfamily living observed earlier for those living in the South is the result of a combination of early marriage *and* low levels of expected nonfamily living, net of expected marriage age; the high level of nonfamily living observed in both the New England and Pacific regions shows the opposite pattern. When marriage age is controlled, then, these regions remain distinctive from the middle portion of the country, but the contrasts become less distinctive.

The regions with higher levels of expectations for nonfamily living, however, were not distinctive in terms of behavior. These two areas of the country may be those where attitudes toward nonfamily living had become entrenched earliest; high rents, coupled with the difficulties young people have experienced in the labor market in the early 1980s, may have had more impact on young adults in these regions than in other areas. While there appear to be broad regional patterns of premarital residential independence, more detailed community-level information is necessary to sharpen our understanding of these effects.

The reversals that characterize Asians and blacks also occur among Catholics, who are as much or more likely to expect and experience non-family living as are Protestants among those becoming residentially independent. Once the very late marriage age of Catholics is taken into account, however, Catholics are less likely to expect or achieve nonfamily living than are Protestants. The difference is particularly striking for Catholics from southern Europe, whose strong avoidance of nonfamily living had been nearly totally masked by their late marriage timing. Clearly, Catholic families, like Asian and black families, maintain prolonged residential dependence in the parental home, both as a result of delayed marriage and of avoidance of nonfamily living.

Fundamentalist Protestants (Baptists and "other" Protestant groups) and those of "other" religious affiliations show the same configuration on these dimensions as southern young adults. Each group planned not only to marry early but also to avoid nonfamily living, relative to the less fundamentalist Protestants, and did so. The results are less fully consistent for those of other religions, whose low levels of expecting nonfamily living turned out not to translate into significantly lower actual patterns.

Our understanding of those with no religious affiliation is also not altered. Those who report that they have no religious affiliation expected high levels of nonfamily living but did not realize them behaviorally before marriage was taken into account. When the exit rates are considered, the expectations of the nonreligiously affiliated remain distinctive—they expect both late marriage and high level of nonfamily living—but their behavior becomes average—both in terms of marriage and in terms of premarital residential independence. This further reinforces our interpretation that the denial of religious affiliation among teenagers may mean relatively little for their later lives (chap. 5).

In contrast, Jews show quite different patterns of nonfamily living once marriage ages are included in the analysis. In at least some of our earlier analyses (particularly in chaps. 4 and 5), Jews appeared to expect and experience high levels of nonfamily living. Controlling for marriage patterns, however, eliminates this effect entirely for expectations,[12] although not for behavior. Jews carry through on their plans for late marriage (few had married by 1986) and experience very high levels of premarital residential independence.

CHANGES IN THE EFFECTS OF ETHNICITY, RELIGIOSITY, AND FAMILY ATTITUDES

Taking marriage into account clarifies and strengthens our analysis of ethnic process variables. Use of a foreign language, which strongly reduced premarital residential independence expectations and behavior, operates wholly via nonfamily living. (See upper central portion of fig. 7.1.) Living in the region in which fellow group members are most strongly concentrated has an even stronger effect on inhibiting nonfamily living than our original results had suggested, since regional concentration also encourages earlier marriages, perhaps by providing a larger marriage market than is available to those living in more ethnically dispersed settings. Generation in the United States also increases nonfamily living, an effect that had not appeared when marriage ages were not taken into account. Those closest to the immigrant generation brought with them not only an avoidance of nonfamily living but also a later age at marriage than the dominant American culture. Their distinctive marriage timing had been obscuring their avoidance of nonfamily living. Thus, the children of the foreign born have room to assimilate on two dimensions, not just one: they maintain both a later age at marriage and a lower likelihood of expecting nonfamily living than later generations.

The level of religious service attendance appears to have its effects solely through its effect on nonfamily living (and then, only for women), since those who attend frequently expect to marry and actually do so in ways that are comparable to those who attend less often. Personal religiosity also only affects nonfamily living, not marriage, at least in terms of expectations for nonfamily living. However, unlike expectations, young women with high levels of personal religiosity actually ended up experiencing relatively little nonfamily living *both* because they married somewhat early and because, even given their early marriage, they avoided nonfamily living.[13]

The effect of attending Catholic schools is clarified and sharpened by considering the timing of marriage as a route to residential independence. Much like the children of foreign-born parents, those who attended Catholic schools are indeed less likely to leave home—or to expect to—via premarital residential independence when marriage is taken into account. Since they also expect to and actually marry relatively late, our earlier analyses suggested only that Catholic school attendance encouraged nonfamily living. Now it is clear that this is the net result of marrying late, leaving young people who attended Catholic schools with extra time for leaving home before marriage. Some of them take advantage of it, although not as many as would be the case among those who did not attend Catholic schools.

Introducing exit rates in the familism analysis reveals an interesting pattern. We interpreted rating the importance of living close to parents and relatives highly as reflecting a pro-family stance that focuses on relationships between parents and children, which should have implications for male-female relationships and thus marriage (chap. 6). We contrasted this measure with two measures of gender role attitudes. One we interpreted as the least familistic, since it devalues family life by emphasizing the importance of work roles over family roles for women (NONFAM); the other we interpreted as more familistic, since it took family life for granted for both men and women but focuses on rebalancing men's and women's division of labor within the home to match that outside the home (EGALFAM).

In their expectations about the timing of marriage and residential independence, those rating living close to parents and relatives very important were focusing on nonfamily living rather than marriage. Such feelings had no effect on when they expected to marry, so that taking expected marriage ages into account made no difference; all the effect of parent-child closeness on expectations operated directly through a general aversion to leaving home prior to marriage. When the time came to establish an independent residence, however, young adults who rated this value highly turned out both to avoid nonfamily living and to delay marriage, relative to those who felt such closeness to be unimportant. Thus, such close relationships may be delaying the entrance into marriage—or it may be that an important portion of early marriages are a response to a difficult home situation. We will investigate this issue further when we examine the effects of family structure, particularly parental remarriage, on residential independence.

At the other extreme is NONFAM. Those who feel that marital and family roles are relatively unimportant for women are indeed familistic on neither the parent-child nor the male-female dimension, delaying marriage and experiencing high levels of nonfamily living, even taking into account their late marriage pattern. Their attitudes and behavior are consistent. However, those holding egalitarian attitudes about the husband-wife division of labor in the home resemble those high on NONFAM in terms of expectations (although differences are not as large) but did not rush into residential independence in early adulthood. All of the increased likelihood of experiencing nonfamily living among those holding egalitarian attitudes resulted from their delayed marriage. So, even with regard to nonfamily living, they were more family oriented than those who value family roles less than work roles.

PATHWAYS OUT OF THE HOME

We have now introduced an important set of considerations for the analysis of leaving home and marriage. Up to this point, we had examined the routes out of the home in terms of nonfamily living relative to total resi-

111

dential independence, the route ratio. This approach does not, however, take into account the timing of marriage and its effect on the likelihood of nonfamily living. Later marriage, we have argued, allows more time for nonfamily living, and therefore, the timing of marriage needs to be explicitly included. We have done so by introducing the concept of "exit rates" that measure the rate of leaving home to an independent residence via either marriage or nonfamily living.

When we first identified nonfamily living as a new phenomenon, the language describing it was and remains awkward. We have also struggled with the distinction between the route ratio and the exit rates we introduced in this chapter, attempting to capture the importance of marriage timing in this approach to analyzing premarital residential independence. Metaphorically, this distinction resembles that between the mix of hot and cold water issuing from a water tap and the volume or flow of water. When we focus on the route ratio, it is similar to the relative balance of hot and cold water, independent of the size of the flow. The exit rates parallel the volume of flows of hot and cold. Hence, the route ratio focuses on destinations; the exit rates, in contrast, focus attention on the speed of movement away from the origin, in this case, the parental home.

Does it matter whether we analyze nonfamily living in the context of route ratios or exit rates? The results in this chapter have shown that the timing of marriage has a very important impact on eventual residential independence, since many groups differ in their marriage timing, often reflecting long-established patterns. Taking expected marriage timing into account is particularly important, since young adults are even more likely to follow through on their expectations with regard to marriage than they are with regard to nonfamily living. In the analyses that follow, we will build on these insights, first by focusing even more closely on the timing of events in early adulthood—marriage, schooling, and parenthood—that can reinforce or frustrate young people's plans for residential independence before they marry. When we turn to considering the role of the parental family, we will document that the share of nonfamily living in the leaving home process—the route ratio—remains reliable for answering most questions. Considering exit rates to marriage further enriches our understanding of the role of nonfamily living in young adulthood and unravels puzzles that remain, in particular, the impact of stepparent families on leaving home.

112

8

Expectations and the Unexpected

Nonfamily residential autonomy has become normative in the transition to adulthood; it is expected and experienced by a majority of young adults. Thus, it is not surprising that the factors that increase nonfamily living are those that reflect the major structural divisions of social life—gender, social class, race, ethnic origin, and religious affiliation—with nonfamily living more frequent among those in the dominant, or more powerful, positions in the social structure. Controlling for the timing of marriage, being male, white, Protestant, and a member of an ethnic group resident for a long time in the United States increases the likelihood of both *expecting* and *experiencing* nonfamily living. These two processes are undoubtedly linked, since young adults generally take into account their likely paths in forming their expectations—such as to higher education and thus deferred marriage—so that the same forces that shape their lives become incorporated into their plans.

However, other forces are likely to influence their expectations. Young adults also dream. Their aspirations are influenced by their friends and teachers and movies, books, and television idols. As a result, they often form expectations that are not consistent with their real opportunities and constraints, and often these plans are difficult to realize. Young women may aspire to malelike careers and educational paths but later find that their gender is more of a barrier than they had expected, limiting their access to sources of funds to support their plans, either because their parents prefer to invest more in sons' educational expenses (Goldscheider and Goldscheider 1991) or because other funding sources, such as those available for military training programs, are less available to them. Similarly, young men who planned to stay home until marriage may find that the opportunities to leave and be independent are too good to pass up or that the social pressures from family or friends to leave home (which are likely to be greater on males than on females) are more than they can tolerate.

Once expectations are formed, they should also create a momentum of

113

their own, since expectations in many cases result in serious planning by young adults, leading to preparations and actions consistent with realizing them. Whatever factors led to the development of these expectations, the expectations themselves and the planning based on them influence the actual experience of nonfamily living (chap. 3). Planning thus makes a difference to later behavior. But for whom should planning have a stronger influence? Normally, those with more resources or greater power should be better able to carry out their plans. We anticipated that males, non-Hispanic whites, and those from families with higher socioeconomic status would be better able to follow through on their expectations about routes to residential independence. But as we will show, we encountered some surprises.

In addition, events may occur during the first several years after high school that were not anticipated at the time expectations about leaving home were being formed. These unexpected events, particularly those associated with critical life course changes, could also have an impact on the translation of expectations into behavior. Earlier than expected marriage is likely to have a catastrophic effect on nonfamily living, and experiencing longer than planned continuation in school or unplanned pregnancy could also affect residential decisions. Unexpected or poorly planned events should interfere with the simple connection between expectations and behavior, either by increasing the probability of the alternatives to nonfamily living—marriage or remaining residentially dependent—or by facilitating an unexpected leaving home to set up an independent residence before marriage. Therefore, the living arrangement choices young adults make result from a wide range of factors, including their background characteristics (i.e., the structural contexts of decision making), their expectations, their abilities to translate expectations into behavior, and the extent to which they are able to overcome the challenges of unexpected life course changes.

In this chapter, we consider two features of the complex linkages between expectations and behavior. We examine first the contexts in which the plans of young adults are made and in which expectations for nonfamily living are carried out. We specify the groups that have stronger linkages between expectations and behavior and identify those characterized by poor planning (where expectations and behavior are only weakly related). We then look at how events in the transition to adulthood might intervene to upset expectations. In particular, we examine how unanticipated events—those associated with marriage, parenthood, and education—block the realization of expectations about residential autonomy prior to marriage. Both analyses draw on the dynamic, longitudinal nature of the HSB survey to assess the connections between the expectations of seniors in high school and their choices during the subsequent six years.

THE "POOR PLANNERS"

Most of those who expected to leave home to establish an independent household before marriage were able to carry out their plans between 1980 and 1986, that is, within six years after their last year of high school (chap. 2). Whether or not their timing was off (and for many, residential independence came much later than they had expected in the spring of their senior year in high school), they were continuing to follow the route they had charted at that time. Many of the rest are likely to realize their plans eventually. However, there is a substantial minority who by 1986 had already followed a route different from the one they anticipated, who either experienced nonfamily living when they had expected to remain residentially dependent until marriage or who short-circuited their original plan for nonfamily living and married, achieving residential independence in the process. (Given the two-year interval between surveys, some of these might actually have experienced a brief period of nonfamily living by taking an apartment and then marrying during the same interval.) Those who have not yet achieved residential independence may change their plans as well.

On balance, however, expecting residential independence prior to marriage had a strong effect on achieving it. Even when the factors that affect both expecting and achieving nonfamily living were taken into account, such as parental resources and gender, those who expected nonfamily living were 25 percentage points more likely to achieve an independent household while unmarried than those who did not expect it—75 percent versus 50 percent (chap. 3).[1]

This pattern reflects the overall effect of expectations for the group as a whole. It is likely that some young adults were more on target and some were less. At one extreme, those whose expectations depended on plans already well in hand, like early marriage, probably planned their residential pathway very accurately. At the other extreme, those who did not take the task of filling out a questionnaire on the ages they expected to do things very seriously probably had lives with little connection to the responses they marked. We have no way to test the seriousness of their responses, but we can look at our measures of gender, class, and race/ethnicity to see whether there are important differences in the effects of some young adults' plans on their route out of the home. This analysis should give us some first clues about the forces that intervene between expectations and the eventual decisions young adults make about residential independence.

The first surprising finding when we examined the influence of class, gender, and race on the extent to which young adults were able to realize their expectations for nonfamily living was that having more resources (high parental socioeconomic status) provided almost no boost toward residential independence before marriage.[2] Those from wealthier backgrounds in general are more likely to expect and experience nonfamily living, but resources provided little additional impetus to residential independence before marriage for those who expected nonfamily living than for those who did not. Even though setting up an independent residence is expensive, those with fewer resources apparently can make a difference through planning. This suggests that dreams, and the plans based on them, are the key determinants in realizing expectations for nonfamily living, whatever the level of parental resources.

This interpretation is reinforced by the gender differences that emerged. Young women are significantly more likely to carry through their plans for nonfamily living than are young men, despite young men's greater ability to earn money early in adulthood. Figure 8.1 shows this result among those who achieved residential independence: the route ra-

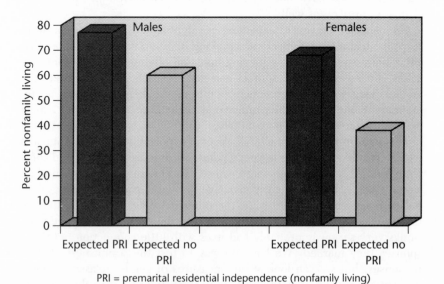

Fig. 8.1.   Percent nonfamily living by gender and expected route out of the home

116

Table 8.1. Relative odds of premarital residential independence and marriage as routes to residential independence for young men and women by their expectations

Gender and plan	PRI[a]	Marriage
Men expecting PRI	1.39	0.30
Men not expecting PRI	1.10	0.46
Women expecting PRI	1.43	0.44
Women not expecting PRI	1.00	1.00

[a] PRI = premarital residential independence

tio favors premarital residential independence for males (because they marry later) more than for females, but the difference between males who did and did not expect nonfamily living is much less than that for females. (See table B8.1 for the detailed statistical results.) Among young men who expected nonfamily residential autonomy, 76 percent of those who achieved residential independence did so prior to marriage, compared with 60 percent of otherwise comparable young men who expected residential independence with marriage—a difference of 16 percentage points. In contrast, 68 percent of young women who achieved residential independence did so prior to marriage among those who expected it, while barely one-third (38%) did so among those who did not expect it—a difference of 30 percentage points.

What explains the greater planning precision of young women? Part of the answer undoubtedly lies in the fact that women expect and do marry earlier than men, so that they are planning for a closer target, which should increase their chances of hitting it. Table 8.1 presents the relative odds of actually marrying or experiencing nonfamily living as the first stage of residential independence for young men and women who did and did not expect nonfamily living. The data show that the biggest difference among those who did and did not expect premarital residential independence is that young women planning marriage as their route out of the home were much more likely to actually follow through by 1986 than either males or females who were planning nonfamily living as their first residential independence. Young men, no matter what their plans, and those young women planning nonfamily living were less than half as likely to marry over the six-year period after high school as were young women planning marriage as their route to residential independence.

But that is not the whole story. Young women expecting nonfamily living were *more* likely to actually experience it than young men, even young men who expected it, although the differences are small. This finding suggests that the social forces that structure young adults' lives, forces that give average young men time to experience nonfamily living (so that

117

they can drift into it even if they did not expect it), can be overcome by determined young women. Women have the power to defer marriage, as we documented, and can also take the initiative to leave home before they marry to set up an independent residence. Hence, although young women overall are less likely than young men to plan for or experience nonfamily living, they can catch up to young men if they plan to.

In contrast, the racial differences in planning success are in the opposite direction: the group with the lower likelihood of experiencing nonfamily living, blacks, are least likely to carry through on their expectations. Part of this racial difference seems to reflect the same process as the gender difference—the much later marriage timing of blacks than other groups. Young white adults (i.e., nonblack, non-Asian, non-Hispanic) are more likely than young blacks to experience residential autonomy before they marry whether or not they expected it. But it is also the case that the effect of planning for nonfamily living is much greater for young white adults than for young black adults, among whom planning has essentially no effect (table 8.2).

The likelihood of achieving premarital residential independence for those who expected it among whites is 43 percent greater than for those who did not expect it. In contrast, the difference in achieving nonfamily living between blacks who did and did not expect it is very small. (The odds of achieving premarital residential independence among blacks who did not expect it were 76%, and the odds of those who did were 83%, the level of whites who did not expect it). Young blacks who expected residential autonomy before marriage show even lower odds of marrying over the six years after graduating from high school than those expecting to establish a new residence at marriage. The odds for both of these black groups are not very high: 27 percent of the level for whites not expecting premarital residential independence among blacks who also do not expect it, and 17 percent of that level among blacks who do expect it.

However, differences in marriage timing are unlikely to be the whole story, since Hispanics plan about as well as whites, despite their later marriage age. Further, the effect of expecting premarital residential independence is significantly greater for young Asian-Americans than for the majority of white adults, despite their much later marriage age. Unlike other groups, young Asian-Americans' plans for nonfamily living had no effect on their very low likelihood of marriage; marriage is so late for them that those planning nonfamily living do not have to defer marriage further to realize their plans for living independently before marriage.

The results are surprising—greater planning prowess of young women and Asians, poor planning of young blacks, and inability of parental resources to help young adults realize their plans. Part, but clearly not all,

Table 8.2. Relative odds of premarital residential independence and marriage as routes to residential independence for young adults by race and expectations

Race and plan	PRI[a]	Marriage
Whites expecting PRI	1.43	0.50
Whites not expecting PRI	1.00	1.00
Blacks expecting PRI	0.83	0.17
Blacks not expecting PRI	0.76	0.27
Hispanics expecting PRI	0.76	0.31
Hispanics not expecting PRI	0.53	0.55
Asians expecting PRI	0.99	0.25
Asians not expecting PRI	0.51	0.27

[a] PRI = premarital residential independence

of the answer is associated with the timing of these events in the life course. An additional possibility is that these patterns result from differences among these groups in their ability to plan other dimensions of their lives among the densely packed transitions of young adulthood.

UNEXPECTED EVENTS: MARRIAGE, CHILDBEARING, AND SCHOOLING SURPRISES

An important consideration in young people's ability to carry out their plans for residential independence is likely to be their progress on the rest of the schedule they set for themselves. Whether a young adult expects to leave home before marriage is strongly influenced by the age marriage is expected (chap. 7). This could mean that those whose plans for marriage were delayed might well increase their likelihood of experiencing nonfamily living. They would have more time to do so; further, their early marriage plans might well have been linked to wanting early residential independence, causing them to substitute one route out of the home (nonfamily living) for the other (marriage). While marrying *before* one expected to is likely to have a calamitous effect on the likelihood of experiencing nonfamily living, becoming a parent prior to the time expected could also propel young adults into residential independence. Earlier than expected parenthood and changes in marriage plans, then, may be important intervening events in the transition to adulthood and in the establishment of an independent residence.

When young people plan to complete school may also be an important component of their plans for residential independence. Those who drop out of school earlier than they anticipated might well want to move out—

119

and may perhaps be less welcome in the parental home; those who decide to extend their schooling beyond their original plans might also change their route to residential independence. Poor planning on all these dimensions—marriage, parenthood, and education—might therefore account for some of the discrepancy between the original expectations young adults have for residential autonomy before they marry and later patterns of leaving home.

To examine whether planning efficacy in these other areas of young adulthood might be influencing who achieves nonfamily living, we calculated a series of measures based on comparing the ages young adults said they expected to marry, become parents, and finish school with what they were actually doing on these dimensions at those ages (to the extent we could observe them). Thus, if we observe a young person who became a parent at age 20 but who had expected to do so at age 23, we know that he or she became a parent earlier than expected. If instead we see no evidence of parenthood even at age 24, we know that parenthood was delayed for that person relative to expectations. Among those who expected to be a parent at some age later than we could observe, for example, 25 or older, however, we could only tell if it happened earlier than expected but not if it happened on time or late. Therefore, those who marry or become parents or leave school "late" are generally those who expected relatively early transitions in these areas. Nevertheless, our observations extend well past the median age of expecting to finish school and to about the median age of expecting to marry; only those who experienced "late parenthood" are seriously biased toward those expecting unusually early parenthood.

Keeping this caveat in mind, we can now ask, Who plans their progress toward new family roles and educational attainment well, and who plans poorly? Are the patterns the same as for successful planning to leave home before marriage?

Overall, about 20 percent of young adults were off course in their plans for marriage and school by 1986, while only 9 percent were off schedule in terms of plans for parenthood (table 8.3). These young people had been "optimistic" both about marriage and about school, planning earlier marriage and longer schooling than they experienced. Two-thirds of those off their anticipated marriage timing experienced delay; 78 percent of those who were not on their educational trajectory had dropped out of school earlier than they had planned at the end of high school. Only a little over a fifth remained in school longer than they had expected.

These are substantial life course changes, which could easily account for discrepancies between expectations for nonfamily living and its real-

Table 8.3. Percentages experiencing marriage, parenthood, and school termination earlier or later than expected (unweighted)

	Total off-schedule	Percentage early	Percentage late
Marriage	20.4	33.0	67.0
Parenthood	8.6	51.7	48.3
School termination	19.7	78.0	22.0

ization. However, they really do not seem to be an important part of the explanation. Taking into account planning status in these three realms—marriage, parenthood, and schooling—did not alter in any way the relationship between expectations and behavior. Moreover, those who are poor planners about their route to residential independence are not necessarily poor planners in these other transitions in adulthood. For example, although young women seem to plan for nonfamily living better than young men, they are actually more likely to marry earlier than planned, much more likely to become a parent earlier than planned, and even somewhat more likely to leave school earlier than planned, compared with young men.[3]

The black-white difference in expecting and achieving premarital residential independence also does not seem to be linked to similar patterns on these other life course dimensions. Young blacks are more likely than whites to become parents earlier than they originally planned, but for both groups, only a few are involved, with unexpectedly early parenthood characterizing 4.5 percent of whites[4] compared with 7.4 percent of young blacks. Black-white differences in school trajectories are small, and blacks are less likely, not more likely, to be off schedule in terms of their expectations about marriage.

The opposite pattern characterizes Hispanics. Young Hispanics resembled white non-Hispanics in their level of planning accuracy for leaving home before marriage but were much less accurate in their plans for marriage, parenthood, or schooling. Hispanics married, became parents, and left school earlier than they expected far more often than non-Hispanic whites, with differences most dramatic for schooling. High school dropout rates are well known to be higher among Hispanics than other groups in the United States, but these data suggest that even among those completing high school, Hispanics were half again as likely not to meet their goals for higher education as non-Hispanic whites.

Only two groups link on-target expectations for nonfamily living with careful planning in these other realms—Asian-Americans and Jews.[5] Both were particularly unlikely to marry or become parents earlier than they planned (just 2% of young Asians and less than 1% of the Jews experienced unexpectedly early parenthood). Asians were somewhat less likely than average to drop out of school earlier than expected (13% vs. 15%), and only 8 percent of Jews experienced this unexpected outcome. Nevertheless, these are very small groups. It is clear, overall, that there is little relationship between planning successfully for leaving home before marriage and carrying out plans in these other domains of early adulthood.

We also examined the reverse question: Do those who plan for nonfamily living plan their other transitions well? Premarital residential independence as a route out of the parental home needs to be carefully placed between childhood and new family formation, which are both more clearly established life course stages than nest leaving. We found that in most respects, those who expected nonfamily residential independence resembled fairly closely those who did not in terms of their planning success for marriage and parenthood. The later marriage plans of those expecting nonfamily living meant that they were less likely to be behind schedule in their timing of marriage and parenthood.

But they differed quite substantially in terms of school planning. Young adults who planned to leave home before marriage were considerably more likely to terminate schooling earlier than expected (19% for those expecting nonfamily living compared with 11% for those not expecting it). This finding suggests that when young adults are confronted with a trade-off between resources needed to continue in school and resources needed to maintain an independent residence, those who expected nonfamily living are more likely to make the choice to drop out of school earlier than they planned rather than forgo residential independence. If so, nonfamily living may not only be financially expensive for young adults in the short term. If it causes them to compromise their eventual earning capacity, because many choose to leave school earlier than they had planned, nonfamily living might be even more expensive in the long term. This possibility should be examined in future research.

UNEXPECTED EVENTS AND NONFAMILY LIVING

Failing to realize other plans early in adulthood, whether or not they relate to expecting to leave home before marriage, should nevertheless have an effect on actually achieving it. The most obvious example is marriage, which, if it occurs earlier than planned, could well preclude nonfamily living. But delayed marriage could increase nonfamily living, if

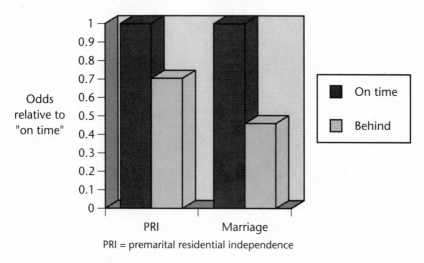

PRI = premarital residential independence

Fig. 8.2. Effect of marriage delay on route to residential autonomy

those expecting early marriage decide to move out of the parental home anyway when marriage does not materialize.

MISTIMED MARRIAGES

What we find, however, is the opposite: those who had not married by the age they had expected to were only 71 percent as likely to move out of the parental home to nonfamily living as those who were still on time in terms of marriage plans (fig. 8.2, table B8.3). (They were also less likely to establish residential independence via marriage, which is not very surprising.) Far from moving out of the parental home anyway, these young people, who had planned early marriage but not achieved it, were still residentially dependent. This finding suggests that some of the recent increase in young adults' living with parents has resulted directly from the delay in marriage, a delay that not even the young people themselves expected.

MISTIMED PARENTHOOD

Most young people link their expected timing of parenthood quite closely to their expected timing of marriage. As a result, those who were behind on their parenthood timing resemble those who were behind in terms of marriage, at least with regard to nonfamily living (fig. 8.3, table B8.3). This suggests that a significant segment of those who experienced delayed parenthood were those who had not married when they expected to.

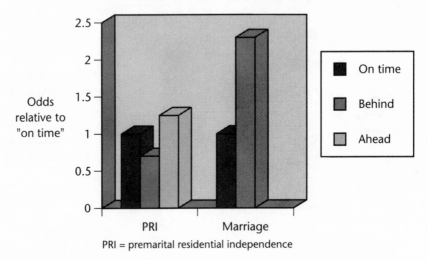

PRI = premarital residential independence

Fig. 8.3. Effect of parenthood mistiming on route to residential independence

However, many of those who experienced delayed parenthood actually did marry, following through on that part of their plan, but evidently decided not to have children so quickly.[6]

Those who found parenthood occurring earlier than expected show a similar pattern: for many, early parenthood was linked to marriage,[7] suggesting a "shotgun" effect still operated in the 1980s. For many others, the link between marriage and parenthood turned out to be more distant. The linkage between early parenthood and marriage was stronger at higher levels of parental socioeconomic status, as well as for Asian-Americans, Hispanics, and non-Hispanic Catholics, groups that may be less accepting of unmarried parenthood. In contrast, early parenthood was only half as likely to be linked with marriage among blacks (data not presented).

Those who did not marry when they became parents earlier than they expected were more likely to establish a nonfamily independent residence than those on time (and much more likely than those who were behind their schedules). These unexpectedly early parents who establish residential independence as unmarried persons are not, of course, experiencing nonfamily living in the pure sense, since in most cases the child moved with them, establishing a single-parent household. Interestingly, this effect was considerably *weaker* among those who had expected nonfamily living; they were less likely to move out to unmarried residential independence on becoming a parent than those who had not expected nonfamily living. This suggests that those expecting nonmarital residential independence had not planned it to come with unmarried parenthood.

When we consider changes in school plans directly, it becomes clear that remaining in school beyond the age expected has a dampening effect on both routes out of the parental home—before and with marriage (table B8.3). Those who were still in school at ages after they had expected to be no longer in school, whether because achieving their desired level took longer or because remaining in school became more feasible or desirable, were only 82 percent as likely to achieve an independent residence before marriage as those on the schooling schedule they had expected and only 66 percent as likely to marry (fig. 8.4). This relationship between extended schooling and delay of residential independence was characteristic of both sexes and all racial, ethnic, and religious groups; however, at higher levels of parental socioeconomic status, staying longer in school proved to be much less of a hindrance to marriage.

In contrast, those dropping out, that is, ending schooling earlier than originally planned, were very likely to marry, although there was no overall effect on nonfamily living. When an independent residence comes with marriage, remaining in school may be less feasible than when an independent residence occurs before marriage; so that they dropped out

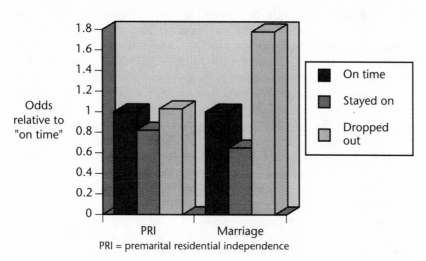

PRI = premarital residential independence

Fig. 8.4.   Effect of school mistiming on route to residential independence

125

of school to achieve an independent residence—via marriage. These patterns varied sharply by sex, however. Predictably, the relationship between dropping out and marriage was much stronger for young women than for young men, consistent with what we know about the greater incompatibility of the married and student roles for women than for men (Goldscheider and Waite 1991).

There was also a strong link between ending school early and leaving home *before* marriage among young women but not among young men (data not presented). The effect is not dramatic: young women who left school early were only 13 percent more likely to experience nonfamily living than those on time. The gender difference suggests that girls experience sharper trade-offs than boys, not only between marriage and student status but also between nonfamily living and student status. Married men are often able to stay in school because their spouse—or less commonly, their parents—subsidize their continuing education, which is much less likely for wives. These results suggest that *parents* are more likely to subsidize their sons so that they can remain in school and in an independent residence before they marry than they are to subsidize their daughters. Young women have to leave school to be residentially autonomous, while young men do not.

PLANNING AND NONFAMILY LIVING

This analysis highlights the importance of plans and expectations in young adulthood. The plans of young adults matter for nonfamily living, even among those who cannot expect much help from their surroundings. Although some aspects of context can reinforce their plans, those from families with low socioeconomic status have as much of a chance to realize their plans for nonfamily living as those from higher-status families; young women are more rather than less likely to meet their own expectations than young men, despite the greater social support young men receive for independent residence. Most important, the connection between plans and expectations in young adulthood and nonfamily living suggests that nonfamily living does not just happen but is often the result of deliberate planning and expectations among young adults who are integrating their residential autonomy in the contexts of marriage, education, and parenthood plans in the transition to adulthood.

Consistent with our finding in chapter 7 that marriage expectations appear to be followed through more consistently than expectations for nonfamily living, we have documented that poor planning for marriage, parenthood, or school is not very closely linked to planning for nonfamily living. Those who marriage plans did not work out do not change their plans to achieve a substitute route out of the home. Some young people confronting unexpectedly young parenthood may be forced out of the parental home to unmarried independence as a result. One troubling exception emerged, however, which is the link between dropping out of school early and nonfamily living, particularly among young women. Living in the parental home is an efficient subsidy for higher education, so that if plans for residential autonomy are taking precedence over plans for additional schooling, the gains in independence may be coming at a high cost.

However, so far we have only looked at the influence of the plans of young adults and their expectations for nonfamily living. There may be other pressures on them that they did not take into account in forming their plans, pressures from their families and *their* expectations about what should happen next in the transition to adulthood. In the next chapters, we will turn our attention to the family context specifically and consider how family structure (particularly parental divorce and remarriage), family resources (particularly those provided to the children directly—or obtained from them), and parental expectations per se influence pathways to residential independence.

9

Family Structure

Our discussions to this point have focused on young adults—their attitudes and values (about family closeness and sex roles) and their life course progress (marriage, parenthood, and schooling). However, they did not come to adulthood in a vacuum; the parental family should also be taken into account. It provides a context (like an ethnic or racial group or a region of the country) within which young adults form their attitudes and values. The family is also a group of related individuals—primarily the parents and their children—whose decisions affect each others' lives. Parents provide the resources that increase the likelihood both of expecting and of experiencing nonfamily living, and, of particular interest in this chapter, they also make many decisions that could influence their children's *desires* to leave home, so that they no longer *want* to remain in their parents' home. Why might this be the case?

One implication of the decision to defer independent residence and continue to live in the parental home is that young adults participate in face-to-face relationships with the others who live there as dependents of their parents: sharing space in the public areas of their parents' homes and in household amenities (e.g., the refrigerator and, often, the television and car) and, in turn, acknowledging their parents' rules and authority. These relationships are ordinarily positive, in that children normally love and respect their parents. Living at home can be supportive and helpful for young adults, providing them with useful guidance in the multiple decisions they face during these years. It can also confer major economic advantages, giving them greater access to their parents' resources and life-style than would be possible on their own.

Such relationships can become problematic in late adolescence and early adulthood as young adults begin to feel the need to be independent and assert their adult status. If so, they are likely to feel that their parents are demanding a great deal from them, perhaps asking for too much financial or emotional support or perhaps simply far too much obedience. Or they may simply find their parents' meddling—or even their lack of in-

128

terest—too difficult to handle on a daily basis. In many contemporary American homes, it is likely that these relationships have become even more problematic. Many parents socialize their children to be independent rather than obedient from a very early age (Alwin 1988). For them, residential independence has become part of the conception of what "adulthood" means.

The relationships between older adolescents and their parents can also become a problem if young people do not feel that this is still *their family*, for example, those who have gone through the divorce revolution in the United States, as their parents have divorced and remarried and shared the experience with their children. For children, divorce means living for some period of time in a mother-only family; remarriage means acquiring a stepparent, often accompanied by stepsiblings and perhaps even followed by half siblings in a "blended" family. Thus, many of these young adults spent some portion of their early years growing up in households that did not contain the simple nuclear family. This experience has been particularly common in black families—and particularly uncommon in Asian-American families.

Experiencing these family forms in childhood may affect the decisions of young adults about leaving the parental home. Part of the support provided in nuclear families may be less available in reconstituted or mother-only families. Blended families, for example, have weak institutional and normative supports for step relationships, thereby leading to strains between the generations (Cherlin 1978); stepparents provide to their stepchildren less *parental* support in terms of supervision and involvement than biological parents do to their "own" children (Schwebel, Fine, and Renner 1991). They also provide less financial support when the stepchildren are in college (Goldscheider and Goldscheider 1991). Children with only one resident parent (typically their mother), who has thus been raising them alone, might also feel that one parent is not much better than none, depending on how well she has met her disproportionate parental responsibility. Research has also shown that the presence of stepchildren often results in family conflict and therefore may lead to stepchildren leaving home earlier than other children (White and Booth 1985; Mitchell, Wister, and Burch 1989; Aquilino 1990).

Thus, the changing structure of families is likely to have an influence on young adults' plans and decisions about nonfamily living, either through an increase in generational conflict or the absence of many of the benefits that might offset continuing dependence. Although their painful experiences with the parents' marriages may make them reluctant to marry at an early age, they are likely to want to get away from homes filled with conflict and not feel it terribly important to remain close to a family that can provide little support for them in what might be a long interval before marriage. Specifically, we expect that children in mother-only households and those in families with a stepparent will be less likely to wait for marriage (or to plan to do so) before establishing an independent residence.

The structure of the parental family may have particular significance for the nonfamily living patterns of ethnic and racial groups. For example, the structure of the black family may be a key to understanding the high level of expected nonfamily living among young black adults and their delayed marriage. Perhaps other ethnic and religious differences in routes to residential independence in young adulthood can also be clarified by introducing family structural considerations.

The decision to leave the parental home before marriage may, therefore, not only be the outcome of young adults' own characteristics but also may reflect the *kinds* of families that they grew up in, the structure of these families, and the likely history of relationships within them. To study the context within which young adults make their decisions about residential independence, we focus on this family and household context more concretely. Specifically, we examine how the structure of the family influences whether young adults expect residential autonomy before marriage and whether they experience it. Our primary questions are: (1) How does living in a mother-only family, a reconstructed family, or a nuclear family influence nonfamily living? Do the effects of parental family structure operate primarily through marriage or through nonfamily living? (2) Is the influence of family structure on nonfamily living similar for daughters and sons? (3) Do differences in parental family structure help us understand racial, ethnic, and religious differences in patterns of nonfamily living among young adults?

THE EFFECTS OF FAMILY STRUCTURE
ON NONFAMILY LIVING AND MARRIAGE

Three family structure types were delineated, indicating whether the respondent's family (1) was mother-only, (2) included a stepparent, or (3) was of some other sort. The construction was based on responses to a series of questions about the presence or absence in the household of various household members, including mother, father, male guardian, female guardian, and other potential household members. A mother-only family was defined as a family in which no father or male guardian was present (or where information on male relatives was missing) and the student's household included a mother or female guardian.[1] A stepparent family

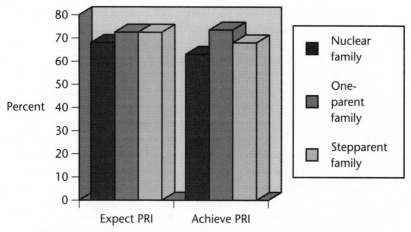

Fig. 9.1.   Effect of family structure on expecting and experiencing nonfamily living

included a parent of one sex and a "guardian" of the other. Most of the remaining families (93%) had both a mother and a father (but not a male or female guardian) present. Hence we shall refer to these families as "nuclear" families.[2]

Those living in mother-only families or in stepparent families are more likely than those in nuclear families to expect and experience nonfamily living rather than marriage as their route out of the home (fig. 9.1, table B9.1).[3] These effects are somewhat stronger for actual behavior than for expectations; the effect of living in one-parent families is also stronger than the effect of living in stepfamilies. Both those in mother-only families and those in stepfamilies were about 6 percentage points more likely to expect nonfamily living than those in nuclear families (73% vs. 67%). Among those actually experiencing residential independence, 67 percent of young adults from stepfamilies did so while not married and 74 percent of those from mother-only families did so via that route, compared with only 63 percent of those from nuclear families.

We had expected that at least part of the effect of family structure would be mediated by whether young adults attached importance to family closeness, which we documented greatly reduced their likelihood of expecting or achieving nonfamily living (chap. 6). It seemed reasonable to postulate that if children in stepparent families expect residential independence before marriage, it would be associated with greater conflict in these families, which would be reflected in the importance young adults attach to family closeness. If those in stepparent or mother-only families

131

feel that their family provides them with little social and emotional support, this should be reflected in feeling that remaining close to their families is not very important, even in the absence of conflict.

However, this was not the case (data not presented). There were no changes in the results when we included the measure of family closeness in the same analysis with the measures of family structure. This is because there are surprisingly few differences among mother-only, stepparent, and nuclear families in the importance young adults attach to being close to their parents and relatives. Young adults in mother-only families give responses to the question on the importance of living close to parents and relatives that are almost identical to those given by young adults in nuclear families (scoring 0.83 compared with 0.85 on the scale, in which 0 = not at all important, 1 = somewhat important, and 2 = very important), and those in stepparent families score only somewhat lower (0.78). Evidently, even if such families are conflict-ridden, there will be *some* family member with whom it is important for young adults to remain close.

We also tested whether the effects of family closeness on nonfamily living would be greater among stepfamilies and mother-only families, since family conflict would have a stronger effect on tenuously bound families than on those in more strongly institutionalized families. This also was not the case (data not presented). There were no significant differences in the effect of family closeness by family type; feeling that living close to parents was not important had no more effect on nonfamily living among young adults from mother-only or stepparent families than it did among those from nuclear families.[4] Thus, the higher probability that young adults from stepparent families or from mother-only families leave home before marriage reflects something about the contexts of those families and how these contexts influence the attitudes of young adults toward the two routes out of the home—before and at marriage. The influence of these structural family contexts on how young adults choose to establish their own home appears unaffected by any particular importance they attach to feeling close to their parent(s).

Many studies have found that experiencing nonnuclear families in childhood affects a wide range of family-related behaviors in early adulthood, including sexual behavior, out-of-wedlock parenthood, and age at marriage (Goldscheider and Waite 1991, Thornton 1991). We have now documented that such experiences also influence nonfamily living. However, parental family structure influences the age children marry, and, in turn, we have documented that the timing of marriage has an important influence on nonfamily living (chap. 7). Do experiences of living in mother-only or stepparent families affect leaving home only through marriage timing, or do these experiences have effects independent of the timing of marriage?

Timing of marriage

Odds of PRI	Early	Moderate	Late
Low	South	-------	Blacks Asians Catholics Hispanics
Average	-------	(Prot 2, female, white, central region, nuclear)	Males (B) Northeast & Pacific (B) Jews (E)*
High	Stepfamily (B)	Stepfamily (E)	Males (E) Socioeconomic status* Northeast & Pacific (E) Jews (B) Mother only

E = Expectations
B = Behavior
* = females only
PRI = Premarital residential independence

Fig. 9.2. Influence of family structure on the timing of marriage and premarital residential independence

The data show that experiencing nonnuclear family structures influences nonfamily living both through early leaving home and through marriage delay. The effects of living in a mother-only family during the high school senior year differ substantially from those of living in a stepfamily at that age and are not fully consistent in their effects on expectations and later behavior. (Detailed data are presented in table C9.1.) Figure 9.2 shows how the effects of family structure influence expectations and behavior and how their effects compare with those from our basic model. (We follow the format developed in chap. 7.)

Those living in a mother-only family increase their orientation toward nonfamily living both by delaying marriage and by leaving home earlier than those in nuclear families. This places them in the lower right-hand corner of figure 9.2 in terms of both expectations and behavior. This pattern is similar to, but even more consistent than, that of males relative to females (which only applies to expectations) and young adults from higher socioeconomic status families compared with those in lower socioeconomic status families (which applies to both expectations and behavior only for females).

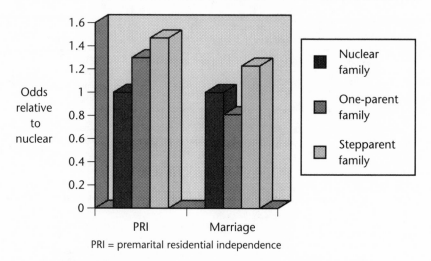

Fig. 9.3.   Effect of family structure on routes to residential autonomy

The precise size of this effect is shown in figure 9.3 for behavior, but the same pattern characterizes expectations. Young adults living in a mother-only household are more than 30 percent more likely to establish an independent household while unmarried than they are to remain residentially dependent, compared with those living in nuclear families; they are also only 82 percent *as likely* to marry as their peers living in two-parent nuclear families. These results are consistent with their expectations, since their greater likelihood of expecting nonfamily living is substantially (but by no means fully) reduced when their later expected marriage age is taken into account.

Young adults from stepparent families have a distinctive pattern in terms of actual nonfamily living. In our previous analyses, we were not able to identify any group of young adults that both married early *and* left home before marriage (fig. 7.2). The lower left quadrant, indicating rapid exit rates both to marriage and to nonfamily living, remained empty. But young adults from stepfamilies leave their families at an accelerated rate via both routes. Figure 9.3 shows that although they are substantially more likely to leave for residential independence before marriage (46%) than at marriage (22%) compared with those in nuclear families, the effect on early marriage is a strong one. (A similar linkage between stepfamilies and early marriage was found by Thornton [1991].)

These results indicate that the effect of living in a stepparent family was seriously underestimated in figure 9.1, where stepparenthood appeared to have less impact on nonfamily living than living in a mother-only family. The data in figure 9.1, based on comparing the proportion leaving to independent residence before marriage with those leaving to marriage *among those establishing an independent household,* missed much of the effect of stepparent families on nest leaving, since this family structure increases leaving by both routes.

These two results—late marriage for those in one-parent families, early marriage for those in stepfamilies—appear unusual, especially when those living in stepfamilies ordinarily spend some time, an average estimated to be about five years (Bumpass, Sweet, and Martin 1989), in a mother-only family. Clearly, things changed substantially as a result of their mothers' remarriages. Moreover, young adults living in stepparent families did not anticipate early marriage. Their pattern of expected marriage placed them in the lower middle square of figure 9.2, since they expected to marry at about the same time as those from nuclear families—even a little later (although not so late as those living in mother-only families). Together these findings suggest that some young people from stepfamilies are reacting to immediate conditions in their stepparental family by leaving home any way they can. If the resources to leave home while unmarried are not available, then some other way is found to support their residential independence. In contrast, young people from mother-only families are responding to their experiences by delaying marriage, not leaving their mother's household much earlier than those in two-parent families. Their greater likelihood of leaving home to nonfamily living is offset by their reduced propensity to leave to marriage.

What is it, then, that leads young people in mother-only and stepparent families to plan for residential independence prior to marriage? Is it only young women who are escaping a stepparent family via marriage, or do young men also try to form a new family early in adulthood? Are there differences by social class in these patterns, so that poverty reinforces the difficulties of mother-only and stepfamilies, or do these patterns characterize such families at all levels of socioeconomic status? How do these family structure effects on residential autonomy clarify the racial and ethnic differences we have observed in nonfamily living in young adulthood? The rest of this chapter focuses on these questions.

SONS AND DAUGHTERS IN BLENDED
AND MOTHER-ONLY FAMILIES

Given contemporary patterns of child custody after divorce or separation (and the growth of out-of-wedlock parenthood), many have expected that sons would be affected more than daughters by nonnuclear family experiences, since their relationships with their same-sex parent are likely to have been more damaged than their sisters' relationships have been.

135

However, the lesson that marriage is not forever may be more *salient* for young women, whose roles have been normally focused more on investments in marital relationships than young men's. Does family structure shape the nonfamily living expectations and experiences of one gender more than the other?

Our results show that the effect on the likelihood of marriage both of having a stepfamily and of living in a mother-only household are much greater for young women than for young men (table B9.2). The unexpectedly high level of marriage out of stepfamilies turns out only to characterize daughters. The marriage delay associated with mother-only families only characterizes daughters as well.

These patterns strongly suggest an interpretation of maternal role modeling, in which the recent experiences of mothers are having specific effects on critical choices of their daughters. It appears that in many cases, the negative experiences mothers have of raising children alone discourages daughters from marrying. In contrast, seeing their mothers as "new" brides evidently reinforces the positive aspects of marriage.

Furthermore, these results direct our attention to resource differences between mother-only and stepfamilies. Daughters whose mothers did not remarry (and whose families are thus likely to have fewer resources than they had prior to divorce) may well have learned that marriage is economically problematic for women, since in many cases it led their mothers to neglect developing their own abilities to support themselves and instead to trust their husbands (mistakenly, it turned out) to do so. Sons rarely learn such a hard lesson, since their fathers normally benefit financially by divorce. In contrast, daughters whose mothers remarried learned directly that remarriage confers substantial economic benefits (Hoffman and Duncan 1988) and are therefore likely to be very receptive to marriage for themselves.

This latter interpretation is reinforced by the finding that the negative effect on marriage of having a mother-only family compared with a nuclear family is greatest for those at the lowest levels of current socioeconomic status. These are the families that suffered the most from marital breakup and in which the lesson of self-support would be most dramatically learned. In contrast, in high socioeconomic status families, the effect of the negative lessons of living in mother-only families on the likelihood of marriage would be much less, compared with living in nuclear families.

FAMILY STRUCTURE AND ETHNIC FAMILIES

Could the introduction of family structural factors clarify the racial and ethnic differences in nonfamily living documented in chapter 4? It is

Table 9.1. Family measures for basic groups (unweighted)

Family variables	Total	Asians	Blacks	Hispanics
Mother-only family	16.6	9.1	34.0	16.1
Stepparent family	7.1	4.1	9.4	6.4
Nuclear family	76.3	86.8	56.6	77.5

widely known, for example, that higher proportions of blacks than whites live in female-headed households (Sweet and Bumpass 1987). Does the greater likelihood of nonfamily living among black Americans—and their lower marriage propensities—reflect their very different family structures? Similarly, we have documented that Asians and Hispanics have lower levels of nonfamily living. Are these patterns the result of their greater concentration in nuclear families? These questions address the links between group differences in nonfamily residential independence and group patterns of family structure. We also test whether the impact of family structure on premarital residential independence differs within racial and ethnic groups. For example, is the black pattern of higher levels of residential independence more characteristic of those in mother-only households? Are the effects of race on nonfamily living reduced among those living in nuclear families, such that blacks in nuclear families have patterns of residential autonomy comparable to whites?

Data in table 9.1 begin to address these questions by displaying the differences among blacks, Asians, and Hispanics in the proportions living in nuclear, mother-only, and stepfamilies. Overall, more than three-fourths of these young adults were living in nonremarried nuclear families; of those who were not, about twice as many lived in mother-only as lived in stepfamilies. Asians are distinctive in their high proportions living in nuclear families, while blacks have an extraordinary high proportion of young adults who are not, primarily because they are living in mother-only families. Further, young blacks in two-parent families are more likely to be in stepfamilies than are non-Hispanic whites. This suggests strongly that differences in family structure may have been influencing the patterns of differences in nonfamily living among these groups that we observed earlier (chaps. 3 and 4).

THE BLACK FAMILY

We turn first to one of the great puzzles of the American family—the uniqueness of black family structure. A wide range of explanations have been suggested for the extraordinarily high proportions of female-headed families found in black communities, including the cultural heritage of customs from their West African origins (Morgan and Kramerow 1992), the disruptions of American slavery in the United States (Moynihan 1965), migration out of the South, residential segregation (Massey and Denton 1987), discrimination against black men leading to high rates of unemployment (Wilson 1987), and the chain linking poverty to welfare dependence and thus the forced exclusion of males from the household to qualify for aid (Ross and Sawhill 1976). Whatever the reasons, however, conspicuous family structural differences between black and white Americans remain: young black adults grow up with quite different experiences of family structure than do others, and these differences—of father absence, sometimes followed by mother's remarriage—are likely to have effects on their expectations for nonfamily living and their actual patterns.

If we assumed that the effects of family structure were the same for young blacks as for other young adults, this great difference in family structure would indeed appear to account for the delay in marriage experienced by black young adults and the opportunity this gives them to experience nonfamily living. However, when we tested this assumption, we found that expectations for and experience of nonfamily living among blacks are both much less sensitive to the effects of family structure than is the case for other groups. There are no differences either in the likelihood of marrying or of forming an independent residence before marriage between black young adults in stepparent families, mother-only families, or nuclear families and very little difference in their expectations. Young black adults living in all types of family structures marry very late and leave at a late age to nonfamily households (but expect and experience proportionately somewhat more nonfamily living as a result of their high marriage age).

It may be that nonblacks show stronger effects of family structure than blacks because divorce, mother-only, and blended families are relatively "new" experiences for them, experiences for which they have had little preparation by observing the families of their friends and relatives. Blacks, in contrast, have had longer to adjust to these family structural experiences and may have adapted to them by finding family surrogates and family networks that substitute and compensate for an absent parent. While not living in the same households, parents and relatives may be nearby and accessible in the local neighborhood for support and assistance. If so, this might account for our finding that black young adults' expectations for and experiences of nonfamily living are less influenced by growing up in one-parent families and stepfamilies than whites.

It is also the case that blacks are less affected by several other factors that have played a role in our analysis of the process of leaving home

before marriage. Living in the South or the North made much less difference for blacks than for whites (chap. 4); and being a Protestant or a
Catholic was much more important for whites than for blacks (chap. 5). It
may be that the ubiquity of segregation, the shared experiences among
blacks, and, in turn, the closer ties among blacks than among whites result in the absence of differentiation within the black community.

ASIAN-AMERICAN AND HISPANIC-AMERICAN FAMILIES

Nonnuclear family experiences are much less common among Hispanic
young adults and especially uncommon among Asian young adults. Only
a very small proportion of Asian young adults live in mother-only families
or with a stepparent. This suggests that the lower level of nonfamily living
among Asians, both in terms of residential expectations and behavior,
might primarily be a function of their high concentration in nuclear families. This turns out to be the case, since when family structure variables
are considered, the distinctively low likelihood that Asians will experience nonfamily living becomes much less exceptional, and the Asian difference is no longer statistically significant for expectations.

Although there are only a few young Asian adults who were not living
with both parents, the effect of family structure on their nonfamily living
experience was considerably exaggerated, compared with the overall effect for non-Hispanic whites. Asians in stepfamilies were significantly
more likely to leave home by both routes—before they married and at
marriage—than others in stepfamilies, completely offsetting their "normal" low levels of marriage and residential autonomy before marriage.
This reinforces our interpretation of the lack of impact of family structure
on nonfamily living among black families, since the Asian pattern is the
opposite side of the same coin: the group where these family structural
patterns are very rare is the most responsive to the effects of family structure on the routes selected out of the parental home.

In contrast to blacks and Asians, there are no differences between the
effects of family structure on either nonfamily residential autonomy or
marriage between Hispanics and non-Hispanic whites. This may reflect
the similarity in family structure of Hispanics and the majority population; if so, this reinforces our interpretation above that having an unusually high (or low) proportion of nuclear families influences how much impact family structure has on young adults' transitions to residential
independence. It may also be that the family values of Hispanics, particularly gender-differentiated roles and generational closeness, are the key
factors shaping their nonfamily living expectations and behavior and not
the structure of the family per se.

CONCLUSION

Both children and their parents are involved in the decision of whether children should continue to live in the parental household until they marry or should move out and establish an independent residence before marriage. Since this is a family decision involving both the child and the parents, it reflects and affects the relationships between the generations. As an emerging family phenomenon, nonfamily living is associated with less intergenerational sharing and greater independence from the kind of face-to-face monitoring that continued coresidence into adulthood implies for both generations.

Much more research needs to be directed to uncovering the basis of generational consensus and conflict over the patterns of nonfamily living. This is particularly important given the family nature of the decision to leave home and establish an independent household. We shall further examine these relationships in chapter 11 when we contrast the factors that affect the expectations of parents with those that affect the expectations of their children. We also consider who "wins" when disagreement characterizes the generations and investigate whose expectations for the timing of nest leaving are more predictive of the actual patterns of leaving home before marriage. Parents and children are likely to surprise each other, as each proceeds along their joint and separate life courses.

10

Education, Income, and Generational Resource Flows

One of the broader implications of the importance of family structure on nonfamily living is that circumstances in the home in which young adults are raised have an impact on their transition to adulthood. The focus on the parental home shifts our attention toward the parents and the family and the processes linking the generations, building another layer onto our analysis of individual and life course effects on nonfamily living. It also redirects our attention to social class as a context shaping the relationships between the generations in the household decisions about residential independence. In this chapter, we disentangle the components of social class by separately examining parental income and education and by analyzing directly the access young adults have to the resources they are likely to need to support residential independence.

Many view increasing affluence as the central cause of the shift from family-based living arrangements toward nonfamily living. Historically, rising income and intergenerational social mobility have been linked to the decline in family orientation and the growing independence and autonomy of young adults. Families increasingly lost direct control over economic production and consumption as a result of the processes that separated family and economic spheres of activities. The result of these processes was to move economic activities out of the family and reduce its control over economic resources and their distribution (chap. 1).

The argument that rising income is primarily responsible for the increases in living alone (nonfamily living) derives from a theory of consumer demand. It compares living arrangements decisions to other decisions such as the purchase of coffee. In this approach, unmarried persons are assumed to prefer privacy to companionship in their living arrangements; separate living—privacy—is more expensive than sharing a home, and thus higher income enables them to afford the privacy that comes from living alone, while those with lower incomes must share living arrangements (Michael, Fuchs, and Scott 1980).

This logic also suggests that over time, as the economic conditions of

141

individuals improved, more resources were available to purchase privacy and autonomy. Young adults increasingly gained access to resources, either through their own newly acquired incomes or through the support of their parents and other family members. Hence they became able to use these resources to purchase residential independence, even before they married and acquired any new family responsibilities.

While young adults may find compelling reasons for using their newly acquired resources to purchase privacy and independence through non-family living, it is less clear why parents or other family members would subsidize such use. It is easier to maintain parental control when the children are living at home, where parents can supervise their activities more efficiently. Hence those parents concerned about being able to supervise their children should be motivated to use their resources to keep their children at home until marriage. However, continuing coresidence can reduce the parents' own independence and privacy. If so, those parents concerned about the effects of their children's presence on their own privacy would use their resources to subsidize their children's residential independence. How parents use their resources therefore reflects their preferences about control relative to privacy.

In more traditional families, parent-child relationships are likely to be highly unequal; children expect to obey parents, and parents expect to be obeyed "as long as they are under my roof," a phrase to be found in many languages. In such families, children are expected to do as they are told and to be seen and not heard. In this situation, parental control is greater under coresidence, and parental privacy is minimally infringed. But in more contemporary families, children are not socialized to be obedient (Alwin 1988) and frequently compete with their parents both for space and for facilities as well as for authority (arguing that *they* know better about many issues). In such families, parents have little to gain from coresidence in terms of control over their children's behavior and much to gain in terms of privacy by their departure. Modern parents who have the resources are therefore more likely to subsidize the independence of their children, since in the process they too acquire privacy and independence in their middle age.[1]

Treating premarital residential independence within a consumer demand model requires that we consider how tastes have changed with increasing affluence. Those who have taken this broad view have suggested that it is only since the middle of the twentieth century that increases in income have been used for privacy rather than for other goods (Beresford and Rivlin 1966; Michael, Fuchs, and Scott 1980). Previously, increases in affluence apparently did not lead to changes in the proportion living in nonfamily households. Changes in preferences were necessary before income would be used to increase the probability of living alone (Pampel 1983).

Hence it is necessary to separate the effects of increasing affluence from those of changing tastes to understand how each set of factors operates to influence changes in nonfamily living. Such a separation is particularly necessary when we move from considering the broad processes connecting changing aggregate income levels, values, and rates of nonfamily living to analyze individuals and their families and the factors associated with nonfamily living among young adults in the 1980s. For a country as a whole, nonfamily living is likely to increase both as a result of increases in income, which increase resources for the purchase of privacy, and as a result of increases in education, which increase the demand for privacy. Having access to more income should increase nonfamily living among those with higher than lower levels of education, since the additional funds would be more likely to be used to purchase privacy, either for parents or children, among those with more than among those with less education.

In previous chapters, we have examined "tastes" indirectly, by analyzing ethnicity and religiosity, and directly, through measures of parent-child closeness and sex role attitudes. We have shown that at similar levels of socioeconomic status, there are major variations in nonfamily living among racial, ethnic, and religious groups. We have interpreted these variations, when socioeconomic status is controlled, as reflecting structural and cultural factors, or in our current terms, variation in tastes of a particular kind. We disentangled these racial, ethnic, and religious taste variables further by examining the intensity of these affiliations; we investigated taste factors reflected in differences in nonfamily living for young women and men along with gender role attitudes. We were using as our measure of resources the aggregate measure of socioeconomic status, which combines taste and resources, mixing education and income (together with consumption patterns, described in Appendix B). We will now separate these components and examine directly the access parents and children actually have to each others' resources to realize their often disparate goals.

INCOME AND EDUCATION

The socioeconomic status (SES) scale captures in a general way the ranking of individual families on a broad interrelated range of factors, some tapping financial resources per se and others reflecting the tastes and lifestyles associated with them. As a generic summary measure and as a basis

143

for a first approximation of social class, this scale is very useful, particularly as a control variable, in our analyses. However, for the specific purposes of disentangling the dimensions of resources and related tastes intertwined within the SES scale, we need to separate the income from the nonincome aspects of socioeconomic levels.

Education is a key component of the SES scale for the parental household, which has both a relatively moderate relationship to income[2] and a theoretical interpretation that more closely approximates "tastes." Higher levels of education normally mean greater exposure to new values, openness to new ideas and influences, and contact with a network of people who are also open to new ideas. So when income is controlled, these specific aspects of education should increase orientations toward nonfamily living. Since our focus is on high school seniors, all having the same level of education at the beginning of the survey, we use parental education to reflect the home environment in which these young adults have been socialized.[3]

We begin by investigating the basic relationship between premarital residential independence and these two socioeconomic measures, total family income and average parental education, controlling for the other elements in our basic model. The results indicate that each measure has a significant positive impact on expectations for nonfamily living and actual behavior. The higher the family income and the higher the level of parental education, the more likely it is that young adults will expect to leave home before marriage and the more likely it is that they will experience nonfamily living. Parental characteristics have much stronger effects on the residential decisions than on the expectations and plans of their children. The effect of income is strongest at high levels of parental education, with little or no effect among those whose parents have little education; the effects of education are substantial at all levels of parental income (fig. 10.1, table B10.1).

Starting with the first two bars for expectations, the figure shows that among those whose parents had a low educational level (only grammar school), young adults from families with low income ($7,500 per year) are about as likely to expect nonfamily living as young adults from families with high incomes (earning $50,000)—64 percent. In the next two bars, the effect of differential parental income on nonfamily living among young adults whose parents have a high educational level (postgraduate) is more substantial: 69 percent for those whose parents' incomes are low compared with 76 percent for those whose parents' incomes are high.[4]

In contrast, differences in parental education made a considerable difference at all levels of parental income. This can be seen by comparing bars with similar shading. The darker shading indicates low parental income, while the lighter shades indicate high parental income. Thus, the

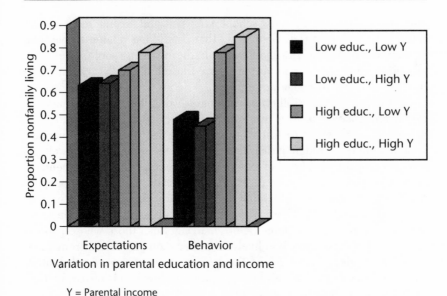

Y = Parental income

Fig. 10.1. Effects of parental education and income on expecting and experiencing non-family living

effect of education can be seen by comparing the pairs of darker shades (same, low income, education differs) and the pairs of lighter shades (same, high income, education differs). Higher levels of education increase expectations for nonfamily living both among those with low parental incomes and those with high parental incomes, although the difference is somewhat greater for those with high parental incomes. This suggests that parental education indicates preferences: among those with low parental education, adding income does not lead to greater use of resources for independent residence; among those with high parental education, who thus have a preference for residential independence, having more resources does increase nonfamily living. But, clearly, more than resources is operating. Even among those with the lowest parental incomes, high parental education results in higher expectations for nonfamily living. Somehow the means to establish an independent residence are found when nonfamily living is a priority.

All these patterns are much more dramatic for the actual routes to residential independence followed by these young people in the first six years after finishing high school. The effect of differences in parental education is particularly dramatic. A much higher proportion of those achieving residential independence did so independent of marriage among those whose parents had a postgraduate education than among those whose parents only completed grammar school, with parental income making relatively little difference. This suggests that something related to parental education is making a critical difference in these young people's lives early in adulthood that seems to become more muted in later years. The likeliest difference is marriage timing.

To consider this possibility, we distinguish the effects of parental education and income on the two separate routes to residential independence. This allows us to test whether their effects operate to increase nonfamily living through increasing marriage ages or whether their effects also increase the likelihood of experiencing nonfamily living independent of the age at marriage (fig. 10.2). Parental education affects young people's likelihood of experiencing nonfamily living through both routes to residential independence. Those whose parents had high levels of education are more likely to leave home before marriage than those whose parents had little education and less likely to marry, compared with remaining residentially dependent. All of these differences are quite substantial, with the least impact of parental education at low levels of parental income and then, only for leaving home before marriage.

Parental income also reduces the likelihood of marriage at these young ages, compared with living at home, although its effects are much less than those of parental education. The first two bars on the "marriage"

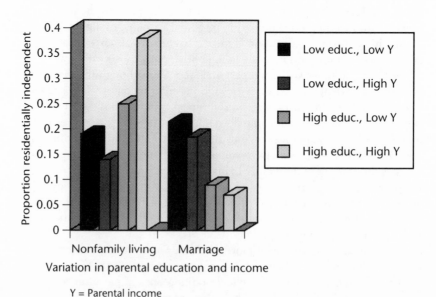

Y = Parental income

Fig. 10.2. Effects of parental education and income on experiencing residential independence before and at marriage

side of figure 10.2 show that among those with low parental education, moving from low to high parental income slightly reduces the likelihood of marriage; the same picture emerges from comparing the last pair of bars.

The story changes when we consider leaving home before marriage. At high levels of parental education (the right-hand pair of nonfamily living bars), parental income has the effects of increasing residential independence before marriage. However, at low levels of parental education (the first pair of bars), higher parental income actually *reduces* premarital residential independence, keeping young adults in the parental home. Parents with less education may use their income to keep their children at home prior to age 24, perhaps using coresidence to maintain supervision over their children better than those with high levels of education.

Those with more educated parents are less likely to establish an independent residence by getting married and more likely to do so while still unmarried. Having a higher parental income, in contrast, appears to influence the route to residential independence in these early years after high school primarily by decreasing the likelihood of independence via marriage, *with no significant difference by income level* in whether young adults establish an independent residence while still unmarried or remain living at home or in some form of group quarters. This result is consistent with the lack of effect of parental resources in helping young adults achieve their expectations for independent residence (chap. 8). Income evidently matters much less for nonfamily living than most would imagine, given a consumer demand model of living arrangements in young adulthood.

These findings are consistent with the argument that income and education represent two somewhat different types of effects on nonfamily living—resources and tastes. Combining income and education into one measure, as in the SES scale, strengthens the relationship between socioeconomic status and premarital residential independence more than if one or the other was included individually. Nevertheless, it is important to understand the mechanisms that link socioeconomic status to nonfamily living that are operating in families, and these reflect the different meanings of education and income.

INTERGENERATIONAL FINANCIAL FLOWS

All of the analyses of the effects of parental education and family income we have presented take for granted that young adults have access to the resources that these characteristics reflect. Assuming that parents spend time with their children when they are growing up, parental values, pref-

erences, and world views resulting from the education they attained become part of the values and attitudes of their children. The mechanism is
socialization. The financial mechanism can operate differently. Although
parents who have more financial resources normally provide their children with an equivalent life-style of investment and consumption, from
education to health care, not all do. There are Cinderellas; some children
have little access to the resources of their parents.

Generally, children do well. Parents in contemporary American society
are expected to support their children monetarily for long periods of time
into adulthood. Children are rarely expected to provide financial contributions to their parents, whether during high school or in adulthood, with
perhaps some exception near the very end of their parents' lives. This
economic flow from parents to children has become central in the stratification system, since most American children require substantial parental subsidies to continue their education beyond high school, and children
who work and contribute to family support during either the high school
or the college years are likely to be at an educational disadvantage. The
flow of income from parents to children may also be a key feature in patterns of nonfamily living, so that young adults who can count on their
parents' subsidies will be more likely to expect residential independence
before marriage than those who cannot. Similarly, those whose parents
expect them to contribute to the family economy are likely to need to
defer residential independence until they marry.

As children approach young adulthood, the extent to which parents
provide them access to their resources cannot be assumed from measures
of family income. Parents vary substantially on the extent they subsidize
their children's lives in young adulthood even among those with the same
levels of income and education (Goldscheider and Goldscheider 1991).
Hence, where possible, we should study the access to financial resources
directly rather than as an inference from family income.

To study the relationship between intergenerational financial flows
and nonfamily living, we use parents' reports about their contributions
to their children and their children's contributions to the household
economy. Because we use data reported by the parents, this greatly reduced the size of the sample we have available for analysis, since only
10 percent of parents were directly questioned. The data on intergenerational flows are also limited to the senior cohort, further reducing the size
of the sample.[5] Nevertheless, these data are particularly valuable, since
students cannot report such information nearly as accurately as their parents (Rosenthal et al. 1983) and since they provide a unique opportunity
to examine the issue of intergenerational financial flows at this critical
segment of the life course.

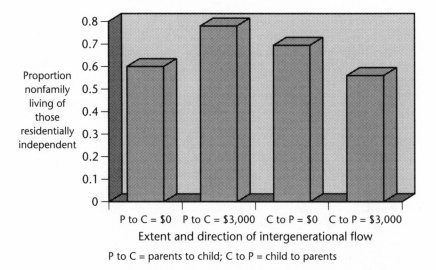

Extent and direction of intergenerational flow

P to C = parents to child; C to P = child to parents

Fig. 10.3. Effects of intergenerational financial flows on experiencing nonfamily living

Nearly half (45%) of parents reported providing some support for their child's tuition and living expenses for 1980–81, the academic year after high school graduation; however, the amounts reported seem quite small.[6] Only one-sixth of parents reported providing more than $1,200. Since the family incomes reported by these parents are not severely underestimated, it is likely that these numbers are also estimated reasonably accurately.

For the analysis of the flow from children to parents, we used a question that asked parents to estimate the dollar amount that the child was expected to contribute to the parental household during 1980–81.[7] Only 18 percent of the parents reported receiving any support at all, and nearly three-fourths of those reporting that their child contributed to the expenses of the household reported amounts of less than $1,000. Although it is possible that this is a substantial underestimate of children's contributions, since it is reported by parents rather than children, nevertheless, it suggests that even among young adults who are not in school and not living at home, few make much if any financial contribution.[8]

Nevertheless, the extent to which parents subsidize their children's educations and the extent to which young adults supplement their parental family income influence nonfamily living. Greater flows from parents to children—and smaller flows from children to parents—increase young adults' likelihood of achieving residential independence before they marry (fig. 10.3). Parental help seems to make somewhat more dif-

149

ference than do child contributions,[9] with a difference of 17 percentage points in the proportions who left home taking the route before marriage between those receiving no parental help and those receiving the maximum (61% vs. 78%), while there is only a difference of 11 percentage points for reverse flows from children to parent (57% vs. 68%). Young adults seem to know something about these flows and to take them into account at least in part in forming their expectations about routes to residential independence, since the same patterns characterize their expectations about nonfamily living. In each case, the effects are considerably weaker for expectations than for behavior. Consistent with the pattern that emerged for parental income and education, young adults underestimate the importance of the financial requirements of an independent residence before marriage.[10]

The major impact of financial flows on routes out of the home is via marriage (fig. 10.4). Financial flows from children *to* parents have all of their effects on marriage timing and almost none on residential independence prior to marriage, so that the more young adults support their parents, the more likely they are to marry early. This pattern primarily reflects the behavior of young women, not young men. Financial flows between parents and daughters have much more impact on expectations

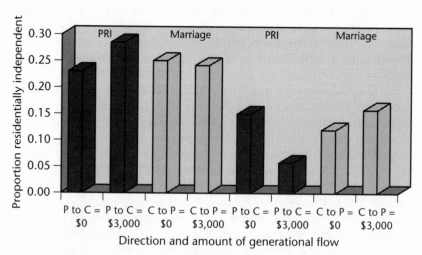

P to C = parents to child; C to P = child to parents
PRI = premarital residential independence

Fig. 10.4. Effects of intergenerational financial flows on experiencing residential independence before and at marriage

and eventual independence than flows between parents and sons, for whom they have no effect at all.

More detailed investigation of these results showed that this is almost entirely a Hispanic pattern (data not presented). Young Hispanics are more likely than non-Hispanics to contribute to their families' incomes holding constant differences in family structure and family income than are non-Hispanics (Goldscheider and Goldscheider 1991). Our analysis here shows that the more they do, the more likely they are to marry early. It may be that both for young women and for Hispanics, the obligation to help their parents ends with marriage. Sons and non-Hispanics generally may be supporting their families because they have a personal obligation to do so, one that continues whether or not they live at home or have taken on the financial obligations of marriage. If daughters' financial obligations to parents end at marriage, since husbands traditionally support their wives, this may provide some incentive to marriage for young women. The early marriage timing of Hispanics relative to other Catholics might also be the result of these reverse financial flows. However, both these effects may also reflect the presence of strongly held family values, both of intergenerational pooling of incomes and of early marriage.

In contrast to the pattern shown by flows to parents, which is restricted to the marriage route, the effects of flows *to children* operate via both routes—increasing premarital residence independence relative to remaining dependent and reducing marriage—with a net result that greater parental financial support increases the likelihood of residential independence of the nonmarried (fig. 10.4).

Which situations might enhance or mute the effect of financial flows from parents to children? We found two interesting patterns. First, flows from parents to children have more effect on enhancing nonfamily living among daughters than they do among sons (data not presented). This result is almost parallel to the gender pattern in the reverse flows, in that the gender difference in the effects of parent to children financial flows appears about equally for those who leave home before and at marriage. There is no gender difference in the extent to which parents subsidize their sons versus their daughters, although sons do contribute somewhat more to their parents' family income (Goldscheider and Goldscheider 1991). The impact of the parental subsidy, however, is greater for daughters, fostering greater residential independence—and less dependence on marriage as a route to that independence.

A seond interesting pattern involves stepparent families, among whom parent to child flows reduce expectations for nonfamily living (data not presented). Although young adults in stepparent families are more likely to expect and experience premarital residential independence than those in nuclear families, this difference is muted among those whose parents provide financial help to them in young adulthood. This pattern works more strongly for expectations than in practice: the extent to which parents provide financial help makes less difference for nonfamily living among young adults in stepparent families than among those in other family structures,[11] but somehow, young adults *expect it to*. It may be that young adults who know that their parents and stepparents are planning to contribute to their education feel less pressure to leave home early than do children in this situation whose family will not contribute. There are no differences in expectations for nonfamily living between intact and stepfamilies where the level of parental contribution is high.

We had anticipated that the quality of relations in stepfamilies could be gauged by our measure about the importance of living close to parents (chap. 6): among those who wanted to be close to their parents, having a stepfamily would not increase early residential independence; only among those who felt family unimportant would stepparents particularly impel young people out of the home. This turned out not to be the case. However, parental financial contributions *do* operate in this fashion. Evidently, the expectation of such subsidies is a better indicator that the stepfamily is functioning like a nuclear family, providing what adolescents need and preventing an early separation by leaving home before marriage, than measures such as "importance of living near family." We interpret these findings in the context that most of the children in stepparent families are living with their mother and stepfather and that most of the resources in these families are provided by the stepfather. The relative avoidance of nonfamily living in families with greater financial flows from parents to children suggests father-stepchild bonds in these families and less need for the children to escape an unsupportive environment. At least, this seems to characterize their expectations.

Three paths to increasing nonfamily living seem to be reflected in these patterns: (1) the continuation of higher education among young adults with parental subsidies facilitates the residential independence of children (while, of course, increasing their financial dependence); (2) continuing education operates to delay marriage, hence lengthening the exposure to the probabilities of moving out of the parental home before marriage; and (3) parental support and the resultant greater exposure to college education should result in the greater independence of children from the control of their parents and change the norms toward increasing independent residence. These paths are more likely to affect actual patterns of leaving home than expectations as expressed during the senior year of high school. Thus, both from the point of view of the mechanisms that are operating to connect financial flows to nonfamily living and from the measurement problems associated with the timing of the expectations indicator relative to financial flows, the effects on behavior are greater than on norms.

11

Parents and Their Children
Who Wins?

We have documented that young people's expectations about their routes to residential independence are influenced by their own characteristics: their family-related attitudes and the measures we link to differences in values and preferences. Their actual decisions are also influenced by these factors (although not always in the same way) as well as by events that occurred after their high school senior year. Further, we have shown that several characteristics of their parents matter both for young adults' expectations and behavior: parents' educational and income levels as well as their histories of marriage and remarriage. Young people's expectations continue to have an impact on their behavior, even after taking into account the factors that shape both their expected sequence of marriage and leaving home and their actual decisions about both of these life course transitions.

What about parents' expectations for their children? Whether unmarried children establish an independent residence before they get married or wait until marriage to do so may well be a family decision, involving parents as well as children. It is, after all, the "parental" home that they are leaving.[1]

Both parties—parents and children—share the expectation that an eventual residential split is appropriate. It should normally occur by the time of marriage, since family extension has generally been rare in the United States (Laslett 1973, Pryor 1972); remaining in the parental home after marriage has normally been reserved for short-term and emergency situations (Cherlin 1979). In contrast, leaving home to establish an independent residence *before* marriage is a recent phenomenon. It had become normative by the 1980s, a component of the plans of a substantial majority of young adults, but as likely testimony to its recency, substantially fewer parents, barely a majority, expected it for their children (chap. 2).

From the child's point of view, living or not living in the parental household is obviously an important decision; but whether or not the child leaves or remains also makes a difference to parents. Clearly, the leaving of the last child is critical, since it marks the parents' passage to the "empty nest" stage of their lives, but every child has an effect, adding to (or alternatively, detracting from) the quality of life in the household. Emotionally, a given child can burden marital relationships or can provide bridges of communication that smooth over the strains. Financially, children can contribute (chap. 10) or be a drain (although that can continue, and become even greater, when they leave the household). Thus, both children and parents have an interest in this decision and may have quite different views on whether independence before marriage is desirable.

In particular, parents' own experiences may have shaped their views about their children's life course decisions. These parents reached adulthood in the years before the greatest period of change in young adults' living arrangements; thus, they were unlikely to have observed or followed such a pattern themselves and might discourage it for that reason. Many, however, may welcome this new life course pattern for their children, since in many ways their lives have changed as much or more than their children's. They bore their children before fertility commenced its sharpest declines in the late 1960s but raised them in its midst, subject to all the pressures that led their younger peers to delay or forgo parenthood. By the 1980s, they may have viewed early nest leaving less as a departure from previous norms than as an opportunity to reduce parental responsibility in favor of a more adult-oriented life-style. This may particularly be the case among parents who experienced divorce and remarriage; their children are very likely to establish an early independent residence (chap. 9). This might result as much from the parents' preference to live cohesively in their newly re-formed family as from the children's need to leave.

Parental marital histories and parental resources and resource flows could be thought of as "happening" to the young adults, part of the context in which they were growing up, like race or region. But education and income, the experiences of marriage, divorce, and remarriage, as well as religion, ethnicity, and race have also been shaping *the parents'* views of life and of the life course patterns they would like their children to follow. Their views could thus be influencing the actual residential decision, which young adults might not have always taken into account in shaping their own expectations. We documented considerable differences between the expectations of parents and their children (chap. 2). Parents were less likely to expect nonfamily residential autonomy for their children than their children expected for themselves, and parents' expectations did seem to affect their children's decisions, even after the children's own expectations were taken into account.

In this chapter, we examine three sets of questions. First, do the factors we have shown are important for young adults' expectations also shape the parents' expectations and, if so, is their relative impact similar? Second, do parental expectations make any difference in their children's routes to residential independence? Finally, does having the support of a parent who expects the young adult to experience nonfamily living (or to remain dependent until marriage) increase the likelihood that he or she will follow the path the parent expects? And if there is no parental support—if the young adult expects a segment of nonfamily living but the parent expects continued residential dependence or if the young adult expects to stay home until marriage and the parent expects an early departure, even without benefit of marriage—who wins?

We are able to exploit again the unique data collected on the parents of these young adults.[2] Like their children, parents were asked at what age they expected the children to marry and what age they expected them to achieve an independent residence, allowing us to construct a measure of residential expectations for parents parallel to that for young adults. These data allow us to examine the expectations of parents for the residential independence of their children.

WHAT AFFECTS PARENTAL EXPECTATIONS?

Overall, the factors influencing parental expectations about their children's routes to residential independence are similar to those that affect the young adults' expectations, but their impacts are generally larger. (Compare tables B11.1 and B3.1.) Parents are more likely to expect nonfamily living for their sons than their daughters and more likely to expect nonfamily living if they have attained a relatively high level of socioeconomic status than if their social status is low.[3] There is a larger gender difference among parents than among the young adults themselves, but the generational difference is not great (fig. 11.1). The difference between parents' expectations for their sons and their daughters is 10 percentage points compared with a gender difference among the young adults of 8 percentage points.

Parental resources make a considerably greater difference for parents than they do for their children. Whereas moving up from the lowest decile of socioeconomic status to the highest decile increases the proportion of young adults who expect nonfamily autonomy by 15 percent (from 0.64 to 0.74), among parents, such a move increases the proportion of parents who expect nonfamily living for their children by more than 25 percent (from 0.49 to 0.63). The gap between the expectations of parents and children is considerably greater among families with low socioeconomic status.[4]

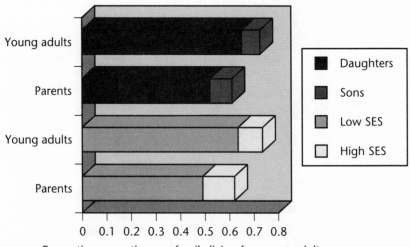

Fig. 11.1. Generational differences in nonfamily living expectations by gender and socioeconomic status

The ethnic patterns show even greater differences between parents and young adults and suggest that the potential for generational disagreement is quite high among some groups. The overall ranking of groups is basically similar for parents and young adults (fig. 11.2). Among whites, high proportions of those in Jewish and Protestant families expected a segment of nonfamily autonomy.[5] As with their children, there is very little difference between the routes to residential independence expected by Jewish and Protestant parents (66% among Jews and 64% among Protestants), and their likelihood of expecting nonfamily living is not very much less than their children's. Parents in Asian and Hispanic families were much less likely to expect unmarried residential autonomy for their children than parents in other groups, consistent with the ranking of these groups among their children. But the very high likelihood of expecting nonfamily living among young black adults (higher than any group) is not characteristic of their parents, who are considerably less likely to expect such a life course stage for their children than either Jews or Protestants. This results in a considerable gap between the generations in the black community.

Parent-child differences are also large in (white) Catholic, Hispanic, and Asian-American families. Among the young adults, Catholics were as likely to expect nonfamily living as were Protestants or Jews; however, this was not the case with Catholic parents, creating a generational gap

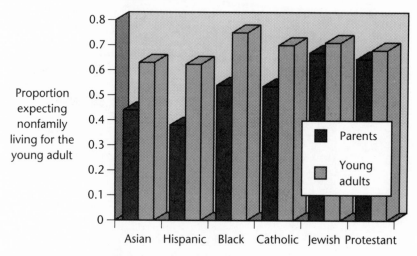

Fig. 11.2.   Generational differences in nonfamily living expectations by race, ethnicity, and religion

among Catholics more than four times as great as among Protestants or Jews. The generation gap is even more dramatic for Hispanic and Asian communities. Among these two groups, considerably less than half of the parents were anticipating nonfamily living for their children—44 percent among Asian parents and only 38 percent among Hispanic parents—while in each group more than 60 percent of the young adults were expecting it for themselves.

Hence although the general pattern of factors influencing parental expectations about the pathways their children would take out of the home resembles the patterns we have discussed among the young adults themselves, there are much greater differences among parents than among their children. Some groups of parents have expectations about nonfamily autonomy that approach the high levels of their children (with two-thirds of Protestant and Jewish parents expecting nonfamily living), but others have barely accepted this new living pattern as a potential route out of the home (Hispanic and Asian parents). Both the higher level of expecting nonfamily living and the smaller group differences for young adults compared with their parents suggest that this new nonfamily pattern is more broadly normative among the younger generation. They are more likely to be sharing their expectations with each other than are their parents and, as a result, have reinforced each others' orientations toward nonfamily autonomy. This is consistent with our argument that expectations can be thought of as norms among high school students in the 1980s. These norms are much less widely shared among their parents for their children, reflecting the extent of cohort increases in nonfamily living during the second half of the twentieth century. The generation gap in these expectations is least among those of high socioeconomic status, Protestants, and Jews, implying that families in these groups have been in the forefront of this revolution.

These are aggregate generational patterns; they do not tell us anything about the level of agreement in particular households. But if the level of intergenerational disagreement at the group level translates into disagreement at the family level, the potential for conflict between parents and children in particular groups is great. If parental expectations matter, then the parental reaction when young adults first begin communicating their plans for establishing an independent residence prior to marriage could turn out to be an unexpected intervening event producing barriers to realizing their expectations.

DO PARENTAL EXPECTATIONS MATTER?

Before taking other factors into account which might affect routes to residential independence, parental expectations seemed to be *more* closely linked to young adults' later residential behavior than those of the young adults themselves (chap. 2). However, this connection might reflect other factors. For example, at least in families with good intergenerational communication, the expectations of children, while not identical, are likely to be closely related to parental expectations. Adding the other factors that influence living arrangements, such as resources and group membership (race, ethnicity, and religion), might greatly weaken the impact of parental expectations on young adults' routes to residential independence, especially since the parents' expectations are so much more closely linked to these background factors than their children's are.

In fact, parental and young adults' expectations seem to have essentially identical impacts on the likelihood that the route to residential independence is via nonfamily autonomy once other factors in the basic model, as well as their children's expectations, are taken into account. When either generation expected the nonfamily route, about 75 percent of young adults experienced this route to residential independence, controlling for the expectations of the other (data not presented). Parental expectations clearly matter, even after taking into account their children's expectations and the other factors that influence living arrangements.

PARENTAL SUPPORT OR DISAGREEMENT

What if parents and their children are in agreement, supporting each other in the expectation of achieving residential independence either before or at marriage? Does having parental support strengthen young people's ability to translate their expectations into reality? And what happens when they disagree, with one generation expecting nonfamily autonomy and the other expecting continued residential dependence until marriage? Is nonfamily living more likely if it is what *the young adults* expect, even though their parents do not; or more likely when it is what *their parents* expect, even though the young adults themselves had anticipated remaining dependent until marriage. Who wins?

To address these issues, we constructed a fourfold categorization of expectations about leaving home based on combinations of the expectations of parents and their children. The first two categories distinguish the two types of generational agreement: both the parent and the young adult expect nonfamily autonomy; neither the parent nor the child does so, each assuming residential dependence until marriage. These two categories reflect situations of parental support for their children's expectations and thus no generational conflict. For the two situations where there is generational disagreement, either the young adult expects the nonfamily route while the parent expects the child to remain residentially dependent until marriage or the parent expects the nonfamily route while the young adult expects to remain dependent until marriage.[6]

These two situations of generational conflict in expectations about the young adult's route out of the parental home are potentially quite different. In families in which young adults expect to establish an independent residence before marriage even though their parents do not expect them to do so, it seems that the children are eager to leave home, even though their parents are reluctant. In embracing this new phenomenon of nonfamily living, the new generation is in the forefront of social change, while their parents have not yet accepted this new living arrangement norm. In the context of actual families, then, in which young adults expect nonfamily autonomy and their parents do not, social change is emerging from below, and we will refer to them as "child innovative" families. In contrast, when parents expect nonfamily living and their children do not, social change is being worked out from above, from the parental generation, and we will call them "parent innovative" families.

There is agreement between parents and their children in 65 percent of the cases: in 40 percent parents and their children expect some segment of nonfamily living, and in 25 percent parents and their children agree that the child should remain home until marriage. In 35 percent of the cases, there were generational differences in expectations. About two-thirds of these cases were child innovative families, in that children expected to leave home while still unmarried and parents expected them to wait until marriage (23% and 12%).

160

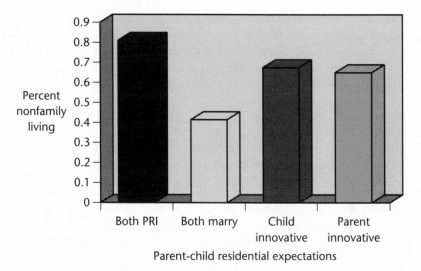

Fig. 11.3.   Effect of generational agreement about nonfamily living on its realization

Our first analytic question is, How does parental support affect leaving home? When both young adults and parents expect that the young adult will leave home before marriage, the nonfamily route is very likely. Of those who established an independent residence in the six years after high school, fully 81 percent did so via nonfamily living (fig. 11.3, table B11.2). In contrast, when both generations expect that residential independence will be deferred until marriage, only 42 percent took the nonfamily route among those who established an independent residence. This is barely half the odds of nonfamily living that results when both generations expect this route and far below the 69 percent overall proportion who experience nonfamily autonomy after leaving home. When only the expectations of the young adults were taken into account, the proportion experiencing nonfamily living among those who expected it was 75 percent, compared with 51 percent among those who did not (chap. 3). This is a difference of 24 percentage points compared with the difference of 39 percentage points where young adults have parental support for their expected route to residential independence.

Thus, parental support is a key factor strengthening the relationship between young adults' expectations and their eventual decisions about residential independence, a context that facilitates young adults' realizing their expectations. This contrasts with our earlier finding that greater parental socioeconomic status per se *did not* facilitate young adults' achieving their expected route to residential independence (chap. 8). Together,

161

these findings reinforce our view that parental resources need not matter very much in routes to residential independence, particularly when parents do not provide them to their children. The keys to understanding the role of parents in the nest-leaving patterns of young adults are parental support and the access to parental resources this is likely to provide.

WHO WINS?

The importance of parental support through their expectations about nonfamily autonomy raises a follow-up question about the consequences for experiencing this new life course stage when there is disagreement within the household. How is generational conflict in expectations resolved over the transition to adulthood? The evidence suggests that when families have conflicting expectations about routes out of the home, it does not matter which generation expects which route. Among those becoming residentially independent, 67 percent of those establishing an independent residence did so via nonfamily living in child innovative families; this occurred in 65 percent of those in parent innovative families (fig. 11.3). Thus, there appears to be little difference in the processes underlying residential dependence in child innovative and parent innovative families. Since leaving home is a household decision, in which the expectations of both generations matter, when one expects the nonfamily route and the other does not, the result of the conflict appears to be a tie.

However, we have shown that occasionally, this view of the process does not reveal the whole story. In addition to route ratios, we need also to examine exit rates (chap. 7). When some factor is increasing both routes out of the home, such as living in a stepparent family (chap. 9), simply comparing routes misses part of what is really happening, and our explanation can shift drastically when we consider each route relative to remaining residentially dependent. When we take this view of parent-child disagreement, important differences between parent innovative and child innovative situations appear.

In parent innovative families, the proportion achieving nonfamily autonomy relative to remaining residentially dependent is 29 percent greater than in child innovative families (fig. 11.4). The parents' expectations clearly have a stronger effect on the nonfamily route than their children's, leading to earlier residential autonomy for young adults when only the parents expect such a route than when only the young adults expect it. Perhaps the parents can predict what will happen better than their children can, based on their experience and judgment.[7] It may also be that parents can make nonfamily autonomy happen in ways their children

162

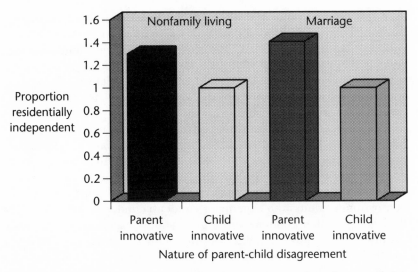

Fig. 11.4.   Generational disagreement and achieving residential independence via nonfamily living and via marriage

cannot, by providing resources, encouragement, or even pressure to achieve this outcome.

When it comes to marrying in the first six years after high school graduation, however, the young adults' expectations seem to dominate over those of their parents. Young adults are 41 percent more likely to achieve residential independence by marrying when only they expected this route than when only their parents expected it. In the area of marriage, then, young adults who were not expecting the nonfamily route seem to have fairly concrete plans, plans that their parents might not know about, and to be able to carry them out, even though their parents expected nonfamily autonomy as the route out of the home.

Thus, for nonfamily residential independence, the parents' expectations dominate—they win—and many of their children, who expected to remain dependent until marriage, leave home to nonfamily living. When we consider leaving home to marriage, however, in the same configuration, that is, parent innovative families, it seems that more of the young adults win, achieving the route they expected, but their parents did not. In short, when there is conflict, parental influence is felt primarily on young adults' leaving home unmarried, while their children have greater control over marriage.

What is particularly interesting about parent innovative families is that each generation's "winning" leads to greater residential independence for the young adults. Some young people realize their expectations and become residentially independent as a married person, while others become residentially independent while still unmarried. When parents expect nonfamily autonomy and their children do not, relatively few young adults remain in the parental home. Like children in stepparent households, they seem to leave home any way they can.

These results suggest that parent-child support or disagreement might be influencing the overall rate of leaving home. Nonfamily autonomy is generally a faster route to residential independence than leaving home via marriage, when tends to occur at a later age (chap. 2). When both the parents and their children expect this new life course stage, the proportion of young adults who experience residential independence is higher than for any other combination of generational expectations, primarily because so many young adults take the nonfamily route (fig. 11.5). In families in which both generations expect residential independence to be delayed until marriage, only 92 percent as many had achieved residential independence via one route or the other, in this case, because so many were delaying leaving home until marriage.

In families with disagreement over the expected route to residential independence, we showed that the proportions taking one or the other route barely differed. Nevertheless, overall residential independence is quite high where only parents expected the nonfamily route, nearly as great (97%) as when both generations expected it. Evidently, those young adults who were winning by achieving residential independence via marriage, despite their parents' expectations, were marrying at unusually young ages. Parents who expect nonfamily autonomy, the early route out of the home, have children who leave home early, even if they do not take that route.

In contrast, in families in which just the children expected nonfamily autonomy, only 88 percent as many achieved residential independence as when both were expecting this route. Both marriage and residential independence were delayed. In this case, the conflict between young adults and their parents is apparently often resolved by young adults *postponing* their decision to leave home. This allows parents to feel that their children will remain residentially dependent until marriage, while the young adult can continue to plan for nonfamily living but at some later time. In child innovative families, the conflict between the different expectations of parents and their children is resolved by delayed nest leaving, with young adults putting off the nonfamily independence that they are expecting while their parents continue to expect residential dependence until marriage.

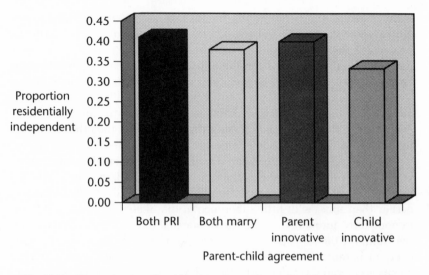

Fig. 11.5. Generational residential expectations and overall residential independence

Hence unlike parental support, which simply reinforced the effects of young adults' expectations, the effects of parent-child disagreement differ considerably, depending both on how we look at it and on the direction of disagreement—which generation expected which route. The relative weight of the nonfamily route is the same in both situations, but when only young adults expect nonfamily autonomy, overall nest leaving is delayed, while when only parents expect this route, it is considerably accelerated. Delay thus characterizes the majority of cases of parent-child expectations' conflict, since child innovative families are considerably more common than parent innovative families. This suggests that increasing parental support for nonfamily living for their children is very important in the trend toward earlier residential independence, and as the level of support for this new life course segment among parents reaches that of the generation of young adults, the age at leaving home should continue to fall.

CONFLICT IN CONTEXT

This is a fascinating result, given the light it sheds on conflict within the family—and on the future. To sharpen and expand this analysis, we ask whether there are differing contexts that influence these outcomes of parent-child disagreement. We have already shown the importance of group membership, leading to differences among ethnic and racial groups and between young men and women. Where there is intergenerational conflict about routes out of the home, are parents more likely to win among some groups than among others? Are young adults with particular characteristics, for example, women or blacks, more able than others to carry out their expectations in the absence of parental support? In some families, does conflict in expectations accelerate leaving home by any route or delay it even longer? Although these are difficult questions to answer with the information we have, in part because the number of cases available for analysis is much smaller than for most of the other issues we investigate in this study, some important patterns emerge.

Our first discovery is that parent-child disagreement has much more powerful effects on daughters than on sons, particularly when only the parents expect nonfamily living (table B11.3). Generally, daughters marry earlier than sons, with little difference in the likelihood of leaving home to nonfamily autonomy among the unmarried (chap. 7). In child innovative families, the same pattern emerges (lower portion of fig. 11.6). However, in parent innovative families, which we showed above generally means accelerated residential independence, daughters avoid this type of conflict dramatically more than sons: young women leave home via the

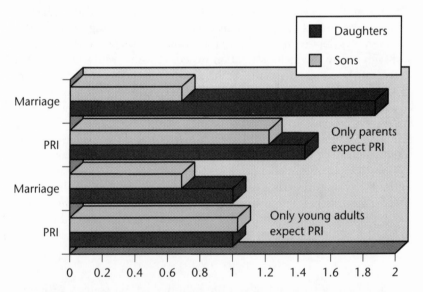

Relative odds of achieving residential independence via given route
(Daughters in families in which only young adults expect PRI = 1.00)
PRI = premarital residential independence (nonfamily living)

Fig. 11.6.   Gender differences in the effects of parent-child disagreement

nonfamily route considerably more rapidly than young men, and even more rapidly via marriage. If only parents expect nonfamily autonomy, daughters are 16 percent more likely to establish an independent residence via this way than are sons and 150 percent more likely to do so via marriage.

This result is consistent with the gender differences in the effects of residential expectations on later behavior that we observed earlier (chap. 8). There, we showed that expectations had less effect on young men's later behavior than did young women's; here, it is the parent's expectations that sons are less responsive to rather than their own. One consequence of this pattern is that daughters who remain residentially dependent are considerably more likely to live in homes in which parents expect their daughters to remain home until marriage (even if they, themselves, do not). These daughters are probably providing major domestic services to the parental household (Goldscheider and Waite 1991). Sons remaining at home are much more likely to have parents who had been expecting nonfamily autonomy for them and might be frustrated by their continuing residential dependence and their noninvolvement in most cases in the domestic activities of the family.

A similar set of patterns emerged when we considered differences in the effects of parent-child disagreement by levels of socioeconomic status (table B11.3). In this case, families at high socioeconomic status levels resemble families with sons, and those with low socioeconomic status resemble families with daughters. This resemblance includes difference in participation in domestic activities, since children share much more in the tasks of the household in families with lower than higher socioeconomic status (Goldscheider and Waite 1991; chap. 9). Hence there is likely to be greater conflict over routes to residential independence when children remain home in high status families, which are also more likely to be parent innovative families.

There were no stable differences in the effects of parent-child disagreement by race, ethnicity, or religion. In each of the groups, whatever the generational conflicts over the route expected, there are no distinctive subgroup patterns of resolving them in terms of either exit rates or routes to residential independence. While the number of cases on which this conclusion is based is relatively small for many of these groups, other findings (chap. 10) have emerged. Since the absence of subgroup differences is likely to be real, the results suggest that family generational conflict is more powerful a context for decision making about residential transitions than are specific group norms or values. Perhaps the effects of ethnic, racial, and religious differences are experienced primarily in the prevention of such generational conflicts rather than in how they are resolved. In all child innovative families, young adults remain residentially dependent for a longer period of time; in parent innovative families, they leave disproportionately early. Parents' expectations about their children's transition to adulthood matter in all families, at least for routes to residential independence.

12

Nonfamily Living in Context
Households, the Life Course, and Family Values

Residential independence before marriage has emerged from these analyses as a complex new phenomenon, one that is negotiated between parents and their maturing children over the transition to adulthood. Fundamentally, nonfamily living is about whether *marriage* and new family formation should continue to be the primary basis for adulthood and residential independence. As such, leaving home before or at marriage reflects key values about the meaning of families and the family roles of young adults in the late twentieth century.

What should be the status of young adults in their late teen years or twenties when they are *unmarried?* Should they be dependent "children" in the parental home? This is the situation implied for those who expect residential independence for themselves or for their children to occur only at the time they marry.[1] Or should unmarried young persons be considered autonomous adults who incidentally happen not to be married? If so, young people should pursue residential independence, and their parents should facilitate it—and/or insist on it—at an early age. These are very different views of early adulthood, which may link to a wide range of personal, family, and social issues and have a powerful impact on the later stages of the life course.

We have documented that the second definition of independence, which separates it from marriage, has begun to take precedence in the last decades of the twentieth century in the United States. A high proportion of young adults expect and plan for residential independence for some period before marriage (70%). However, it is likely to be a new definition, since barely half their parents subscribe to it. It is also a fuzzy definition, since it is unclear when, in the period between high school graduation and marriage, it should begin. There is a wide range of expected ages at residential independence, both by parents and children, although most expected the young adult to achieve residential independence within six years after high school. It is thus not surprising, given its newness and its fuzziness, that it is also a *fragile* definition, since many

169

return to residential dependence sometime during young adulthood, and the return to the parental home is primarily from nonfamily living, not marriage. Despite the growing fragility of marriage in young adulthood, nonfamily living is much, much more fragile.

As an emergent, normatively "required" stage in young adulthood, nonfamily living may have greater costs than most have considered. As the capstone defining the transformation of young adulthood, it is a direct substitute for marriage as the quintessential symbol of autonomy and independence. In addition to the effect of nonfamily living on decreasing the likelihood of marriage, particularly for young women (Goldscheider and Waite 1991), we have shown that those planning for it are more likely to end schooling prematurely. Young people may be ranking immediate residential independence higher than these other, longer-run uses of resources, since nonfamily living, family formation, and education beyond high school all involve considerable financial expenditures. The continuing trade-offs between residential independence, education, and marriage in the transition to adulthood are areas where clearly more research is needed.

PARENTS AND NONFAMILY LIVING

Increasingly, parents may be aiding and abetting this new definition of young adulthood, often by using their scarce resources to increase their own privacy. An important result of our analysis is that parents play a key role in young people's expectations and particularly in their decisions about residential independence, indicating that the decision about when and under what circumstances young adults leave their parents' home to establish one of their own is not simply the private calculation of the young adult. While parental characteristics, such as social class and ethnicity, have fairly weak direct effects on young people's expectations, they have a much stronger impact on the expectations of the parents. In turn, parents' expectations matter even more for most elements of young people's residential decisions than do the expectations of the young people themselves. We have shown clearly that young adults' expectations about nonfamily living have an important effect on whether they subsequently experience it; when parents have the same expectations about the sequence of marriage and residential independence that their child holds, their support greatly strengthens the link between expectations and later behavior. Most young adults who became residentially independent followed the route they expected of themselves and that their parents expected for them.

170

However, when parents and their children disagree about the role of marriage in residential independence, that is, when either only the parents expect their child to leave home before marriage or only the young people do, the evidence shows that while the route taken out of the household is largely unaffected, the *timing* of residential independence is greatly altered. When parents expect residential independence *prior* to marriage but their child does not, very early residential independence occurs. In some of these families, young people marry very early, and in others, young people leave home before marriage. This combination suggests that parents who expect their children to leave home before marriage really want independence from their children and achieve it one way or the other. They either facilitate early nest leaving even if their children are not expecting it or do little to prevent early marriages, if that is what their children are planning. In contrast, when parents expect residential independence to wait until marriage but their children were expecting to leave home before marriage, intergenerational coresidence is prolonged. Parents are comfortable with this outcome, since they expect coresidence to continue, even if they had not expected it for so long, but a rupture is prevented, presumably at the risk of some discomfort on the part of the young adults.

These results confirm that living arrangements decisions are really household-level rather than individual-level decisions. As such, research should consider the points of view of the relevant decision makers in the household. There are a wide range of living arrangements decisions, from marital and parent-child to roommate arrangements, that involve at least two parties. Few studies of living arrangements take more than one point of view, and not many more collect much information from the respondent about others in the household.[2] The need for considering the variety of points of view is particularly acute for living arrangements decisions in which, as in this case, one of the parties (the parents) has been traditionally defined as the responsible authority vis-à-vis the behavior and well-being of the others (their children).

The active role parents have in the nest-leaving process is further evidenced by the impact of parental contributions on residential independence. Although parental education, not income, was the critical element of parental socioeconomic status in young people's likelihood of expecting and experiencing nonfamily living (among parents with low levels of education, increased parental income actually decreased the likelihood that their children left home before marriage), when parents actually transfer part of their resources to children for education, the child is more likely to leave home before marriage, either in conjunction with or after schooling.

171

The importance of parental decisions in their children's move to residential independence also appeared in the powerful impact of parental marital history on their children's later behavior. Parents who remarry, introducing a stepparent into the household and their child's life, strongly increased the likelihood that the child would leave home, both before and at marriage. This is one of the strongest effects to emerge in our study, and it is one that merits much more detailed and focused research. It is particularly interesting in light of the fact that things would have been very different if a remarriage had not occurred: a parent raising children alone can anticipate that while their children will in most cases leave home prior to marriage, this is not likely to occur very early in adulthood. Marriage for those growing up in one-parent families occurs later than in intact families, while when a remarriage occurs, the marriage of the younger generation is accelerated. Evidently, things can change fast in families, with considerable impact on both generations involved.

EXPECTATIONS AND BEHAVIOR OVER THE LIFE COURSE

The vast majority of the factors that we examined to explain variation in nonfamily living influenced the expectations of the young adults (and those of their parents), as well as their subsequent behavior, in much the same ways. This was surprising, given the extent of change in the lives of these young adults during the four to six years after their high school senior year and given the newness of the phenomenon we were examining. This overall result suggests that the analysis of measures of expectations, at least those expressed during a salient segment of the life course, can be a valuable proxy for measures of behavior for researchers trying to understand the forces underlying variation in some behaviors. Evidently, the end of high school is a good point in the life course for measuring these expectations. Few young adults had yet *become* residentially independent, but many had already given it some thought and were evidently making plans on which basis they could form expectations about the sequence they were likely to follow.[3]

Part of the connection between expectations and behavior results from the fact that the same factors were influencing both. But this result also reflects the fact that young people's expectations are important direct predictors of their later behavior. Indeed, one of the strongest measures predicting whether young adults will leave home before marriage was the expectation young adults expressed about it, measured in most cases quite a few years before the actual behavior took place.

It is important to realize, however, that the similarity of patterns explaining expectations and behavior was increased by taking marriage timing into account. Marriage age can distort patterns of residential independence by providing more time to leave home while unmarried, so that even those who did not expect it often fall into it while pursuing some of the other items on the agenda of young adulthood, such as a career ladder job. Similarly, those who marry early need to be examined within the small window prior to their marriage, to see whether they use it to experience nonfamily living or for continued residential dependence.

Of course, these expectations were not very good *absolute* predictors in many ways, and the result noted above should not be overinterpreted. Many individuals who expected one route to residential independence actually took the other. Further, both the parents and (particularly) the young adults underestimated *how long* it would take them to become residentially independent. Expectations cannot be used to predict precisely *who* will take one or the other pathway, and guesses about *when* leaving home will occur should be treated with even greater skepticism. It is likely that part of the slippage for this cohort of young adults reflects the rapid changes that were taking place in the U.S. economy during the early 1980s, when these young people were first beginning to navigate into the responsibilities of adulthood. This decade began with a sharp recession, which had barely begun to ease by 1986 (Levy 1987). The period was marked by rapidly increasing housing costs, which neither generation could have predicted when they were first asked about their expectations about residential independence.

Further, not all factors influenced expectations and behavior in the same way. Many young adults responded to factors in their immediate environment that turned out not to matter in the longer run. Others did not take into account at least some of the forces that would later become important influences on their behavior.

The factors that influenced expectations but not behavior were almost entirely attitudinal and were primarily associated with religion. Those who indicated that they had no religious denominational affiliation (None), did not consider themselves religious, or rarely if ever attended religious services also indicated a strong orientation toward nonfamily living but did not follow through. Either religious orientations and behavior are essentially unrelated to residential autonomy, however much they influence expectations about it, or else these elements of religiosity are themselves volatile at these ages. Religiosity and religious self-identification are likely to vary over the life course,[4] so to understand the effect of personal religious orientations on nonfamily living requires indi-

173

cators taken much closer in time to the decision to establish an independent residence. Given the importance of religious affiliation both for expectations and behavior, the connection between religiosity and nonfamily living needs to be carefully disentangled. Longitudinal data measuring changes in living arrangements over the life course need also to assess changes in religious intensity, particularly around the time of new family formation.

The reverse pattern, in which some factors influenced behavior but were not taken into account by young adults in forming their expectations, was linked entirely with parental socioeconomic status and resources. In forming their expectations, young people did not appear to consider carefully the extent to which parental social class (whose influence turned out to be based primarily on parental education) or their parents' contributions to their education [5] would influence their likelihood of actually leaving home before marriage. Other evidence of the relatively small effect of financial resources on nonfamily living is our finding that social class did not help young adults carry through on their expectations in the way one would have expected; expectations for nonfamily living were much more important for actually experiencing it than having a lot of resources.

The social class results also suggest that the effect of parental education is felt disproportionately on the extent to which parents *propel* their children to residential independence, not on the extent to which the young people have internalized their parents' values in forming their own expectations. Even more important, these findings about the weakness of social class and resources in predicting residential independence before marriage shift our attention to isolating and identifying the "taste" factors and the structure of noneconomic preferences that emerge as so important in shaping these patterns.

Overall, the factors that we examined were consistent in their influence on both behavior and expectations. Our measures of parental family structure and, in particular, *all* our measures of ethnicity and ethnic group membership, as well as those relating to religious affiliation, were consistent in their effects on both expectations and behavior. The family structure results are not too surprising. The changes in the household that result from parental divorce and possible remarriage have, if anything, been greatly exaggerated in the personal and public consciousness. It would have been untenable to find family structure having no effect on the emerging patterns of expectations and behavior of young persons in this family-household decision. However, the lack of impact of financial resources, as discussed above, and the sustained effect of values were not anticipated.

VALUES

The power and consistency of the ethnic and religious group membership effects, as well as those of the ethnic process variables (foreign language use, generation, and residential concentration), present a challenge for future research. Many scholars have dismissed these factors as transitional, indicators of social class, or irrelevant in the secular world of American young adults. Such was not the case in this analysis of expectations and decisions about the route to residential independence. Most research of living arrangements changes has highlighted the increase in resources—the rise in affluence over time—far more than changes brought by decreased familism or secularization. Our results suggest that affluence is much less important than values, since they show few and weak relationships between resources and nonfamily living and unambiguously document that nonfamily living has simply not been as well accepted in more familistic ethnic groups and more familistic religious denominations as it has been in the dominant, largely secular culture.

Every measure of the strength of these groups that operates at the group level (unlike the personal religiosity measures) shows strong effects on both the expectations to leave home before marriage and actual nonfamily living. The use of an ethnic language, closeness to the foreign-born generation (even among high school students in the 1980s, most of whom are at least second-generation Americans), and ethnic residential group cohesiveness (even when crudely measured by the data available) all reduce the likelihood that ethnic group members expect and experience nonfamily living. And the more these differentiating factors weaken, particularly when they weaken together (e.g., among those who are both more distant from their immigrant roots and only use English), the more nonfamily living is expected and experienced. These processes characterized both the relatively recent arrivals in the United States (Asians and Hispanics) and some of the older ethnic groups (whites from southern and eastern Europe). However, they were less evident among African-Americans (even the few who were close to their foreign-born roots) or among those from elsewhere in Europe.

Religious affiliation also displayed strong effects on both expectations and behavior. However, it was necessary to subdivide both Protestants and Catholics to discern this result, indicating that these two great world religions are too heterogeneous to be treated as single communities. It was also necessary to parcel out the effects of the distinctive Catholic marriage pattern, which for most Catholics results in the relatively late marriage ages that, other things being equal, allow for nonfamily living to occur somewhat by default. The difference between the results for religious affiliation and for personal religiosity suggests that denominational affiliation is the key to the effects of religious differentiation, one that produces either strongly limiting structures or enduring values. And despite the wealth of studies on denominational change, it seems likely that denominational affiliation is more nearly constant than are indicators of personal religiosity and religious service attendance, at least in the transition to adulthood.

The key to many of these ethnic and religious results is likely to be some aspect of familism. This conclusion is reinforced directly by the "attitude" measures of familism that we examined, which strongly influenced both the expectations and experience of nonfamily living. One measure was the personal statement about the importance of being close to family, which had a strong effect on the extent of nonfamily living in young adulthood. It did not mediate the effects of family structure but was closely linked to several of the ethnic patterns that emerged. The other "familism" attitude, which indexed the importance of nonfamily roles for women, told much the same story. This latter attitude had even stronger effects on nonfamily living than on expectations, and it was much less limited to women in its impact than was the case for gender role attitudes, which focused on gender equality *in* the family.

PROFILES

The patterns we have described apply to young adults as a whole graduating from high school in the early 1980s. More specifically, they apply to white Protestant young adults, the dominant group in American society (and sometimes even more specifically to nonfundamentalist Protestants). Given the strength of ethnic and religious variation throughout this analysis, we profile the various other groups, contrasting them with the dominant group—and often with each other—to see how residential independence strategies tie in with other subgroup patterns in the transition to adulthood.

These profiles do not simply reflect the overlap of race/ethnicity with the social class or the regional concentration of these groups, their characteristic marriage timing, or some other obvious differentiating characteristic, although group differentiation works in some cases through one or more of these axes to produce a special configuration. It is best to understand differences in nonfamily living in the contexts of the communities that these groups represent and the family attitudes, values, and environments that they share. We consider Asian-Americans, African-Americans, and Hispanics as well as Catholics and Jews. Then, although they normally inhabit the same communities, we compare young men and women as they integrate marriage and residential independence into their "separate spheres" over the transition to adulthood.

ASIAN-AMERICANS

Asian-Americans emerge from these analyses as the most cohesively familistic group we examined, with strong two-parent family structures supporting young adults, an emphasis on the value of living close to parents and relatives (which has a powerfully negative effect on nonfamily living), and, as a result, a generally very low level of expected and experienced nonfamily living for both young men and young women. Perhaps because of this strong family support, the plans of these young Asian-Americans are very likely to be carried through, as reflected in the strong links between nonfamily living expectations and behavior. Change cannot easily enter the system with such a strong array of social supports to act as checks. Asian-Americans very rarely marry earlier than they expected, become parents before they expected, or drop out of school before they expected. And when earlier than planned parenthood occurs, it overwhelmingly occurs within the context of marriage, contributing to the strength of family structure in the next generation.[6] Even generational change is largely missing, with generation in America making essentially no difference in the likelihood young Asian-Americans expect or experience nonfamily living.

Like other racial/ethnic groups, convergence toward high levels of nonfamily living occurs as a result of increased use of English and of residential mobility out of the dominant area of settlement (in this case, the Pacific region). But Asian-Americans' armor of familism is also breached in several ways distinctive to them. When the parental marital structure did not hold, there was a very strong movement toward leaving home before marriage, particularly when there was a parental remarriage. In this case, the strong pattern of intergenerational control may backfire, with the younger generation escaping a paternalism that they feel is both personally alien and un-American, resulting in nonfamily living and perhaps a real break from their families. But these cases are rare.

Much more important is the strong effect of increases in socioeconomic status, particularly for young people's expectations about nonfamily living. At the highest levels of socioeconomic status, there are few differences in expectations for nonfamily living between young Asian-Americans and the white Protestant majority. Whether this is a form of emancipation from their group's super-familism or simply a temporary correlate of going away to college (very rare among Asian-Americans, who are likely to commute [Goldscheider and DaVanzo 1989]) would require more detailed analysis to unravel. It is likely that the Asian form of familism can survive distance among its members, as the rich research literature on multinational Asian family corporations, lending societies, and other forms of family coordination suggests (Waldinger, Aldrich, and Ward 1990; Light and Bonacich 1988).

Finally, the Asian community may find itself backing into nonfamily living because of its very late age at marriage. This phenomenon originally created a complex puzzle for our analysis. It appeared that Asian-Americans were unlikely to expect nonfamily living but more likely than average to experience it. It turned out that while nonfamily living is rare among Asian-Americans, it is just not so rare as marriage during the six years of observation included in our survey. Only by taking this characteristic into account could we show the underlying avoidance of nonfamily living. Like increased socioeconomic status, the consequences of delayed marriage are real. Young people observe more of their peers becoming residentially independent before they marry during the early years of adulthood. There is unlikely to be a move toward marriage at younger ages to prevent this effect, since early marriage is not consistent with their other characteristic patterns, particularly longer school enrollment. Simple exposure time among unmarried young Asian-Americans may well contribute to increased nonfamily living among Asian-Americans in the future.

HISPANIC-AMERICANS

While not quite as powerfully familistic as Asian-Americans, Hispanics are the least likely to expect and experience nonfamily living of all the ethnic groups that we examined. Hispanic parents are particularly unlikely to expect nonfamily living for their children. So there is a generational gap, but both generations are at relatively low levels of anticipating nonfamily living compared with others of their generation. They maintain this distinctively low level by continuing high use of Spanish and continued residential concentration (in the Southwest for Mexicans; in Florida and New York for Cubans). Maintaining family closeness as a valued goal also contributes importantly to their intergenerational coresidence. Rating family closeness highly has an unusually strong impact in reducing the likelihood of expecting and experiencing nonfamily living, much as it does for Asian-Americans. Among Hispanics, Cubans stand out as the least likely to experience and expect nonfamily living, but the general Hispanic pattern is consistent across groups, particularly when their relatively late marriage ages—at least compared with white Protestants—are taken into account.

178

Like Asian-Americans, increased English use and moving away from their ethnic region enhance the likelihood that young adults will leave home before they marry. However, Hispanics are also experiencing rapid generational change, particularly among the group that is most highly foreign born, the Cubans.[7]

Hispanics also lack the powerful family structure of Asian-Americans. Although there may be strong sanctions for deviant marital behavior (and in fact, Hispanics, like Asian-Americans, are particularly likely to couple early childbearing with early marriage), parental family structure, with average levels of one-parent families and stepfamilies, is not distinctive. This may be related to the high levels of unexpectedly early transitions to marriage and parenthood and from school that characterize Hispanic communities. While family disruption is disapproved, too many have placed themselves at risk of it to keep levels very low.

In the context of the familism revolutions under way in the United States, Hispanics may be particularly vulnerable on one axis—parent-child—because they are under such pressure on another—gender. Gender differences in nonfamily living are unusually large for Hispanics, in contrast to Asians. This means that although both groups are patriarchal in their sex role attitudes, holding gender-linked attitudes can have very different implications. Asians, unlike Hispanics, deny premarital residential independence to both their sons and their daughters and therefore are under less pressure from the gender revolution among young people.

The nature of familism also appears to be different for these two groups. Familism among Asians appears to include commitment to extended family and strong family support for the children's education and mobility. Over time, this may involve leaving home before marriage, if that is what is needed to achieve the group's educational and career goals. In contrast, Hispanics have a distinctive pattern reinforcing avoidance of nonfamily living—a high level of financial contribution *from* young adults to parents—which also likely serves to reduce social and economic mobility. In ways that are not totally clear, this pattern appears to be linked to early marriage. If Hispanics converge to the general pattern of low to no financial contributions from adult children as well, an additional barrier to nonfamily living will fall.

AFRICAN-AMERICANS

The patterns for African-Americans are quite different from those of both Asian-Americans and Hispanic-Americans. It appears that the major basis for group cohesion for this group is not familism at all but the powerfully unifying effect of discrimination and racism, so that race creates its own distinctiveness, blurring all others. Factors that lead to variation in nonfamily living arrangements in the nonblack community have been shown over and over again in these chapters to have little or no effect among blacks. Living in the South, using a foreign language, being Catholic, Protestant, or of some other religious affiliation, being the child of a foreign-born parent, and even gender make little difference in nonfamily living among young African-Americans. Similarly, expressing feelings about the importance of living close to parents and relatives and growing up in a one-parent or stepparent family had no effect on the likelihood of expecting or experiencing nonfamily living. There are a few exceptions to this pattern, for example, attendance at Catholic schools seems to mark young blacks as it does others, although its effects are different, leading to a convergence of blacks and whites.

Nevertheless, of all the race and ethnic groups that we examined, blacks are most likely to expect and most likely to actually experience premarital residential autonomy as their route out of the parental home. The key factor that helps place the black pattern into perspective is their very late expected and actual age at marriage. Once age at marriage is taken into account, the black pattern of nonfamily living relative to whites reverses itself: blacks are less likely to expect or experience nonfamily living at a given age than white young adults. Just as for Asians, leaving home before marriage is not common among blacks; it is just not as rare as marriage. In the African-American case, the combination appears to be the result of weak family patterns: low rates of marriage lead eventually to nonfamily living by default.

Viewing this pattern as evidence of weak, not strong, family structures is reinforced by the low levels young adults report for feeling it important to live close to parents and relatives as well as by the high level of fragmentary or disrupted parental families, with much higher proportions living in both mother-only and stepfamilies at the end of high school than any of the other groups we studied. Marriage is only weakly connected to parenthood in the younger generation as well, since blacks who become parents at ages earlier than expected are less likely to marry than others who have this experience. This picture of weak family structure is also consistent with the fact that young African-Americans are very unlikely to be able to carry out their planned route to residential independence—at or before marriage. This pattern may indicate a very low level of parental support for their plans—whichever ones they have—since the black parents in this study were much less likely to expect their children to leave home before marriage than their children expected; the level of parent-child conflict in expectations at the family level is also considerably greater among blacks than among any other group (Goldscheider and Goldscheider 1989a).

180

However, young black adults can evidently draw strength from outside their own families in ways that do not appear for other groups. The best evidence for this is the absence of a family structure effect on nonfamily living, indicating that the losses nonblacks experience in this situation are somehow made up within the black community. In addition, ratings of family closeness are not important for nonfamily living among blacks, suggesting that even those who report that family closeness is not of particular importance to them are as comfortable remaining home until marriage—no matter how long it is delayed—as those who rate it highly.

These contrasts with white Protestants would not be complete without considering the two religious groups normally grouped with them as the major religions in the United States[8] as well as the special communities of Protestants. Although our initial glance revealed very little difference in nonfamily living expectations among Protestants, Catholics, and Jews, a closer examination of religious groups, defined more sharply as communities than as categories, particularly taking into account the very different marriage patterns of Protestants, allowed the differences to emerge more clearly.

FUNDAMENTALIST PROTESTANTS

Our primary finding for this group was that they were less likely to expect and actually experience nonfamily living than are other Protestants. This was particularly the case when their younger marriage age was taken into account. The difference between the two groups was quite large: less than half of the more fundamentalist Protestants actually left home before marriage compared with two-thirds of the more liberal Protestants.

Although fundamentalist Protestants are more likely to describe themselves as religious and to attend religious services more regularly, the supports for nonfamily living seem to be less individual and more embedded in the social structures to which they belong. Unlike for Protestants in more liberal denominations, neither the level of personal religious feelings nor the level of service attendance had any effect on the actual patterns of leaving home before marriage.

Fundamentalist Protestant denominations are among the least studied religious groups in the United States. While the effects that we documented take into account differences in social class and region, our profile of them is less complete than those of most other groups. We only focused on them in the context of specifying the religious factor in the living arrangements of young adults and did not consider whether other factors—for example, socioeconomic status, family structure, or parental expectations—influenced their orientations toward nonfamily living differently from other groups. Yet while Protestants all have some distinctive traits, in particular, earlier marriage than any other of the white religious groups or the other racial or ethnic groups, our results for fundamentalist Protestants suggest that for most purposes, taking all Protestants together as a group is not adequate.

CATHOLICS

Recent research on the family-related behavior of American Catholics has shown convergence to the more general (i.e., Protestant) pattern. Despite continuing doctrinal differences and increasingly vocal pronouncements descending the hierachy from Rome, Catholics in the United States no longer have larger families than non-Catholics and have lost most of their distinctive contraceptive and abortion patterns (Goldscheider and Mosher 1991, Jones and Westoff 1979; see also Alba 1990). Their propensity to divorce is also rapidly approaching the Protestant level. Other research that has focused on the values and beliefs of American Catholics has documented continuing differences from Protestants, in part reflecting broader orientations that are religiously and institutionally based (Greeley 1989).

The results of our analysis are consistent with findings documenting the general lack of Catholic distinctiveness within marriage but show at the same time that important differences remain in family building prior to marriage, as do differences in parent-child relationships. Each of these has important implications for nonfamily living. It is also clear from the evidence we presented that these differences are reinforced by specifically Catholic institutions, schools and churches.

Catholics expect to marry a full year later, on average, than do Protestants, and they follow through, with a distinctively lower likelihood of marriage at each age during the six years after high school. This is reinforced among those attending Catholic schools. This pattern is most distinctive among Catholics who are not from southern Europe, suggesting that the Irish pattern of very late marriage still continues (Kennedy 1972, Kobrin and Goldscheider 1978), at least to some extent, more than a century after the major wave of immigration from Ireland.

But this very distinctiveness appears to be opening the way to a rapid increase in nonfamily living and perhaps to a period of conflict in parent-child relationships. The "generation gap" in expectations is very large among Catholics, with far fewer Catholic than Protestant parents expecting nonfamily living for their children. Nevertheless, the traditional late marriage age (which their parents also expect for their children) has allowed this generation of young Catholics who have established an independent residence to experience nonfamily living in almost exactly the same proportions as non-Catholics. If the marriage age of Catholics was the same as for non-Catholics, nonfamily living patterns between the groups would have been significantly different. So the very distinctiveness in one area (marriage age) has resulted in greater similarities between Catholics and non-Catholics in other areas (living arrangements).

JEWS

Young Jewish adults expect and experience nonfamily living more than any other white group in this study and are most distinctive in having *parents* who are most likely to expect it for them as well. As with Catholics, part of this is the result of very late marriage, but there the resemblance ends. Late marriage (and nonfamily living) is paired among Jews with a distinctive pattern of planning efficacy, so that not only do few marry, become parents, or drop out of school earlier than expected but plans for leaving home are also unusually well carried out. In a tantalizing finding, we also documented that Jews who were finding conditions unfavorable to carrying out their planned age *at parenthood* were nevertheless marrying. Jews do not need to marry late to defer childbearing (as many Catholics do) but can combine marriage with delayed childbearing within marriage to achieve educational and career goals (particularly for women).

However, most of our results for Jews were weakened by the very small number of cases in our final analytical sample. It is a population that has been characterized as extremely cohesive, yet it is undergoing rapid change (Goldscheider 1986). The indicators of change available for other groups in the sample (living in an ethnic region, generation, and language use) did not work well for them. Part of the key may lie in religious denominational shifts (from Orthodox to Conservative to Reform), in affiliation with other specifically Jewish organizations, or in other indicators of group cohesiveness, none of which can be examined with these data. Nevertheless, the data reveal that nonfamily living among Jews receives the support of parents and is consistent with their educational and family goals. Together, these patterns imply that familism and family commitments among Jews are consistent with high levels of nonfamily living, probably because living independently is part of a broader family-supported life course trajectory.

YOUNG MEN AND YOUNG WOMEN

Comparing the transitions to adulthood of young men and women normally focuses our attention on the fact that young women are more family oriented than young men. This reflects in part their earlier age at marriage and in part the fact that most consider family roles to be more critical for young women than for young men, since they shape women's financial well-being, social status, and niche in society.[9] It is true that young women in this study expect to, and actually, marry earlier than young men and that this has some impact on young men's greater likelihood of experiencing nonfamily living. But what is fascinating in all these results is that this difference is extraordinarily fragile and that there are many circumstances in which young women's likelihood of nonfamily living approaches and even surpasses that of young men. Young women are much more responsive than young men to variation in the attitudinal and social factors we measure—ethnicity, religion, social class—and hence are much more heterogeneous in their expectations about, and experiences of, nonfamily living as a route to residential independence.

The picture that emerges from a wide range of results can be illustrated with the following example: among families at low levels of socioeconomic status, the likelihood that females will expect or experience nonfamily living is much less than that of males, but at high levels of socioeconomic status there is very little gender difference. To the extent that family socioeconomic status is increasing, then, this cross-sectional finding predicts convergence in the residential patterns of young men and women. Similarly, there is a strikingly consistent pattern linking ethnicity and religion with gender differences. The route to residential independence differs most between young men and women among those speaking a foreign language and among those who live in the region where most of their ethnic group live. These findings suggests that the process of linguistic and residential integration into the broader American society reduces gender differentiation. Similarly, religion reinforces gender differences: young men and women who consider themselves very religious, who frequently attend religious services, and who were enrolled in Catholic school varied more in their nonfamily living patterns than more secular young adults. Hence the forces that are leading to increased affluence and secularism and to decreased familism are also increasing the similarities between the early transition to adulthood of young men and women, that is, egalitarianism.

Nevertheless, substantial gender differences in nonfamily living remain, suggesting that young women who want to experience nonfamily living have to overcome the resistance of their ethnic communities and religious teachers. They also have to deal with parents who make larger gender distinctions than their own generation does. The importance of parents was apparent in the evidence about the parents' expectations, directly (although the generational differences were not great) as well as in the effect of parental contributions to their children's education, which had a stronger effect on the expectations and experience of their daughters than on their sons.

Even so, there was substantial evidence that young women could overcome these structural and family barriers through their own actions. Planning for a later than average marriage age had much more impact on young women's likelihood of nonfamily living than on young men's, greatly reducing the differences between them. And planning directly to leave home before marriage, as evidenced by their expectations at the end of high school, was very successful in increasing young women's likelihood of actually experiencing nonfamily living as their route to residential independence—far more so than such plans did for young men.

This finding should also encourage us to think somewhat more about the lives of young men. They planned for nonfamily living, but their plans had little effect on their attaining it. In the midst of the wealth of studies on how the plans and expectations of women are changing, there is a great paucity of research on men, as they grope their way to adulthood under circumstances of changed male-female roles. Negotiating within these changes may be particularly problematic when the traditional route to male independence, via economic prowess, has been compromised (Easterlin et al. 1992).

However, many young women were also not successful in following through on their plans in young adulthood, and it may be that even for those who were, the costs of nonfamily living were greater than for young men. Daughters were much more likely than sons to experience marriage and parenthood earlier than they expected, which perhaps should not surprise us, given the forces arrayed against any alternative plans by many of their families and religious/ethnic communities. And while the closer linkage between dropping out of school and marriage for females than males is also not surprising, it was also the case that young women were more likely to leave home before marriage by dropping out of school than were young men. This further suggests that the costs of nonfamily living in terms of long-run educational attainment are greater for young women than for young men. Egalitarianism is clearly unfolding in the generation of the 1980s; but there is still a way to go before young men and women proceed in the transition to adulthood without the liabilities and costs of gender.

THE CONTEXTS OF NONFAMILY LIVING

What these results—particularly the group profiles—suggest is that nonfamily living is highly variable across social contexts. It is virtually taken for granted among highly educated Protestants and Jews, both parents and young adults (and hence, most family scholars as well), but it is much less clear among other communities and in other circumstances. The newness of the phenomenon, the fuzziness about when it should start (and end), and its fragility, together with the lack of consensus between parents and children on what are appropriate residential sequences in young adulthood, show that it is not yet clearly institutionalized as a way-station in young adulthood.

It is also likely, although here our evidence is less clear, that the rules underlying the alternative to nonfamily living—the continued coresidence of parents and unmarried children past their late teens and into their twenties—are also becoming fuzzy. It may be that these changes are increasing the pressure on young adults and their parents toward nonfamily living, since parents rarely attempt to incorporate young adults as contributors and responsible persons in the household, while at the same time they resent their "freeloading." Increasing the involvement and responsibilities of children in the parental household—and beginning this process prior to adulthood—could relieve the pressure. This would allow the parental home to serve more extensively as a resource allowing for greater investment for later adulthood, promoting young people's remaining in school longer, increasing the accumulation of human capital, and otherwise saving for an adult future.

Both these paths into young adulthood need further research. We need to learn how young adults feel about the homes they are expecting to establish prior to marriage, and we need to learn more about the domestic basis of parent-child relationships, the strains this imposes, and how these strains can be reduced. We need to go much further to understand the forces underlying the growth in nonfamily living and the costs and benefits the various pathways to residential independence impose on both generations, now and in the future.

Appendices
Notes
References
Index

Appendix A

Strengths and Limitations of the
High School and Beyond Survey

The High School and Beyond (HSB) survey, which provides the core of the information on which we based our study, is a unique body of data on young people just entering adulthood in the 1980s and their parents. Designed and executed by the Center for Educational Statistics (using the survey resources of the National Opinion Research Center), the survey began in spring 1980 with interviews in their high schools of 58,728 sophomores and seniors (divided about equally between the two classes). This group was designed to be representative of young people in the United States as a whole who had remained in school to that point. (Two-thirds of high school dropouts remain in school until spring of their sophomore year [Ensminger and Slusarcick 1992].) They were recontacted every two years (in spring 1982, 1984, and 1986), providing the most recent information about the transition to adulthood currently available, on a wide range of issues for a large sample, well into the mid-1980s.

In fall 1980, parents of a representative subsample of 7,201 students were also queried (primarily via mailed questionnaire) about themselves and the student in the study. Based on information provided by their children, one parent was contacted, 63 percent of whom were mothers. In our analyses, the sex of the parent never influenced the results, and it was dropped from our final equations.

The design included an oversampling of schools with high proportions of Hispanics and of Catholic schools with high proportions of black students, together with several other groups of interest. In addition, the survey collected a considerable amount of information about the ethnic and religious characteristics of the young adults. These elements of the study design greatly strengthen the value of these data for the analyses both of ethnicity and religiosity, central concerns of our study. Below, in our discussion of the measures we constructed from these data, we highlight the strength of the information on non-English-language use.

Thus, HSB is a powerful data set for the analyses of the transitions young adults make after high school, particularly their plans for, and experiences with, living in nonfamily residences or marrying. By providing a longitudinal design, we are able to compare young adults' expectations about living arrangements sequences with their actual choices; by interviewing parents, we can examine the relative weight of both generations on this decision that affects both; and by asking large numbers of young adults detailed questions about ethnicity and religiosity, family values, and family life, we are able to develop a vivid picture of the forces impinging on their decisions as they moved into early adulthood in the 1980s.

Nevertheless, as with all complex sources of information, these data have a number of limitations. We will discuss the most critical of these below, noting how we have responded to them (when it was possible to do so) and what concerns remain. The major issues are attrition, item nonresponse, truncation, and the problem of high school dropouts.

ATTRITION

Not everyone participated, and of those who originally did so, some did not continue in the survey throughout all the longitudinal stages to the end.[1] The response rate for the original survey was 82 percent, in part because several high schools were not eventually included. Of those originally interviewed, 94 percent of those targeted for reinterview two years later were reached. Subsequent reinterview percentages were also close to this level (92%, 91%).

These attrition rates are quite low, given the size and scope of the enterprise and the high level of mobility of persons in this age group. There is no satisfactory way to estimate the attrition bias on our analysis, although it does not seem to be great. An analysis of this problem based on a parallel study from the 1970s (NLS72) showed this to be the case (Goldscheider and DaVanzo 1989). In that study, those not interviewed in 1979 were more likely to be married but also more likely to have lived at home in 1973 than those interviewed in 1979, suggesting that such longitudinal studies are not biased against nest leaving as a result of attrition.

NONRESPONSE

As a very large survey, dependent to a great extent on mailed responses, there was a high level of item nonresponse, as respondents simply skipped past questions (either by mistake or because of fatigue or ambivalence) that would have been answered had the design included the far more expensive personal interview method. Again, there are few means for estimating the bias in this source. So that our results would reflect as little of the bias as possible, we included indicator variables for missing values for each set of measures in the analysis (e.g., socioeconomic status, ethnicity, familism attitudes), and the results of these analyses are included in the detailed tables presented in Appendix B.

TRUNCATION

By terminating the survey in 1986, a substantial portion of the transition to adulthood of most of these young people remains unobserved. The seniors were mostly age 23 and 24 at the last interview, and the sophomores were only age 21 and 22. As a result, most had not married, and many had never left home to establish an independent residence. We "correct" for this bias to the extent possible by using techniques that are the most robust in the face of such right censoring, predicting how the proportions experiencing a given event differ depending on their values on the set of independent variables, rather than, say, predicting variation in "age at" marriage or leaving home. This allows those who have not yet made one of these transitions, those who are the most extreme, to contribute their information.

Nevertheless, it is quite possible that the processes that influence marriage and the attainment of independent residence change over the transition to adulthood. Very few data sets allow analysts even to consider this question, and most have not examined it. A recent report (Avery, Goldscheider, and Speare 1992) suggests that the effects of parental social class change over children's age, going from delaying marriage (as we observe in this analysis) to having no effect by their children's late 20s; other effects (gender, race) were stable over the age range 18 to 29. Hence, we are more confident that the effects we estimated represent the experiences of those having early transitions than the experiences of those who deferred them to later ages.

DROPOUTS

The question of truncation links to our final and most central concern, which is that we have limited our analysis to those who graduated from high school by the next survey (for seniors) and by the second survey (for sophomores). This was necessary for the senior cohort, who were surveyed in the spring of their final year in high school (although about 1% managed not to have graduated two years later and were dropped from the analysis). However, we had the opportunity to study the 11 percent of the original sophomore class who dropped out prior to completing high school and chose not to do so. Why did we do this, and what effect did it have on our analysis?

Our major concern with the dropouts was that to include them in our entire analysis would cause considerable difficulty with *left censoring*. We had learned from prior analyses of other data that remaining in high school for the vast majority of teenagers in the United States forestalls progress on the major family dimensions of adulthood. Although many hold jobs while in school, almost none are married, parents, or living independently of their own parents while still in high school (Kobrin 1981). To include with the other students those known to be dropping out and to see how their characteristics and expectations predicted later behavior would have meant that for the vast majority who did not drop out, we would be trying to predict behavior after high school based on their attitudes and expectations measured two full years prior to the onset of any of these transitions. And in fact, the sophomores had extraordinary difficulty answering questions about the timing of their transitions, with levels of nonresponse approaching one-third.

The only alternative that would have allowed us to retain them in our study

191

would have been to take an approach to "time" that would have had the clock start two years earlier for the dropouts. This would mean that while we would measure attitudes, expectations, and characteristics as of the senior year for most of the sample (both those who started as seniors and those who continued to the senior year among sophomores), we would use parallel information for the dropouts as of the sophomore year and then measure their behavior as if they were seniors, looking at their marital status and living arrangements in 1982. However, this would have meant treating continuation in school differently for the dropout group (the vast majority of whom were not in school) than the nondropout group, many of whom continued in school throughout the study.

The more we struggled with this problem, the more it became clear that answering questions about the transition to residential independence among high school dropouts would require a separate study, which we have not done. Nevertheless, it is important to assess the extent of bias this has introduced into our study. Below we perform some of the analyses that are presented in chapter 2 (when did they expect to leave home and marry and by what route and then, what happened) for dropouts and nondropouts.

DROPPING OUT OF HIGH SCHOOL
AND RESIDENTIAL INDEPENDENCE

Overall, those who did not complete high school were less likely to expect to leave home unmarried. This is primarily because many of them expected to and did marry relatively early, suggesting that for this group, the decisions relating school and marriage timing were unusually interrelated. However, among the unmarried, the differences between dropouts and nondropouts are less, particularly when we combine those living with parents and those in other forms of not-yet-independent housing, dormitories and barracks. Table A.1 shows weighted proportions expecting and experiencing these events, by school completion status.

INDEPENDENT VARIABLES

Below (table A.2) we present definitions, short acronyms, and descriptive statistics for the variables we used to predict expectations and experiences of nonfamily living. Most of the variables used in this analysis are straightforward (gender, education, race, family structure). Among those that are not, one, socioeconomic status (SES), was constructed by others, and the construction of most of the others is discussed in the relevant chapter (ethnic region, gender role attitudes, family structure). The only exception is our language scale. This was a summary of the answers to ten questions asking about non-English-language use in a variety of contexts: with mother, father, other relatives, in school, at work, with peers, and so forth. We first divided these realms into family, school/peer, and community, where the effects of language might differ in reinforcing ethnic values. However, there seemed to be no differences in the effects of non-English-language use, with each adding its separate, approximately equal, effect to our nonfamily living measures. As a result, we combined them additively.

Table A.1. Residential transitions and high school completion (weighted)

Residential transitions	High school status	
	Dropout	Complete
Expected nonfamily autonomy	58	68
Age expected to marry (median)	20	22
Age expected residential independence (median)	19	21
Living arrangements at two years[a]		
Unmarried independence	22	16
Semiautonomous	3	18
With parents	53	56
Married independence	22	10
Total	100	100
Living arrangements at four years[b]		
Unmarried independence	34	40
Semiautonomous or parents	36	39
Married independence	30	21
Total	100	100

[a] Two years after high school completion, i.e., two years after the dropouts would have completed had they not dropped out.
[b] Four years after high school completion, i.e., four years after the dropouts would have completed had they not dropped out.

Table A.2. Descriptive statistics for the independent variables used in the analysis (unweighted)

Variables	Definitions	Means	Standard deviations
MALE	Male	.473	—
SES	Scale based on parental education, father's occupation, family income, and household consumption	−.113	.755
SOUTH	Census region = South	.222	—
NEWPAC	Census region = New England or Pacific	.190	—
BLACK	Race = black	.173	—
BLKCATH	Black and religion = Catholic	.022	—
BLKPROT	Black and religion = Protestant	.096	—
BLKOTH	Black and religion other	.055	—
ASIAN	Nonblack and origin = Asia	.031	—
HISPANIC	Nonblack and Hispanic	.172	
PRICAN	Hispanic and Puerto Rican	.019	—
MEXICAN	Hispanic and Mexican	.092	—
CUBAN	Hispanic and Cuban	.023	—
OTHHISP	Hispanic and other origin	.038	—
CATHOLIC	Catholic, nonblack, non-Asian, non-Hispanic	.214	—

(table continued on following page)

Table A.2. Descriptive statistics for the independent variables used in the
analysis (unweighted) *(continued)*

Variables	Definitions	Means	Standard deviations
CATHSEUR	Catholic, origin Greece, Italy, Portugal, or Spain	.034	—
MODCATH	Catholic, non-Cathseur	.180	—
JEW	Jewish, nonblack, non-Asian, non-Hispanic	.012	—
PROTESTANT	Protestant, nonblack, non-Asian, non-Hispanic	.305	—
PROTFUND	Protestant, Baptist or "other" Protestant denomination	.094	—
PROT2	Protestant, non-PROTF	.211	—
OTHREL	Other religion, nonblack, non-Asian, non-Hispanic	.041	—
NONE	No religion, nonblack, non-Asian, non-Hispanic	.023	—
PARFB	One or more parents non-U.S. born	.204	—
LANG	Scale based on average use level of non-English language (0 = never, 4 = always)	.407	.887
ETHREG	Residence in ethnic region	.091	—
CHURCHATT	Times per year attend services	28.796	27.136
RELIPER	Self-defined as a "religious person" (0 = not at all; 2 = very much)	.844	.626
FAMCLOSE	Rating of importance of being near family (0 = not imp.; 2 = very imp.)	.804	.674
EGALFAM	Attitude that men work, women at home (reverse coded, range 0–5)	2.423	1.132
NONFAM	Attitude that family not necessary for women's happiness (range 0–5)	2.464	1.110
LNEXMAR	Expected marriage age (log)	1.866	.443
LOGINC	Total family income (log)	9.921	.707
PARED	Average parental education	12.733	2.124
PARPAY	Actual parental contribution to child	$1,043	$1,161
CONTRIB	Actual child's contribution to parents	$325	$680
MOTHONLY	Mother-only family	.164	—
STEPFAM	Parent and guardian of the opposite sex	.070	—
BOTHPRI	Parent and child expect nonfamily living	.400	—
BOTHMAR	Neither expect nonfamily living	.250	—
PARPRI	Only parent expects nonfamily living	.230	—

194

Appendix B

Detailed Tables

Table B3.1.   Basic model predicting premarital residential independence (PRI)

Variables	Expecting PRI	Leaving to PRI	Leaving to marriage
MALE	0.081**	0.042[†]	−0.593**[a]
SES	0.042**	0.267**	−0.393**[a]
ASIAN	−0.048**	−0.444**	−0.911**[a]
HISPANIC	−0.057**	−0.610**	−0.514**
BLACK	0.066**	−0.428**	−1.193**[a]
CATHOLIC	0.019**	−0.287**	−0.746**[a]
JEWS	0.032	0.334**	−0.805**[a]
SOUTH	−0.049**	−0.204**	0.081*[a]
NEWPAC	0.061**	0.017	−0.285**[a]
Missing SES	−0.042**	0.033	0.368**[a]
Missing ethnicity	−0.000	−0.441**	−0.647**[a]
YEAR	—	0.403**	0.295**[a]
NOPRI	—	−1.698**	—
PRI	—	—	−1.698**
INTERCEPT	0.647**	−1.989**	−1.882**[a]
DEP MEAN	0.685	0.232	.123
R-SQUARE	0.025	.097	.085
MULT K =	—	6.209	10.129
N =	35,136	41,063	41,063
OMITGRP N =	—	26,466	26,466
MODEL DF	11	13	13

2-sided P values: ** = $P \leq .01$ * = $.01 \leq P \leq .05$ † = $.05 \leq P \leq .10$
(tested against remaining residentially dependent)
[a] Significant at $P < .05$, tested against leaving to PRI

195

Table B4.1. Hispanics and premarital residential independence (PRI)

Variables	Expecting PRI	Leaving to PRI	Leaving to marriage
MEX	−0.044**	−0.530**	−0.430**
CUBAN	−0.200**	−1.063**	−0.756**
PUERTO RICAN	−0.013	−0.699**	−0.776**
OTHHISP	−0.013	−0.467**	−0.428**
MALE	0.080**	0.038	−0.596**[a]
SES	0.044**	0.273**	−0.391**[a]
ASIAN	−0.046**	−0.436**	−0.904**[a]
BLACK	0.065**	−0.433**	−1.197**[a]
CATHOLIC	0.021**	−0.282**	−0.743**[a]
JEWS	0.032	0.334**	−0.803**[a]
SOUTH	−0.036**	−0.169**	0.100*[a]
NEWPAC	0.059**	0.007	−0.297**[a]
YEAR	—	0.403**	0.295**[a]
NOPRI	—	−1.702**	—
PRI	—	—	−1.702**
Missing SES	−0.042**	0.034	0.369**[a]
Missing ethnicity	0.001	−0.439**	−0.646**
INTERCEPT	0.644**	−1.997**	−1.884**[a]
DEP MEAN	0.685	0.232	.123
R-SQUARE	0.028	.098	.085
MULT K =	—	6.215	10.132
N =	35,136	41,063	41,063
OMITGRP N =	—	26,466	26,466
MODEL DF	14	16	16

2-sided P values: ** = P ≤ .01   * = .01 ≤ P ≤ .05
  (tested against remaining residentially dependent)
[a] Significant at P < .05, tested against leaving to PRI

Table B4.2.   Measures of ethnicity and premarital residential independence (PRI)

Variables	Expecting PRI	Leaving to PRI	Leaving to marriage
GENERATION	0.001	−0.070[†]	−0.183**
LANGUAGE	−0.045**	−0.112**	0.002[a]
MALE	0.079**	0.036	−0.599**[a]
SES	0.039**	0.258**	−0.394**[a]
ASIAN	−0.006	−0.262**	−0.798**[a]
MEX	−0.016	−0.367**	−0.392**
CUBAN	−0.095**	−0.749**	−0.610**
PUERTO RICAN	−0.057**	−0.493**	−0.681**
OTHHISP	0.023*	−0.359**	−0.380**
BLACK	0.062**	−0.437**	−1.189**[a]
CATHOLIC	0.025**	−0.272**	−0.739**[a]
JEWS	0.041[†]	0.357**	−0.784**[a]
SOUTH	−0.041**	−0.180**	0.101*[a]
NEWPAC	0.059**	0.010	−0.283**[a]
YEAR	—	0.405**	0.295**[a]
NOPRI	—	−1.705**	—
PRI	—	—	−1.705**
Missing SES	−0.035*	0.024	0.381**[a]
Missing ethnicity	0.015	−0.440**	−0.606*
Missing generation	−0.088*	0.034	−0.093
Missing language	0.014	0.065	0.259
INTERCEPT	0.649**	−1.984**	−1.871**[a]
DEP MEAN	0.685	0.233	.123
R-SQUARE	0.032	.099	.085
MULT K =	—	6.222	10.135
N =	35,117	41,044	41,044
OMITGRP N =	—	26,452	26,452
MODEL DF	18	20	20

2-sided P values: ** = P ≤ = .01   * = .01 ≤ P ≤ .05   † = .05 ≤ P ≤ .10
(tested against remaining residentially dependent)
[a] Significant at P < .05, tested against leaving to PRI

197

Table B4.3.   Measures of ethnicity and premarital residential independence (PRI): Interactions by SES and ethnic origins (separate regressions)

Variables	Expecting PRI	Leaving to PRI	Leaving to marriage
LANG	−0.021**	−0.049[+]	0.089*[a]
PARFB	0.029**	0.005	−0.083
LANG · PARFB	−0.044**	−0.116**	−0.162**
LANG	0.044**	−0.129**	0.030[a]
SES	0.037**	0.272**	−0.418**[a]
LANG · SES	0.003	−0.035[+]	0.058[+][a]
PARFB	0.025**	−0.008	−0.119[+]
ASIAN	0.006	−0.529**	−0.801**
ASIAN · FB	−0.026	0.321*	−0.088
MEX	0.036**	−0.350**	−0.393**
MEX · FB	−0.087**	−0.098	−0.124
CUBAN	−0.004	−0.330	−0.627[+]
CUBAN · FB	−0.126**	−0.514[+]	−0.090
PUERTO RICAN	0.029	−0.446**	−0.713**
PUERTO RICAN · FB	0.015	−0.125	−0.055
OTHHISP	0.033*	−0.268**	−0.066
OTHHISP · FB	−0.049[+]	−0.290*	−0.927**[a]
BLACK	0.064**	−0.416**	−1.211**[a]
BLACK · FB	−0.022	−0.169[+]	0.121
SES	0.029**	0.237**	−0.434**[a]
PARFB	0.008	−0.052	−0.149**
SES · FB	0.043**	0.101*	0.194**
ASIAN	−0.052**	−0.440**	−0.941**[a]
SES	0.048**	0.347**	−0.511**[a]
ASIAN · SES	0.038*	−0.021	0.292*
LANG	−0.029**	−0.110**	−0.060
ETHREG	0.035[+]	−0.218*	0.156[a]
LANG · ETHREG	−0.047**	0.041	0.144
BLACK	−0.029**	−0.388**	−0.966**[a]
SOUTH	0.035[+]	−0.197**	0.192**[a]
BLACK · SOUTH	−0.047**	0.111	−0.240**[a]

2-sided P values: ** = P ≤ .01   * = .01 ≤ P ≤ .05   [+] = .05 ≤ P ≤ .10
(tested against remaining residentially dependent)
[a]Significant at P < .05, tested against leaving to PRI

Table B5.1.　Religious denominations and premarital residential independence (PRI)

Variables	Expecting PRI	Leaving to PRI	Leaving to marriage
CATHOTH	0.011	−0.312**	−0.487** [a]
CATHSEUR	−0.061**	−0.624**	−0.719**
PROTFUND	−0.053**	−0.210**	0.464** [a]
NONE	0.093**	0.051	−0.163
OTHRELIG	−0.080**	−0.104	0.557** [a]
JEWS	0.012	0.257*	−0.591** [a]
BLACKC	0.051**	−0.682**	−0.882**
BLACKP	0.034**	−0.444**	−0.980** [a]
BLACKO	0.047**	−0.582**	−0.966** [a]
MALE	0.079**	0.040	−0.597** [a]
SES	0.042**	0.269**	−0.379** [a]
ASIAN	−0.067**	−0.519**	−0.684**
MEX	−0.066**	−0.613**	−0.201** [a]
CUBAN	−0.225**	−1.150**	−0.517** [a]
PUERTO RICAN	−0.036*	−0.783**	−0.545**
OTHHISP	−0.035**	−0.550**	−0.200* [a]
SOUTH	−0.031**	−0.160**	0.072[†][a]
NEWPAC	0.059**	0.014	−0.301** [a]
YEAR	—	0.403**	0.297** [a]
NOPRI	—	−1.697**	—
PRI	—	—	−1.670**
Missing SES	−0.042*	0.035	0.367** [a]
Missing ethnicity	−0.021	−0.523**	−0.418**
INTERCEPT	0.665**	−1.923**	−2.115** [a]
DEP MEAN	0.685	0.232	.123
R-SQUARE	0.032	.099	.087
MULT K =	—	6.222	10.153
N =	35,136	41,063	41,063
OMITGRP N =	—	26,466	26,466
MODEL DF	20	22	22

2-sided P values: ** = $P \leq .01$　　* = $.01 \leq P \leq .05$　　† = $.05 \leq P \leq .10$
(tested against remaining residentially dependent)
[a] Significant at $P < .05$, tested against leaving to PRI

Table B5.2. Measures of religiosity and premarital residential independence (PRI)

Variables	Expecting PRI	Leaving to PRI	Leaving to marriage
CATH SCHOOL	0.015*	−0.289**	−0.482**[a]
RELIPER	−0.048**	−0.024	0.022
CHFREQ	−0.001**	−0.001	0.001
CATHOTH	0.023**	−0.207**	−0.329**
CATHSEUR	−0.053**	−0.508**	−0.542**
PROTFUND	−0.035**	−0.197**	0.467**[a]
NONE	0.034*	0.032	−0.123
OTHRELIG	−0.055**	−0.087	0.557**[a]
JEWS	−0.023	0.231[+]	−0.593**[a]
BLACKC	0.053**	−0.526**	−0.633**
BLACKP	0.043**	−0.412**	−0.939**[a]
BLACKO	0.057**	−0.548**	−0.919**[a]
MALE	0.072**	0.028	−0.608**[a]
SES	0.046**	0.292**	−0.347**[a]
ASIAN	−0.070**	−0.490**	−0.631**
MEX	−0.050**	−0.556**	−0.127[+a]
CUBAN	−0.233**	−1.010**	−0.283*[a]
PUERTO RICAN	−0.037*	−0.713**	−0.433**
OTHHISP	−0.029*	−0.498**	−0.122[a]
SOUTH	−0.028**	−0.170**	0.051[a]
NEWPAC	0.050**	−0.000	−0.312**[a]
YEAR	—	0.403**	0.296**[a]
NOPRI	—	−1.712**	—
PRI	—	—	−1.712**
Missing RELIPER	−0.064**	−0.074	0.049
Missing CHFREQ	0.003	−0.161	−0.145
Missing SES	−0.047**	0.023	0.345**[a]
Missing ethnicity	−0.039[+]	−0.310**	−0.240[+]
INTERCEPT	0.752**	−1.871**	−2.137**[a]
DEP MEAN	0.685	0.232	.123
R-SQUARE	0.044	.101	.089
MULT K =	—	6.232	10.178
N =	35,136	41,063	41,063
OMITGRP N =	—	26,466	26,466
MODEL DF	25	27	27

2-sided P values: ** = P ≤ .01   * = .01 ≤ P ≤ .05   [+] = .05 ≤ P ≤ .10
(tested against remaining residentially dependent)
[a] Significant at P < .05, tested against leaving to PRI

Table B5.3. Measures of religiosity and premarital residential independence (PRI): Interactions by religious denomination (separate regressions)

Variables	Expecting PRI	Leaving to PRI	Leaving to marriage
RELIPER	−0.050**	−0.070*	0.060[a]
BLACKC	0.064[†]	−0.739**	−0.283
BLACKC · RELI	−0.010	0.217	−0.357[†]
BLACKP	0.013	−0.479**	−0.943**[a]
BLACKP · RELI	0.034**	0.069	0.003
CATHOTH	0.022[†]	−0.304**	−0.202*
CATHO · RELI	0.011	0.101	−0.134
CATHSEUR	0.038	−0.679**	−0.361[†]
CATHSEUR · RELI	−0.061**	0.176	−0.186
PROTFUND	−0.010	−0.237*	0.569**[a]
PROTF · RELI	−0.024[†]	0.042	−0.102
NONE	0.016	−0.023	−0.149
NONE · RELI	0.058[†]	0.049	0.164
OTHREL	−0.020	−0.276*	0.499**[a]
OTHREL · RELI	−0.032[†]	0.180[†]	0.050
JEWS	0.017	0.402*	−0.659**[a]
JEWS · RELI	−0.064*	−0.284	0.118
CHURCHATT	−0.002**	−0.001[†]	0.001
BLACKC	0.060*	−0.594**	−0.858**
BLACKC · CHATT	−0.000	0.002	0.007
BLACKP	0.020	−0.513**	−0.910**[a]
BLACKP · CHATT	0.001*	0.003[†]	−0.001
CATHOTH	0.016	−0.265**	−0.235**
CATHO · CHATT	0.000	0.002	0.003
CATHSEUR	−0.093**	−0.566**	−0.647**
CATHSEUR · CHATT	0.001*	0.002	0.003
PROTFUND	−0.027[†]	−0.224**	0.499**[a]
PROTF · CHATT	−0.000	0.001	−0.001
NONE	0.027	0.016	−0.112
NONE · CHATT	0.001	−0.001	−0.003
OTHREL	−0.028	−0.076	0.371**[a]
OTHREL · CHATT	−0.001[†]	−0.000	0.005[†]
JEWS	−0.025	0.246[†]	−0.741**[a]
JEWS · CHATT	0.000	−0.002	0.011
CATHSCH	0.008	−0.315**	−0.546**[a]
BLACK	0.065**	−0.401**	−1.192**[a]
BLCK · CSCH	0.027	0.110	0.475**

2-sided P values: ** = P ≤ .01   * = .01 ≤ P ≤ .05   † = .05 ≤ P ≤ .10
(tested against remaining residentially dependent)
[a] Significant at P < .05, tested against leaving to PRI

Table B6.1. Gender and premarital residential independence (PRI): Interactions by religiosity (separate regressions)

Variables	Expecting PRI	Leaving to PRI	Leaving to marriage
MALE	0.078**	0.043[†]	−0.575**[a]
SES	0.055**	0.258**	−0.474**[a]
SES · MALE	−0.029**	0.018**	0.172**[a]
MALE	0.087**	−0.017	−0.850**[a]
ASIAN	−0.007	−0.457**	−1.082**[a]
ASIAN · MALE	−0.085**	0.028	0.358[†]
BLACK	0.085**	−0.477**	−1.491**[a]
BLACK · MALE	−0.046**	0.107	0.676**[a]
HISPANIC	−0.089**	−0.687**	−0.636**
HISP · MALE	0.071**	0.164*	0.251**
CATHOLIC	0.033**	−0.318**	−0.928**[a]
CATH · MALE	−0.030*	0.064	0.382**[a]
JEW	0.117**	0.475**	−1.042**[a]
JEW · MALE	−0.146**	−0.223	0.448
MALE	0.075**	0.025	−0.602**[a]
ETHREGION	−0.065**	−0.159*	0.299**[a]
REGION · MALE	0.055**	0.126	0.030
MALE	0.064**	−0.001	−0.627**[a]
LANG	−0.063**	−0.159**	−0.034[a]
LANG · MALE	0.036**	0.095**	0.071*
MALE	0.075**	0.015	−0.627**[a]
PARFB	−0.008	−0.121*	−0.250**
PARFB · MALE	0.020[†]	0.111[†]	0.145[†]
MALE	0.054**	−0.003	−0.556**[a]
RELIPER	−0.057**	−0.041	0.051
RELIPER · MALE	0.019*	0.037	−0.063
MALE	0.063**	−0.026	−0.579**[a]
CHATT	−0.002**	−0.001*	0.001
CHATT · MALE	0.000	0.002*	−0.001
MALE	0.069**	0.010	−0.664**[a]
CATHSCH	0.008	−0.342**	−0.640**[a]
CSCH · MALE	0.016	0.122[†]	0.359**

2-sided P values: ** = P ≤ .01   * = .01 ≤ P ≤ .05   [†] = .05 ≤ P ≤ .10
(tested against remaining residentially dependent)
[a] Significant at P < .05, tested against leaving to PRI

Table B6.2.   Gender role attitudes and premarital residential independence (PRI),
sophomore cohort only

Variables	Expecting PRI	Leaving to PRI	Leaving to marriage
INTERCEPT	0.446**	− 3.292**	− 1.640** [a]
NONFAM	0.038**	0.111*	− 0.123** [a]
EGALFAM	0.031**	− 0.016	− 0.082*
MALE	0.106**	0.034	− 0.793** [a]
SES	0.033**	0.273**	− 0.474** [a]
ASIAN	0.039	− 0.436**	− 1.249** [a]
HISPANIC	− 0.026*	− 0.618**	− 0.598**
BLACK	0.078**	− 0.414**	− 1.192** [a]
CATHOLIC	0.032**	− 0.324**	− 0.851** [a]
JEWS	0.032	0.355*	− 0.608** [a]
MISSING SES	0.038*	0.438**	0.110
MISSING ETHNICITY	− 0.009	− 0.455**	− 0.704** [a]
YEAR	—	0.772**	0.414** [a]
NOPRI	—	− 1.760**	—
PRI	—	—	− 1.760**
DEP MEAN	0.698	0.240	0.111
R-SQUARE	0.032	.136	.090
MULT K =	—	6.347	11.107
N =	15,002	19,106	19,106
OMITGRP N =	—	12,396	13,396
MODEL DF	11	13	13

2-sided P values: ** = $P \leq .01$ * = $.01 \leq P \leq .05$
                (tested against remaining residentially dependent)
[a] Significant at $P < .05$, tested against leaving to PRI

Table B6.3. Familism and premarital residential independence (PRI): Interactions with ethnicity and gender (separate regressions)

Variables	Expecting PRI	Leaving to PRI	Leaving to marriage
PARCLOSE	−0.061**	−0.280**	−0.148**a
ASIAN	0.053*	−0.338**	−1.187**a
ASIAN · PARCLOSE	−0.051*	0.006	0.179
PARCLOSE	−0.069**	−0.302**	−0.143**a
BLACK	0.019†	−0.617**	−1.136**a
BLACK · PARCLOSE	0.029**	0.118*	0.006
PARCLOSE	−0.052**	−0.283**	−0.134**a
HISPANIC	0.015	−0.557**	−0.470**
HISP · PARCLOSE	−0.055**	0.015	−0.046
PARCLOSE	−0.063**	−0.261**	−0.134**a
CATHOLIC	0.035**	−0.139**	−0.723**a
CATH · PARCLOSE	0.003	−0.091*	−0.039
PARCLOSE	−0.063**	−0.281**	−0.142**a
JEW	0.141	0.325†	−0.797**a
JEW · PARCLOSE	−0.006	0.039	0.021
EGALFAM	0.049**	−0.025	−0.178**a
MALE	0.206**	−0.014	−1.303**a
MALE · EGALFAM	−0.039**	0.020	0.213**a
NONFAM	0.052**	0.162**	−0.265**a
MALE	0.184**	0.028	−1.121**a
MALE · NONFAM	−0.030**	0.011	0.122**a

2-sided P values: ** = $P \leq .01$ * = $.01 \leq P \leq .05$ † = $.05 \leq P \leq .10$
(tested against remaining residentially dependent)
a Significant at $P < .05$, tested against leaving to PRI

Table B7.1.   Basic model predicting premarital residential independence (PRI)
              expectations (including log of expected age at marriage)

Variables	Expecting PRI
Expected marriage age (logged)	0.420**
Male	0.015**
SES	0.002
Asian	−0.153**
Hispanic	−0.099**
Black	−0.038**
Catholic	−0.034**
Jews	−0.061**
South	−0.037**
New England/Pacific	0.038**
Missing SES	0.035*
Missing ethnicity	−0.043**
Intercept	−0.063**
DEP MEAN	0.685
R-SQUARE	0.169
N =	35,136
MODEL DF	12

2-sided P values: ** = P ≤ .01   * = .01 ≤ P ≤ .05

Table B7.2. Ethnic, religiosity, familism, and parental variables and premarital
residential independence (PRI) expectations, including log of expected
age at marriage (separate regressions)

Variables	Expecting PRI
Parent foreign born	−0.029**
Foreign language use	−0.048**
Ethnic region	−0.027**
Religious self-identification	−0.047**
Religious service attendance	−0.001**
Catholic school enrollment	−0.020**
Family closeness	−0.062**
Egalitarian family attitude	0.018**
Nonfamily attitude	0.013**
Mother-only household	0.032**
Stepfamily household	0.038**
Parents' education	−0.002
Family income	0.008*
Parents' contribution	−0.000
Young adults' contribution	−0.000

2-sided P values: ** = P ≤ .01   * = .01 ≤ P ≤ .05

206

Table B8.1. Premarital residential independence expectations (EPRI): Interactions with SES, gender, and ethnicity, the "poor planners" (separate regressions)

Variables	Leaving to PRI	Leaving to marriage
EPRI	0.314**	−0.627** [a]
SES	0.227*	−0.489** [a]
SES · EPRI	0.055[†]	0.192** [a]
EPRI	0.360**	−0.817** [a]
MALE	0.259**	−0.768** [a]
MALE · EPRI	−0.125*	0.378** [a]
EPRI	0.357**	−0.695** [a]
BLACK	−0.269**	−1.304** [a]
BLACK · EPRI	−0.273**	0.223* [a]
EPRI	0.294**	−0.673** [a]
HISPANIC	−0.630**	−0.599**
HISPANIC · EPRI	0.063	0.096
EPRI	0.293**	−0.675** [a]
ASIAN	−0.664**	−1.319** [a]
ASIAN · EPRI	0.383**	0.619**

2-sided P values: ** = $P \leq .01$ * = $.01 \leq P \leq .05$ † = $.05 \leq P \leq .10$
(tested against remaining residentially dependent)
[a] Significant at $P < .05$, tested against leaving to PRI

Table B8.2.   Who is off-schedule? (unweighted percentages)

| | Percent experiencing event off-schedule | | |
	Before expected	After expected	Total unexpected
		Marriage	
Total	6.7	13.7	20.4
Black	4.5	11.6	16.2
Hispanic	7.7	16.9	24.6
Asian	4.6	7.6	12.3
Catholic	4.7	11.8	16.4
Jews	1.8	4.7	6.6
Males	5.6	10.9	16.5
Expected PRI	6.4	9.9	16.3
		Parenthood	
Total	4.5	4.2	8.6
Black	7.4	5.1	12.5
Hispanic	5.3	5.9	11.2
Asian	2.1	1.9	4.0
Catholic	4.3	4.7	9.0
Jews	0.8	1.0	1.8
Males	3.2	3.9	7.1
Expected PRI	5.2	3.2	8.4
		Leaving school	
Total	15.4	4.3	19.7
Black	17.5	3.6	21.1
Hispanic	18.8	5.3	24.1
Asian	13.1	4.9	18.1
Catholic	14.1	4.8	18.8
Jews	8.0	3.5	11.5
Males	14.8	4.3	19.1
Expected PRI	18.6	5.0	23.7

Table B8.3. Effects of unexpected marriage, parenthood, and schooling (separate regressions)

Variables	Leaving to PRI	Leaving to marriage
Married before X[b]	0.023	19.177**[a]
Married after X	−0.343**	−0.792**[a]
Parent before X	0.204**	4.744**[a]
Parent after X	−0.353**	0.825**[a]
Leave school before X	0.032	0.582**[a]
Leave school after X	−0.194**	−0.413**

2-sided P values: ** = P ≤ .01
(tested against remaining residentially dependent)
[a] Significant at P < .05, tested against leaving to PRI
[b] X = expected

Table B9.1. Family structure and premarital residential independence (PRI)

Variables	Expecting PRI	Leaving to PRI	Leaving to marriage
STEPFAM	0.043**	0.379**	0.200**
MOTHONLY	0.057**	0.265**	−0.197** [a]
PARCLOSE	−0.063**	−0.280**	−0.142** [a]
MALE	0.080**	0.037	−0.599** [a]
SES	0.047**	0.285**	−0.423** [a]
ASIAN	0.002	−0.333**	−1.012** [a]
HISPANIC	−0.037**	−0.543**	−0.512**
BLACK	0.041**	−0.528**	−1.132** [a]
CATHOLIC	0.037**	−0.215**	−0.756** [a]
JEWS	0.036[+]	0.356**	−0.781** [a]
YEAR	—	0.411**	0.299** [a]
NOPRI	—	−1.720**	—
PRI	—	—	−1.720**
Missing SES	−0.025	−0.227*	0.230* [a]
Missing ethnicity	0.004	−0.452**	−0.636** [a]
Missing famstructure	−0.048[+]	0.442**	0.240[+]
Missing parclose	−0.098**	−0.210**	−0.150[+]
INTERCEPT	0.686**	−1.907**	−1.794** [a]
DEP MEAN	0.685	0.232	.123
R-SQUARE	0.030	.103	.085
MULT K =	—	6.251	10.132
N =	35,136	41,063	41,063
OMITGRP N =	—	26,466	26,466
MODEL DF	14	16	16

2-sided P values: ** = P ≤ .01   * = .01 ≤ P ≤ .05   [+] = .05 ≤ P ≤ .10
(tested against remaining residentially dependent)
[a] Significant at P < .05, tested against leaving to PRI

Table B9.2. Family structure and premarital residential independence (PRI): Interactions with gender and ethnicity (separate regressions)

Variables	Expecting PRI	Leaving to PRI	Leaving to marriage
MOTHONLY	0.075**	0.281**	−0.267** [a]
MALE	0.087**	0.043	−0.624** [a]
MALE · MONLY	−0.042**	−0.037	0.156[+]
STEPFAM	0.036**	0.316**	0.315**
MALE	0.079**	0.027	−0.580** [a]
MALE · STEPFAM	−0.017	0.148	−0.269* [a]
MOTHONLY	0.056**	0.256**	−0.208** [a]
ASIAN	−0.003**	−0.371**	−1.064** [a]
ASIAN · MONLY	0.055	0.448[+]	0.610[+]
STEPFAM	0.044**	0.369**	0.175** [a]
ASIAN	0.003	−0.355**	−1.067** [a]
ASIAN · STEPFAM	−0.038	0.514	1.287**
MOTHONLY	0.068**	0.301**	−0.234** [a]
BLACK	0.050**	−0.495**	−1.166** [a]
BLACK · MONLY	−0.034*	−0.122	0.126
STEPFAM	0.056**	0.452**	0.275**
BLACK	0.046**	−0.496**	−1.099** [a]
BLACK · STEPFAM	−0.054*	−0.325**	−0.332*
MOTHONLY	0.053**	0.272**	−0.188** [a]
HISP	−0.040**	−0.537**	−0.505**
HISP · MONLY	0.020	−0.040	−0.046
STEPFAM	0.037**	0.406**	0.168* [a]
HISP	−0.039**	−0.532**	−0.526**
HISP · STEPFAM	0.036	−0.168	0.201

2-sided P values: ** = $P \leq .01$ * = $.01 \leq P \leq .05$ [+] = $.05 \leq P \leq .10$
(tested against remaining residentially dependent)
[a] Significant at $P < .05$, tested against leaving to PRI

211

Table B10.1.   Parental education and income and premarital residential
independence (PRI)

Variables	Expecting PRI	Leaving to PRI	Leaving to marriage
PARED	0.010**	0.096**	−0.117** [a]
LOGINC	0.017**	0.033	−0.105** [a]
MALE	0.080**	0.046[+]	−0.599** [a]
ASIAN	−0.047**	−0.471**	−0.873** [a]
MEXICAN	−0.048**	−0.546**	−0.403**
CUBAN	−0.203**	−1.092**	−0.722** [a]
PRICAN	−0.020	−0.755**	−0.707**
OTHHISP	−0.014	−0.482**	−0.409**
BLACK	0.059**	−0.491**	−1.129** [a]
CATHOLIC	0.022**	−0.277**	−0.750** [a]
JEWS	0.035	0.300**	−0.787** [a]
SOUTH	−0.036**	−0.168**	0.098* [a]
NEWPAC	0.060**	0.010	−0.302** [a]
YEAR	—	0.404**	0.294** [a]
NOPRI	—	−1.697**	—
PRI	—	—	−1.697**
Missing education	−0.022**	−0.079[+]	0.053
Missing income	−0.018**	0.071[+]	0.074
Missing ethnicity	0.000	−0.433**	−0.594**
INTERCEPT	0.349**	−3.572**	0.680** [a]
DEP MEAN	0.685	0.232	.123
R-SQUARE	0.027	.099	.085
MULT K =	—	6.222	10.130
N =	35,136	41,063	41,063
OMITGRP N =	—	26,466	26,466
MODEL DF	16	18	18

2-sided P values: ** = $P \leq .01$ [+] = $.05 \leq P \leq .10$
(tested against remaining residentially dependent)
[a] Significant at $P < .05$, tested against leaving to PRI

Table B10.2.   Intergenerational financial flows and routes to residential independence

Variables	Expecting PRI	Leaving to PRI	Leaving to marriage
PARPAY	0.000[+]	0.000*	−0.000**[a]
CONTRIB	−0.000[+]	−0.000	0.000*
LOGINC	−0.008	−0.051	0.098
PARED	0.010**	0.078**	−0.102**[a]
MALE	0.061**	0.121[+]	−0.562**[a]
ASIAN	−0.041	−0.041	−0.725*
HISPANIC	−0.059**	−0.612**	−0.492**
BLACK	0.075**	−0.364**	−1.199**[a]
CATHOLIC	0.006	−0.253**	−0.715**[a]
JEWS	0.012	0.358	−0.755*[a]
SOUTH	−0.050**	−0.347**	0.050[a]
NEWPAC	0.054**	0.016	−0.473**[a]
YEAR	—	0.334**	0.318**
NOPRI	—	−1.723**	—
PRI	—	—	−1.723**
MISSING INCOME	0.032	−0.051	0.068
MISSING PARED	−0.011	−0.081	−0.071
MISSING ETHNICITY	0.122*	−0.121	−0.838**[a]
MISSING PARPAY	0.004	0.146	0.065
MISSING CONTRB	−0.089*	−0.291[+]	0.157
INTERCEP	0.611**	−2.450**	−1.554**[a]
DEP MEAN	.696	0.252	0.123
R-SQUARE	.023	0.103	0.101
MULT K =	—	5.925	10.344
N =	4,495	4,699	4,699
OMITGRP N =	—	2,941	2,941
MODEL DF	17	19	19

2-sided P values: ** = $P \leq .01$ * = $.01 \leq P \leq .05$ [+] = $.05 \leq P \leq .10$
(tested against remaining residentially dependent)
[a] Significant at $P < .05$, tested against leaving to PRI

Table B11.1.   Ethnic, religiosity, familism, and parental variables and premarital
residential independence (PRI) expectations of parents

Variables	Expect PRI for child
Male	0.097**
SES	0.069**
Asian	−0.126**
Hispanic	−0.211**
Black	0.034
Catholic	−0.050**
Jews	0.104*
South	−0.061**
New England/Pacific region	0.072**
Missing SES	−0.127**
Missing ethnicity	−0.028
Intercept	0.594**
R-square	.058
df	12
N	6,019

2-sided P values: ** = P ≤ .01   * = .01 ≤ P ≤ .05

Table B11.2. Parent-child expectations agreement and routes to residential
independence

Variables[^]	Leaving to PRI	Leaving to marriage
BOTHPRI	0.4875**	−0.1629[a]
BOTHMAR	−0.2308*	0.7219**[a]
PARPRI	0.2575*	0.3420*
MALE	0.0433	−0.4841**[a]
YEAR	0.4578**	0.3555**[a]
SES	0.1775**	−0.4720**[a]
ASIAN	−0.1503	−0.5155[+]
HISPANIC	−0.6273**	−0.6156**
BLACK	−0.4214**	−1.1499**[a]
CATHOLIC	−0.2786**	−0.6420**[a]
JEWS	0.5011**	−0.7618**[a]
SOUTH	−0.2778**	0.1637[+][a]
NEWPAC	0.0009	−0.2519**
INTERCEP	−2.3353	−2.3365**[a]
DEP MEAN	0.256	0.116
R-SQUARE	0.121	0.098
MULT K =	5.977	10.783
N =	8,341	8,341
OMITGRP N =	5,237	5,237
MODEL DF	18	18

[^] Models also included controls for missing values on ethnicity and parental socioeconomic status.

2-sided P values: ** = P ≤ .01   * = .01 ≤ P ≤ .05   [+] = .05 ≤ P ≤ .10
            (tested against remaining residentially dependent)

[a] Significant at P < .05, tested against leaving to PRI

Table B11.3. Generational agreement about nonfamily living expectations: Interactions with gender and SES (separate regressions)

Variables	Leaving to PRI	Leaving to marriage
MALE	0.034	-0.255* [a]
BOTHPRI	0.464**	-0.021 [a]
MALE · BOTHPRI	0.050	-0.323[+]
BOTHMAR	-0.259*	1.002** [a]
MALE · BOTHMAR	0.095	-0.863** [a]
PARPRI	0.349*	0.659**
MALE · PARPRI	-0.178	-0.657*
SES	0.230**	-0.394** [a]
BOTHPRI	0.508**	-0.158 [a]
SES · BOTHPRI	-0.149[+]	-0.086
BOTHMAR	-0.229*	0.711** [a]
SES · BOTHMAR	-0.042	-0.213
PARPRI	0.268*	0.408**
SES · PARPRI	-0.100	-0.478*

2-sided P values: ** = $P \leq .01$ * = $.01 \leq P \leq .05$ [+] = $.05 \leq P \leq .10$
(tested against remaining residentially dependent)
[a] Significant at $P < .05$, tested against leaving to PRI

Notes

CHAPTER 2.   ROUTES TO RESIDENTIAL INDEPENDENCE: EXPECTATIONS AND BEHAVIOR

1.   We use the files of the 1980 High School and Beyond survey of seniors (along with the reinterviews in 1982, 1984, and 1986) and of sophomores who were seniors in 1982 (and their reinterviews in 1984 and 1986). We also use the reduced sample of parents and children for parts of the analysis. For details on the data that we use throughout, see Appendix A. The basic technical issues of sampling and weighting procedures are contained in Calvin Jones et al. (1986).

2.   More than half of those who left to such quarters returned home to live for some period of time (Goldscheider and DaVanzo 1986).

3.   We were also concerned that there might be ambiguity over the precise meaning of "own home or apartment" and that respondents might report semi-autonomous living arrangements such as college dorms and military barracks as their "own home" (see Goldscheider and DaVanzo 1986). To investigate this possibility, we tabulated a separate question on expected living arrangements "next year," which included as options "dorms" and "barracks," by the sequence of residence-marriage expectations (by age). The vast majority of respondents planning to be in dorms or barracks the following year (93%) were not expecting residential independence at that age.

4.   We treat together those expecting residential independence before marriage and those who never expect to marry. In addition, some respondents expected an age at marriage earlier than the age they expected to establish their own home, and a few reported that they never expected to have their own home. We discuss these responses in the Appendix to this chapter, showing how we treated ambiguous responses either from the parent or from the young adult.

5.   This contrast may result from other differences between young adults rather than whether they expect to leave home before marriage. Young adults who expect premarital residential independence may have very different ethnic and social class backgrounds, leading them to defer marriage to finish more education, for example. These factors are controlled in all our analyses in subsequent chapters.

6.   Not all these young adults remained residentially independent and unmar-

NOTES TO PAGES 24–43

ried. Some married after experiencing nonfamily living, and others returned to residential dependence, ordinarily in the parental home, for some period of time. We do not examine transitions subsequent to the first in this analysis.

7. We cannot know from these data how many were actually not living with their parents or some older relative but instead were living in some form of group quarters six years after high school. However, analyses of a nearly comparable data set (members of the high school class of 1972) show almost none were in dormitories or barracks seven years after high school graduation (Goldscheider and DaVanzo 1986).

8. In all these comparisons, it is not clear a priori how "good" these predictions are. Obviously, they are not all making perfect predictions, and it is possible that once we take into account other factors, such as the presence of family resources, that might distinguish between those who expect nonfamily living and those who do not, those factors will predict actual behavior as well as they do expectations. If so, then knowing what was "expected" will tell us little or nothing beyond these other characteristics about eventual behavior. We shall specify in later chapters the strength of these relationships in more precise terms, but it remains unclear whether agreement between parents and children in 65 percent of the families is "high" or "low" or whether the fact that expectations predict actual nonfamily living in over half the families should be described as a "weak" or a "powerful" prediction.

CHAPTER 3. LEAVING HOME BEFORE MARRIAGE:
THE BASIC PATTERNS

1. Some have argued that nuclear families preceded industrialization in England (Laslett 1973; also see the discussion in Kertzer 1991), and others argue that family extension will survive economic development in Japan and Taiwan (Morgan and Hirosima 1983; Kojima 1989; Freedman, Chang, and Sun 1982).

2. Each of the results presented in this chapter shows the pure (or partial) effect of the factor being considered, net of all the other factors we include in our models. So in this case, the possibility that those with higher socioeconomic status come from families that do not (or no longer) belong to immigrant ethnic or religious groups is taken into account through statistical controls. The values presented show the predicted amount of premarital residential independence expected or achieved if all the young adults had the *same values* on all the other variables in the multivariate regression equation (taken at the mean of the sample, for each variable) and only differed on, in this example, the measure of family socioeconomic status. See Appendix B for the detailed regression tables underlying this analysis; these present the complete equations, including statistical significance for individual variables.

3. These groups were defined first by race—blacks and Asians—and then the nonblack, non-Asian group was divided into Hispanics and others.

4. This is a weighted average of the three white religious groups, Protestants, Catholics, and Jews.

5. Our analyses uncovered an interesting result relating these regions to

218

ried. Some married after experiencing nonfamily living, and others returned to residential dependence, ordinarily in the parental home, for some period of time. We do not examine transitions subsequent to the first in this analysis.

7. We cannot know from these data how many were actually not living with their parents or some older relative but instead were living in some form of group quarters six years after high school. However, analyses of a nearly comparable data set (members of the high school class of 1972) show almost none were in dormitories or barracks seven years after high school graduation (Goldscheider and DaVanzo 1986).

8. In all these comparisons, it is not clear a priori how "good" these predictions are. Obviously, they are not all making perfect predictions, and it is possible that once we take into account other factors, such as the presence of family resources, that might distinguish between those who expect nonfamily living and those who do not, those factors will predict actual behavior as well as they do expectations. If so, then knowing what was "expected" will tell us little or nothing beyond these other characteristics about eventual behavior. We shall specify in later chapters the strength of these relationships in more precise terms, but it remains unclear whether agreement between parents and children in 65 percent of the families is "high" or "low" or whether the fact that expectations predict actual nonfamily living in over half the families should be described as a "weak" or a "powerful" prediction.

CHAPTER 3. LEAVING HOME BEFORE MARRIAGE: THE BASIC PATTERNS

1. Some have argued that nuclear families preceded industrialization in England (Laslett 1973; also see the discussion in Kertzer 1991), and others argue that family extension will survive economic development in Japan and Taiwan (Morgan and Hirosima 1983; Kojima 1989; Freedman, Chang, and Sun 1982).

2. Each of the results presented in this chapter shows the pure (or partial) effect of the factor being considered, net of all the other factors we include in our models. So in this case, the possibility that those with higher socioeconomic status come from families that do not (or no longer) belong to immigrant ethnic or religious groups is taken into account through statistical controls. The values presented show the predicted amount of premarital residential independence expected or achieved if all the young adults had the *same values* on all the other variables in the multivariate regression equation (taken at the mean of the sample, for each variable) and only differed on, in this example, the measure of family socioeconomic status. See Appendix B for the detailed regression tables underlying this analysis; these present the complete equations, including statistical significance for individual variables.

3. These groups were defined first by race—blacks and Asians—and then the nonblack, non-Asian group was divided into Hispanics and others.

4. This is a weighted average of the three white religious groups, Protestants, Catholics, and Jews.

5. Our analyses uncovered an interesting result relating these regions to

Notes

CHAPTER 2. ROUTES TO RESIDENTIAL INDEPENDENCE: EXPECTATIONS AND BEHAVIOR

1.   We use the files of the 1980 High School and Beyond survey of seniors (along with the reinterviews in 1982, 1984, and 1986) and of sophomores who were seniors in 1982 (and their reinterviews in 1984 and 1986). We also use the reduced sample of parents and children for parts of the analysis. For details on the data that we use throughout, see Appendix A. The basic technical issues of sampling and weighting procedures are contained in Calvin Jones et al. (1986).

2.   More than half of those who left to such quarters returned home to live for some period of time (Goldscheider and DaVanzo 1986).

3.   We were also concerned that there might be ambiguity over the precise meaning of "own home or apartment" and that respondents might report semi-autonomous living arrangements such as college dorms and military barracks as their "own home" (see Goldscheider and DaVanzo 1986). To investigate this possibility, we tabulated a separate question on expected living arrangements "next year," which included as options "dorms" and "barracks," by the sequence of residence-marriage expectations (by age). The vast majority of respondents planning to be in dorms or barracks the following year (93%) were not expecting residential independence at that age.

4.   We treat together those expecting residential independence before marriage and those who never expect to marry. In addition, some respondents expected an age at marriage earlier than the age they expected to establish their own home, and a few reported that they never expected to have their own home. We discuss these responses in the Appendix to this chapter, showing how we treated ambiguous responses either from the parent or from the young adult.

5.   This contrast may result from other differences between young adults rather than whether they expect to leave home before marriage. Young adults who expect premarital residential independence may have very different ethnic and social class backgrounds, leading them to defer marriage to finish more education, for example. These factors are controlled in all our analyses in subsequent chapters.

6.   Not all these young adults remained residentially independent and unmar-

nicity and religion, however, requires more cases as well as more detailed and different measures of group intensity than are available in this data set. For example, our measures of residential concentration are not appropriate for Jews, and we have no measure of their social or economic networks. These have been shown to be critical for understanding the intensity of their communal life. Moreover, Judaism tends to be a more family-oriented religion than Christianity, with less emphasis on public religious worship, so that regular attendance at religious services has a different meaning for Jews than for Catholics or Protestants, as does the specifics of personal "religious" identification. Jews thus constitute an ethnic as well as a religious community, tending to be more ethnic than religious. (For a more detailed discussion of the patterns of living arrangements among Jews and types of measures that can be used, see Goldscheider 1986.) Hence, in this analysis, we will treat them simply as a small, religious group.

4.   Since the reference group changed from all Protestants to liberal Protestants, the resultant pattern alters these findings slightly.

5.   The categories were "very much," "somewhat," and "not at all."

6.   The specific categories of response were "not at all," "a few times per year," "monthly," "two to three times per month," "weekly," and "more than once a week." We recorded these responses to indicate visits per year.

CHAPTER 6.   FAMILISM: PARENTAL AND GENDER RELATIONSHIPS

1.   Family extension is extremely rare among the families of young adults. In part, this reflects their stage in the family cycle, since the parental generation has had a long time to establish a relationship separate from *their* parents, while few of the young in high school have begun families of their own and thus become at risk of doubling up, themselves. Further, their *grandparents* are primarily in their 60s and 70s, and few have experienced levels of disability requiring coresidence with their adult children and grandchildren. Hence there is little variance in family extension to be used to predict residential pathways, and in preliminary analyses, the rare cases of family extension did not differ from the rest. This data set (as well as others that we are familiar with) contains no measures of parent-child authority patterns.

2.   It is difficult to reconcile this result for blacks with other research suggesting the extreme importance of family ties among American blacks (e.g., Stack 1975). It is possible that strong familism is most characteristic of those in the lowest economic strata, whose children would not be well represented in this high school graduating group; it may also be that these young people are reacting to what may seem to them to be an invidious stereotype.

3.   Each of the results presented in this chapter shows the pure (or partial) effect of the factor being considered, net of all the other factors we include in our models, using the method described in chapter 3, note 7. So in this case, the possibility that those with more traditional attitudes toward parent-child closeness come from families with lower socioeconomic status or belong to more fundamentalist religious denominations is taken into account through statistical controls. The values presented show the predicted amount of nonfamily living expected or

experienced if all the young adults had the *same values* on all the other variables in the multivariate regression equation (taken at the mean of the sample, for each variable) and only differed on, in this example, attitudes toward parent-child closeness. See Appendix B for the detailed regression tables underlying this analysis which give the complete equations, including statistical significance for individual variables. Unless otherwise specified, we only report statistically significant differences.

4. Compare table B3.1 with table B9.1.

5. We will consider this question in more detail when we investigate the effects of expected and actual marriage timing on sex differences in expectations and experience (chap. 7).

6. We found no regional differences in the extent of gender differentiation on expectations (table B6.1). There is no evidence that young men and women differ more in the South than they do in other parts of the country. The extremes of gender role segregation often thought to characterize the South evidently do not apply to residential autonomy; nor do the New England and Pacific regions show greater gender equality, at least on this measure.

7. We are not suggesting that "traditional" implies any long-term historical or biological set of arrangements. There is ample evidence that only late in the nineteenth century did home and children become removed from the concerns of men as they gradually discontinued their productive roles in the home in favor of jobs in a more distant workplace (Demos 1986).

8. This was particularly the case in the early years of the gender role revolution. There was an assumption that the roles of men and women would only become more egalitarian by altering the roles of women to resemble those of men, that is, increasing the commitments of women to the world of work so as to reach equality with men in that realm and decreasing the commitments of women to the family to remove the barriers there that are only in the way of women. There was little concern initially about the ways *men's* work roles act as barriers to men's family roles and obligations. It is possible that later stages of the gender role revolution may involve *increases* in familism, as more men realize the importance of sharing in the tasks of the family if they are to have the supports and gratifications of family life (see Goldscheider and Waite 1991).

9. Further, gender role attitudes should also have more effect on the expectations and behavior of women than of men because the focus of these questions is on *women's* roles. None of the questions require men to be willing to share half their family's domestic tasks to qualify as holding a "modern" gender role attitude.

10. These questions were only included on the sophomore questionnaire. Therefore, we have fewer cases for our analysis, and we are not able to follow their behavior beyond the first four years after high school. The attitudinal data that we examine were obtained in the first reinterview wave of the sophomores, when they were in their senior year, at the same time that the data on expectations about residential independence were obtained. As a result, the proportion who experienced nonfamily living in the analysis is slightly higher than that reported in other analyses, since a somewhat lower proportion of leaving in the very early years is to marriage.

11. Treating these two measures separately is consistent with other work that has found multidimensionality in orientations toward gender roles. Two dimensions normally appear (Mason and Bumpass 1975; Waite, Goldscheider, and Witsberger 1986), with one dimension tapping gender change in the workplace, where men and women are perceived to be increasingly equal in pay, opportunity, and commitment, and the other measuring gender change in the home, an area that has shown much less change (Thornton 1989).

12. Compare table B3.1 with table B6.2.

13. Compare table B3.1 with table B6.2.

CHAPTER 7. EXITING FROM THE HOME: THE TIMING OF MARRIAGE AND RESIDENTIAL AUTONOMY

1. These are major underestimates of total nonfamily living, which also includes all the roommates of the primary individual household heads.

2. The question was, "At what age do you expect to get married?" The options included single ages between 18 and 29, less than age 18, age 30 or more, have already done so, and do not expect to do so. For a discussion of this variable and its role in the measurement of expectations, see chapter 2. We took the natural logarithm of the distribution to reduce skewness.

3. The relationship is extremely strong (.428), accounting for about three-fourths of the explained variance in expectations for nonfamily living. The total explained sum of squares in the equation that did not include the log of expected marriage age is only 23 percent of the explained sum of squares in the equation that does include the log of expected marriage age.

4. Calculated from the values in table B7.1. As in previous chapters, each of the results presented in this chapter shows the pure (or partial) effect of the factor being considered, net of all the other factors we include in our models. The values presented show the predicted amount of nonfamily living expected or achieved if all the young adults had the *same values* on all the other variables in the multivariate regression equation (taken at the mean of the sample, for each variable), based on the method described in chapter 3, note 7.

5. However, the effects of expected marriage age differ substantially by gender. The effect of marriage timing is greater for young women than for young men, with the result that gender differences in nonfamily living are greatest among young people expecting relatively early marriage.

6. We shall investigate the effects of unanticipated marriage (marriage that occurs earlier or later than at the expected age) in the next chapter.

7. It is important to remember, however, that we have a rather truncated set of marriage observations for this cohort, since only 39 percent had married within six years after the senior year in high school, based on unweighted frequencies.

8. For behavior, factors are placed in one of the nine boxes in this figure based on the results of our multinomial logistic regression analyses. For young adults not yet living independently, this analysis shows which factors (1) predict establishing an independent residence before marriage and (2) predict marrying and establishing residential independence (each compared with remaining residen-

tially dependent, unmarried). Our reference category is nonfundamentalist Protestants, such as Methodists, Presbyterians, and Episcopalians. Results for residential expectations are presented in tables B7.1 and B7.2. For actual nonfamily living experiences, the Appendix tables presented for chapters 3 through 6 contain the detailed information (cols. 2 and 3).

9. Of course, if Catholics had been the reference religious group, Protestants would have been to their lower left.

10. Male-female differences in residential independence also reflect gender differences in salary levels and rates of college attendance, both of which increase nonfamily living. In an analysis that took these gender differences into account, men were *less likely* than women to experience nonfamily living (Goldscheider and DaVanzo 1989). That model also suggests that greater parental financial resources do not delay marriage, once the greater likelihood of college attendance among young adults in more affluent families is taken into account; rather, they speed marriage.

11. Some portion of the difference in the effect of socioeconomic status on expectations and behavior may also reflect our greater ability to make distinctions for behavior (i.e., the positive but insignificant effect of socioeconomic status on expecting premarital residential independence, once expected marriage age is controlled, might have been significant with a stronger measure of expectations).

12. In fact, Jewish males turn out to be *less* likely than others, particularly than Jewish females, to expect nonfamily living, once their extremely late expected marriage age was controlled.

13. Neither of these effects separately were significantly different from 0; that is, personal religiosity does not make a significant difference on establishing an independent residence either via nonfamily living or via marriage, compared with remaining residentially dependent. However, the combination of these two effects means that women are significantly more likely to establish an independent residence via marriage than they are via nonfamily living.

CHAPTER 8. EXPECTATIONS AND THE UNEXPECTED

1. The discrepancy appears to be less in these "other things equal" calculations than it was in chapter 2, since part of the reason that those who expect premarital residential independence are able to achieve it is due to their characteristics—gender, class, and race—which lead them to both expect nonfamily living and achieve it. In the multivariate analyses, the effects of these factors have already been taken into account statistically.

2. The coefficient for the interaction of SES and residential expectations on the likelihood of leaving residential dependence before marriage was small and significant only at the .10 level (t = 1.65).

3. This can be seen from table B8.2 by comparing the row for "males" with the total.

4. This is 52 percent of the 8.6 percent shown above in table 8.3.

5. Jews resemble Asians in being good planners of nonfamily living. However, this result did not reach statistical significance, perhaps because of the small num-

ber of cases. Hence they were not discussed in the previous section. For parallel findings indicating that Jews are exceptionally good planners of the number of children they have, see Goldscheider 1986 and Goldscheider and Mosher 1988.

6. This was particularly the case among Jews (data not presented).

7. It increased the likelihood of married independence by 115 times, too much to chart.

CHAPTER 9. FAMILY STRUCTURE

1. Given the complexity of the information that was collected (some students reported living with both a parent and a guardian of the same sex, or reported both that they were living alone and living with siblings), we decided to use this information only to distinguish the two most common alternative family types—mother-only and stepfamilies. We could have measured those living only with their fathers and perhaps other types such as those living only with grandparents, but these are very small groups, and the proportion of reporting errors within categories is likely to have been relatively high.

2. Any of these family types can include additional persons, both relatives and nonrelatives. We are not examining this dimension of family structure (nuclear vs. extended), since extended families are very rare in families of older teenage children. We concentrate instead only on parental structure, which is the most important dimension of family structure, at least in terms of numbers and current policy interest.

3. These are presented with controls for the variables in the basic model in chapter 3.

4. There was a nearly significant coefficient for the likelihood of expecting nonfamily living ($t = 1.7$) for the interaction of family closeness and mother-only families when the log of expected marriage age was controlled, but it was in the direction *opposite* to the hypothesis: feelings about such closeness matter slightly less, not more, in mother-only families than in nuclear families.

CHAPTER 10. EDUCATION, INCOME, AND GENERATIONAL RESOURCE FLOWS

1. This is one of the important reasons the decision of young adults to leave home should be treated in a "household" context, since both the parents and the children are directly involved with it. This view is consistent with the finding that over half of the parents expect their children to leave home before they marry and helps us understand why there is no major intergenerational conflict over children leaving home before marriage (chap. 2).

2. Studies typically find a correlation of about 0.4 between income and education among men (Matras 1984).

3. We constructed two measures: family income, defined as the total family income reported by the student, and parental education. There were seven income categories in the sophomore file and eight in the senior file. We recoded these categories to the midpoints to measure income directly. Consistent with other studies of consumer demand, we have transformed these values by taking a

natural log, since the effects of an additional thousand dollars should be greater at lower than at higher levels of income. Parental education is the average educational level attained by mothers and fathers. For the sample as a whole, average family income was about $25,000, and average educational level attained by parents was 12.8 years.

4. These levels of income and education correspond roughly to the lowest and highest deciles, as in the comparisons based on the SES scale.

5. Moving to the much smaller sample has relatively little difference on the results of the analysis, indicating that the large size of the HSB cohorts is not providing us with significant but quantitatively trivial results.

6. The choices and the percentages selecting each among those who reported any support were: 0–$100 (21%), $100–$199 (12%), $200–$599 (13%), $600–$1,199 (16%), $1,200–$1,999 (12%), and >$2,000 (26%). In addition, 55 percent of the parents reported providing no support at all. We recoded these categories to the midpoint for all but the upper category and used $3,000 as an approximate midpoint for the highest category, since more than a quarter of all parents who reported supporting their children at all marked this category.

7. The choices and the percentages selecting each among those who reported any contribution from their children were: 0–$1,000 (72%), $1,000–$1,999 (20%), $2,000–$2,999 (5%), and an additional four categories for contributions greater than $3,000, which together cumulated 3 percent of those making any contribution. We recoded these categories to the midpoint.

8. For further details on this issue, see Goldscheider and Goldscheider 1991.

9. Higher levels of parental help might make even more difference. Unfortunately, we were not able to observe these values, since the categories with which this information was collected did not allow distinguishing variation at the high end.

10. However, introducing these measures of flows between the generations does not reduce the effects of education and income on nonfamily living.

11. These differences, further, are not statistically significant.

CHAPTER 11.   PARENTS AND THEIR CHILDREN: WHO WINS?

1. In the cases in which young adults establish residential independence after living in group quarters—college dormitories or military barracks—the decision sequence is somewhat different, since in these cases, children are making the decision not to *return home*.

2. We use the same sample we used in chapter 10 for the analyses of financial flows between the two generations—the 10 percent file of parental responses—and were able to include parents of both sophomores and seniors, since the parents of each class were asked their expectations about their children's likely age of residential independence and of marriage. In this case, however, the two cohorts are not as fully parallel as they are for our analyses that focus only on the young adults themselves. For the young adults, nearly all measures of attitudes and characteristics are as of their senior year in high school (or are relatively fixed, such as race). Parents of both sophomores and seniors were surveyed in the fall after the

first children's survey, so that parents of seniors are giving their expectations not only later than those of their children but also after more of them had left home. Parents of sophomores, however, made their reports considerably earlier than those of their children (18 months on average), during the fall of their junior year, and rather early for many parents to have a good idea about marital or residential timing or even to be willing to answer. (The proportion with missing responses on this question approached 30%.)

3. These and subsequent percentages are net of the factors considered in our model and show the patterns when gender, race, ethnicity, socioeconomic status, and residence are controlled statistically. See the discussion in chapter 3, note 7.

4. Much of the socioeconomic status difference results from differences between parents and young adults in the effect of parental education, which is 70 percent stronger for parents than for their children. Each additional four years of parental education increases the expectation of nonfamily living among young adults by 4 percentage points but by 7 percentage points among their parents. There is very little difference between parents and young adults in the effect of parental income.

5. Our measures of race, religion, and ethnicity are based on the reports of the young adults, not their parents.

6. By setting (3) as the reference category, the coefficient on (4) becomes a test of their differences. If the sign is positive, so that nonfamily living is more likely when only the parents expect it than when only the young adult expects it, then the parents win; if it is negative, so that nonfamily living is less likely when only the parents expect it than when only the young adult expects it, then the young adult wins.

7. A similar result has been found with these data for marriage timing (Hogan 1985).

CHAPTER 12.   NONFAMILY LIVING IN CONTEXT: HOUSEHOLDS, THE LIFE COURSE, AND FAMILY VALUES

1. Although the possibility exists, and perhaps should be fostered, that young adults could live with their parents in an interdependent relationship of mutual agreement and respect, few we have mentioned this to consider it feasible, either ever or at least until the child is well past the teenage years.

2. The predecessor data set to HSB, NLS72 (the National Longitudinal Study of the High School Class of 1972) obtained *no* information from the parents of students or from the students about their parents' marital statuses until the reinterview of 1986, 14 years after the original interviews and after most studies of the transition to adulthood had moved on to more recent cohorts of young adults.

3. This result may parallel those of fertility expectations, which are much more likely to be accurate when asked of married than of unmarried women (see the studies in Hendershot and Placek 1981).

4. Religiosity may be influenced by nonfamily living as well as influencing it.

5. It was also the case that the measure of parental contributions was obtained several months *after* the measures from which we constructed expectations for

nonfamily living, so without parental communication, they had no idea whether such support would be forthcoming.

6. When we refer to a "strong" family structure, we do not mean that this is an unambiguously "good thing." Under many circumstances, strong families can seriously inhibit the independence of some or all of their members. However, they can also provide the support their members need to achieve many of their personal goals.

7. Like all cross-sectional inferences, of course, this interpretation could be in error if the Cubans who arrived in the United States at an earlier point, that is, whose high school age children have American-born parents, were very different from the more recent streams of Cuban immigration.

8. Islam may be overtaking Judaism as the "third" largest religion in many portions of the country, but the Jews are clearly ahead in terms of current strength of community and political institutions. Moslems and Mormons, another rapidly growing group, appear in our data as part of the residual "other" religion category. Despite their heterogeneity, members of this group tend to have nonfamily living patterns very similar to Protestant fundamentalists.

9. Of course, those who argue this way tend to ignore the ways in which family roles are, in fact, more important for men than for women, such as for their mental and physical health and survival (Kisker and Goldman 1987; Riessman and Gerstel 1985; Kobrin and Hendershot 1977).

References

Abrahamse, Allan, P. Morrison, and L. Waite. 1988. *Beyond Stereotypes: Who Becomes a Single Teenage Mother?* Santa Monica, Calif.: RAND Corporation.

Alba, Richard. 1976. "Social assimilation among American Catholic national origin groups." *American Sociological Review* 41:1030–1046.

Alba, Richard. 1983. "A preliminary examination of ethnic identification among whites." *American Sociological Review* 48:240–247.

Alba, Richard. 1990. *Ethnic Identity: The Transformation of White America.* New Haven: Yale University Press.

Alwin, Duane. 1988. "From obedience to autonomy: Changes in traits desired in children, 1924–1978." *Public Opinion Quarterly* 52:33–52.

Angel, Ronald, and M. Tienda. 1982. "Determinants of household structure: Cultural patterns or economic need?" *American Journal of Sociology* 87:1360–1383.

Aquilino, William. 1990. "The likelihood of parent-child coresidence: Effects of family structure and parental characteristics." *Journal of Marriage and the Family* 52:405–419.

Avery, Roger, F. Goldscheider, and A. Speare, Jr. 1992. "Feathered nest/gilded cage: The effects of parental resources on young adults' leaving home." *Demography* August 29:375–388.

Bean, Frank, and M. Tienda. 1989. *The Hispanic Population of the United States.* New York: Russell Sage Foundation.

Bellah, Robert, R. Madsen, W. Sullivan, A. Swidler, and S. Tipton. 1985. *Habits of the Heart: Individualism and Commitment in American Life.* Berkeley: University of California Press.

Beresford, John C., and A. Rivlin. 1966. "Privacy, poverty, and old age." *Demography* 3:247–258.

Bumpass, Larry, J. Sweet, and T. Martin. 1989. "Changing patterns of remarriage." *Journal of Marriage and the Family* 52:747–756.

Burch, Thomas, and B. Mathews. 1987. "Household formation in developed countries." *Population and Development Review* 13:495–511.

Castleton, Anne, and F. Goldscheider. 1989. "Religion and family demography: Marriage, fertility, and household headship in California, Rhode Island, and Utah." In F. Goldscheider and C. Goldscheider, eds., *Ethnicity and the New Family Economy.* Boulder: Westview Press.

Cherlin, Andrew. 1978. "Remarriage as an incomplete institution." *American Journal of Sociology* 84:634–650.

Cherlin, Andrew. 1979. "Extended family households in the early years of marriage: Some longitudinal evidence." Paper presented at the annual meeting of the Population Association of America, Philadelphia.

Christian, Patricia. 1989. "Nonfamily households and housing among young adults." In F. Goldscheider and C. Goldscheider, eds., *Ethnicity and the New Family Economy*. Boulder: Westview Press.

Cohen, Steven. 1983. *American Modernity and Jewish Identity*. London: Tavistock.

Cooney, Rosemary. 1979. "Demographic components of growth in white, black and Puerto Rican female-headed families: A comparison of the Cutright and Ross/Sawhill methodologies." *Social Science Research* 8:144–158.

Cowan, Alison Leigh. 1989. "'Parenthood II': The nest won't stay empty." *New York Times* 138 (March 12):1, 30.

D'Antonio, William. 1983. "Family life, religion, and societal values and structures." In W. D'Antonio and J. Aldous, eds., *Families and Religions: Conflict and Change in Modern Society*. Beverly Hills, Calif.: Sage Publications.

DaVanzo, Julie, and F. Goldscheider. 1990. "Coming home again: Returns to the nest in young adulthood." *Population Studies* 44:241–255.

Demos, John. 1986. *Past, Present and Personal: The Family and the Life Course in American History*. New York: Oxford University Press.

Easterlin, Richard A. 1987. "The new age structure of poverty in America: Permanent or transient?" *Population and Development Review* 13:195–208.

Easterlin, Richard, C. Macdonald, D. Macunovich, and E. Crimmins. 1992. "Causes of the change in intergenerational living arrangements of elderly widows in the United States." Paper presented at the Conference on Intergenerational Relations, RAND Corporation, Santa Monica, Calif.

Ensminger, Margaret E., and A. L. Slusarcick. 1992. "Paths to high school graduation or dropout: A longitudinal study of a first-grade cohort." *Sociology of Education* 65:95–113.

Fischer, Arlene. 1986. "Hi, Mom, I'm home . . . again." Redbook: 96–97, 136.

Freedman, Ronald, M. C. Chang, and T. H. Sun. 1982. "Household composition, extended kinship and reproduction in Taiwan: 1973–1980." *Population Studies* 36:395–411.

Goldscheider, Calvin. 1986. *Jewish Continuity and Change: Emerging Patterns in America*. Bloomington: Indiana University Press.

Goldscheider, Calvin, and F. Goldscheider. 1985a. "Family size expectations of young American Jewish adults." *Papers in Jewish Demography*. Jerusalem: The Hebrew University.

Goldscheider, Calvin, and F. Goldscheider. 1985b. "Moving out and marriage: What do young adults expect?" *American Sociological Review* 52:278–285.

Goldscheider, Calvin, and F. Goldscheider. 1988. "Ethnicity, religiosity and leaving home." *Sociological Forum* 3:525–547.

Goldscheider, Calvin, and W. Mosher. 1988. "Religious affiliation and contraceptive usage: Changing American patterns, 1955–82." *Studies in Family Planning* 19:48–57.

Goldscheider, Calvin, and W. Mosher. 1991. "Patterns of contraceptive use in the United States: The importance of religious factors." *Family Planning Perspectives* 23:288–290.

Goldscheider, Frances. 1992. "Family relationships and life course strategies in aging populations." Paper presented at the annual meetings of the Population Association of America, Denver.

Goldscheider, Frances, and J. DaVanzo. 1985. "Living arrangements and the transition to adulthood." *Demography* 22:545–563.

Goldscheider, Frances, and J. DaVanzo. 1986. "Semiautonomy and leaving home in early adulthood." *Social Forces* 65:187–201.

Goldscheider, Frances, and J. DaVanzo. 1989. "Pathways to independent living in early adulthood: Marriage, semiautonomy, and premarital residential independence." *Demography* 26:597–614.

Goldscheider, Frances, and C. Goldscheider. 1989*a*. "Family structure and conflict: Nest-leaving expectations of young adults and their parents." *Journal of Marriage and the Family* 51:87–97.

Goldscheider, Frances, and C. Goldscheider, eds. 1989*b*. *Ethnicity and the New Family Economy*. Boulder: Westview Press.

Goldscheider, Frances, and C. Goldscheider. 1991. "The intergenerational flow of income: Family structure and the status of black Americans." *Journal of Marriage and the Family* 53:499–508.

Goldscheider, Frances, and A. Thornton. 1992. "Expecting parental contributions in young adulthood: A two-generation view." Unpublished paper.

Goldscheider, Frances, and L. Waite. 1991. *New Families, No Families? The Transformation of the American Home*. Berkeley: University of California Press.

Gordon, Milton. 1964. *Assimilation in American Life*. New York: Oxford University Press.

Glazer, Nathan, and D. Moynihan. 1970. *Beyond the Melting Pot*. Cambridge: MIT Press.

Greeley, Andrew. 1989. "Protestant and Catholic: Is the analogical imagination extinct?" *American Sociological Review* 54:485–502.

Gross, Jane. 1991. "More young single men hang onto apron strings: Recession and pampering keep sons at home." *New York Times* 140 (June 16):1, 18.

Haaga, John. 1988. "The revival of breastfeeding in the United States, 1963–81." Unpublished paper. Santa Monica, Calif.: RAND Corporation.

Haggstrom, Gus. 1983. "Logistic regression and discriminant analysis by ordinary least squares." *Journal of Business and Economic Statistics* 1:229–238.

Heer, David, R. W. Hodge, and M. Felson. 1985. "The cluttered nest: Evidence that young adults are more likely to live at home now than in the recent past." *Sociology and Social Research* 69:436–441.

Hendershot, Gerry, and P. Placek, eds. 1981. *Predicting Fertility: Demographic Studies of Birth Expectations*. Lexington, Mass.: Lexington Books.

Herberg, Will. 1955. *Protestant-Catholic-Jew.* New York: Doubleday.

Hernandez, Luis. 1989. "Nonfamily living arrangements among black and Hispanic Americans." In F. Goldscheider and C. Goldscheider, eds., *Ethnicity and the New Family Economy.* Boulder: Westview Press.

Hoffman, Saul, and G. Duncan. 1988. "What are the economic consequences of divorce?" *Demography* 25:641–645.

Hogan, Dennis. 1985. "Parental influences on the timing of early life transitions." In Zena Blau, ed., *Current Perspectives on Aging and the Life Cycle.* Vol. 1. Greenwich, Conn.: JAI Press. Pp. 1–59.

Hogan, Dennis. 1986. "Maternal influences on adolescent family formation." In David Kertzer, ed., *Current Perspectives on Aging and the Life Cycle.* Vol. 2. Greenwich, Conn.: JAI Press. Pp. 147–165.

Jones, Elise, and C. Westoff. 1979. "The end of 'Catholic' fertility." *Demography* 16:209–217.

Jones, Calvin, P. Sebring, J. Crawford, B. Spencer, and M. Butz. 1986. *High School and Beyond: 1980 Senior Cohort, Second Follow-up (1984): Data File Users Manual.* Washington, D.C.: National Center for Education Statistics.

Kanjanapan, Wilawan. 1989. "The Asian-American traditional household." In F. Goldscheider and C. Goldscheider, eds., *Ethnicity and the New Family Economy.* Boulder: Westview Press.

Katz, Michael. 1974. *The People of Hamilton, Canada West.* Cambridge: Harvard University Press.

Kennedy, Robert. 1972. *The Irish.* Berkeley: University of California Press.

Kertzer, David. 1991. "Household history and sociological theory." *Annual Review of Sociology* 17:155–179.

Kisker, Ellen, and N. Goldman. 1987. "Perils of single life and benefits of marriage." *Social Biology* 34:135–140.

Kobrin, Frances E. 1976. "The primary individual and the family: Changes in living arrangements since 1940." *Journal of Marriage and the Family* 38: 233–239.

Kobrin, Frances E. 1981. "High school seniors and high school dropouts: An evaluation of life cycle bias in the National Longitudinal Study of High School Class of 1972." N-1710-NICHD, RAND Corporation.

Kobrin, Frances E., and C. Goldscheider. 1978. *The Ethnic Factor in Family Structure and Mobility.* Cambridge, Mass.: Ballinger.

Kobrin, Frances E., and C. Goldscheider. 1982. "Family extension or nonfamily living." *Western Sociological Review* 13:103–118.

Kobrin, Frances E., and G. Hendershot. 1977. "Do family ties reduce mortality? Evidence from the United States, 1966–1968." *Journal of Marriage and the Family* 39:737–745.

Kojima, Hiroshi. 1989. "Intergenerational household extension in Japan." In F. Goldscheider and C. Goldscheider, eds., *Ethnicity and the New Family Economy.* Boulder: Westview Press.

Kuznets, Simon. 1978. "Size and age structure of family households: Exploratory comparisons." *Population and Development Review* 4:187–233.

Laslett, Barbara. 1973. "The family as a public and private institution: An histori-cal perspective." *Journal of Marriage and the Family* 35:480–494.

Laslett, Peter. 1973. *Households and Families in Past Time.* Cambridge: Cam-bridge University Press.

Leibowitz, Arleen, J. Klerman, and L. Waite. 1992. "Women's employment dur-ing pregnancy and following childbirth." N-3392-DOL/NICHD, RAND Corpo-ration.

Levy, Frank. 1987. *Dollars and Dreams: The Changing American Income Distri-bution.* New York: Russell Sage Foundation.

Levy, Marion. 1965. "Aspects of the analysis of family structure." In Ansley Coale, ed., *Aspects of the Analysis of Family Structure.* Princeton: Princeton Univer-sity Press.

Lieberson, Stanley. 1980. *A Piece of the Pie.* Berkeley: University of California Press.

Light, Ivan, and E. Bonacich. 1988. *Immigrant Entrepreneurs.* Berkeley: Uni-versity of California Press.

Lindsey, Robert. 1984. "A new generation finds it hard to leave the nest." *New York Times,* January 15, 10.

Martinez-Luz, Gloria, and C. Goldscheider. 1988. "Language and the occupa-tional attainment of Asian Americans." Working Paper no. 88-03, Population Studies and Training Center, Brown University.

Mason, Karen O., and L. Bumpass. 1975. "U.S. women's sex-role ideology." *American Journal of Sociology* 80:1212–1219.

Mason, Karen O., J. L. Czajka, and S. Arber. 1976. "Change in U.S. women's sex-role attitudes, 1964–1974." *American Sociological Review* 41:573–596.

Massey, Douglas, and N. Denton. 1987. "Trends in the residential segregation of blacks, Hispanics, and Asians: 1970–1980." *American Sociological Review* 52:802–825.

Massey, Douglas, and N. Denton. 1989. "Hypersegregation in U.S. metropolitan areas: Black and Hispanic segregation along five dimensions." *Demography* 26:373–391.

Matras, Judah. 1984. *Social Inequality, Stratification, and Mobility.* Englewood Cliffs, N.J.: Prentice-Hall.

Michael, Robert, V. Fuchs, and S. Scott. 1980. "Changes in the propensity to live alone: 1950–1976." *Demography* 17:39–56.

Mitchell, Barbara, A. Wister, and T. Burch. 1989. "The family environment and leaving the parental home." *Journal of Marriage and the Family* 61:605–613.

Modell, John. 1989. *Into One's Own: From Youth to Adulthood in the United States, 1920–1975.* Berkeley: University of California Press.

Morgan, S. Philip, and K. Hirosima. 1983. "The persistence of extended family residence in Japan: Anachronism or alternative strategy?" *American Sociologi-cal Review* 48:269–281.

Morgan, S. Philip, and E. Kramerow. 1992. "Stability and change in female head-ship: The United States 1910–1980." Paper presented at the annual meeting of the Population Association of America, Denver.

233

Moynihan, Daniel. 1965. "The Negro family: A case for national action." Washington, D.C.: U.S. Government Printing Office.

Osterud, Nancy Grey. 1980. "Sons, daughters, and the household economy: Generational relationships and economic change in an English manufacturing city." Paper presented at the Annual Meeting of the Social Science History Association, Rochester, New York.

Pampel, Fred. 1983. "Changes in the propensity to live alone: Evidence from consecutive cross-sectional surveys, 1960–1976." *Demography* 20:433–447.

Portes, Alejandro, and R. Bach. 1985. *Latin Journey: Cuban and Mexican Immigrants in the United States.* Berkeley: University of California Press.

Pryor, Edward. 1972. "Rhode Island family structure: 1875 and 1960." In Peter Laslett and Richard Wall, eds., *Household and Family in Past Time.* Cambridge: Cambridge University Press.

Riche, Martha Farnsworth. 1990. "Boomerang age." *American Demographics* 12:25–27, 30, 52–53.

Riessman, Catherine, and N. Gerstel. 1985. "Marital dissolution and health: Do males or females have greater risk?" *Social Science and Medicine* 20:624–630.

Rindfuss, Ron. 1991. "The young adult years: Diversity, structural change, and fertility." *Demography* 28:493–512.

Rodgers, Willard, and A. Thornton. 1985. "Changing patterns of first marriage in the United States." *Demography* 22:265–279.

Rosenmayr, L., and E. Kockeis. 1963. "Propositions for a sociological theory of aging and the family." *International Social Science Journal* 15.

Rosenthal, A., D. Myers, A. Milne, F. Ellman, and A. Ginsberg. 1983. "Failure of student-parent cross-validation in the High School and Beyond Survey." Proceedings of the Social Statistics Section, American Statistical Association, Toronto, Canada.

Ross, Heather, and I. Sawhill. 1976. *Time of Transition: The Growth of Families Headed by Women.* Washington, D.C.: The Urban Institute.

Ruggles, Steven. 1987. *Prolonged Connections: The Rise of the Extended Family in Nineteenth-Century England and America.* Madison: University of Wisconsin Press.

Scanzoni, John H. 1975. *Sex Roles, Life Styles, and Childbearing: Changing Patterns in Marriage and the Family.* New York: Free Press.

Schultz, Theodore. 1975. "The value of the ability to deal with disequilibria." *Journal of Economic Literature* 13:827–846.

Schwebel, Andrew, M. Fine, and M. Renner. 1991. "A study of perceptions of the stepparent role." *Journal of Family Issues* 12:43–57.

Speare, Alden, Jr. 1970. "Home ownership, life cycle stage, and residential mobility." *Demography* 7:449–458.

Stack, Carol. 1975. *All Our Kin: Strategies for Survival in a Black Community.* New York: Harper and Row.

Sweet, James, and L. Bumpass. 1987. *American Families and Households.* New York: Russell Sage Foundation.

Thomson, Elizabeth. 1983. "Individual and couple utility of children." *Demography* 20:507–518.

Thornton, Arland. 1989. "Changing attitudes towards family issues in the United States." *Journal of Marriage and the Family* 51:873–893.

Thornton, Arland. 1991. "Influence of parents' marital history on children." *American Journal of Sociology* 96:868–894.

Thornton, Arland, and D. Camburn. 1987. "The influence of the family on premarital sexual attitudes and behavior." *Demography* 24:323–340.

Thornton, Arland, and D. Camburn. 1989. "Religious participation and adolescent sexual behavior and attitudes." *Journal of Marriage and the Family* 51:641–653.

Thornton, Arland, and T. Fricke. 1989. "Social change and the family." In J. Stycos, ed., *Demography as an Interdiscipline*. New Brunswick, N.J.: Transaction Books.

Thornton, Arland, and H. Lin. Forthcoming. *Social Change and the Family in Taiwan*. Chicago: University of Chicago Press.

Tienda, Marta, and R. Angel. 1982. "Headship and household composition among blacks, Hispanics and other whites." *Social Forces* 61:508–553.

U.S. Bureau of the Census. 1985. Subject Report (table 4).

U.S. News and World Report. 1981. "Why so many families are doubling up." March 9:53–54.

Waite, Linda, F. Goldscheider, and C. Witsberger. 1986. "Nonfamily living and the erosion of traditional family orientations among young adults." *American Sociological Review* 51:541–554.

Waldinger, Roger, H. Aldrich, and R. Ward. 1990. *Ethnic Entrepreneurs*. Beverly Hills, Calif.: Sage.

Wilson, William J. 1987. *The Truly Disadvantaged: The Inner City, the Underclass, and Public Policy*. Chicago: University of Chicago Press.

White, Lynn, and A. Booth. 1985. "The quality and stability of remarriages: The role of stepchildren." *American Sociological Review* 50:689–698.

White, Lynn, and D. Brinkerhoff. 1981. "Children's work in the family." *Journal of Marriage and the Family* 43:789–798.

Yancey, William, E. Ericksen, and R. Juliani. 1976. "Emergent ethnicity: A review and reformulation." *American Sociological Review* 41:391–402.

Young, Christabel. 1987. *Young People Leaving Home in Australia: The Trend Toward Independence*. Canberra, Australia: Department of Demography, Australian National University Printing Press.

Index

Catholic schools, 11, 77–78, 89; and gender, 89; and marriage timing, 110
Catholics, 44, 48, 66–78, 84, 94, 124, 139, 157–158, 182–183; black, 68, 71–72, 74, 78; ethnic groups, 67; and familism, 84; and financial flows, 151; and gender roles, 94–95; Hispanics, 71; and marriage timing, 101, 108, 109; and parenthood planning, 124; southern European, 70, 76, 109; and stepfamilies, 130
Census, 5
Chang, M., 218
Cherlin, A., 129, 154
Christian, P., 100
Church attendance, 75–77, 211 n6
Cohen, S., 67
Cohort, 11, 34, 155, 159. See also Generation
Contraceptive usage, 67, 101
Cooney, R., 52
Cowan, A., 5
Cuban-Americans, 42, 56, 57, 58, 60, 62, 74, 228 n7; and marriage timing, 108
Czajka, J., 42

D'Antonio, W., 67
DaVanzo, J., 4, 5, 18, 52, 97, 100, 178, 190, 217, 218, 224
Demos, J., 222
Denton, N., 63, 138
Discrimination, 52, 54, 138
Divorce, 15, 42, 101, 155
Domestic economy, 17, 42. See also Housework
Dormitories, 17, 217 n3, 218 n7, 226 n1
Duncan, G., 136

Easterlin, R., 25, 185
Education: young adults. See School planning.
Education, parental, 39, 40, 141–147, 225–226 n3; changes in, 141–142; and financial flows, 152–153; and marriage timing, 146–147; and parental income, 143–147
Egalitarianism, 36, 37, 44–46, 49, 50, 82–83. See also Gender roles
Empty nest, 3, 155
England, 60, 218 n1
Ensminger, M., 189

Ericksen, E., 54
Ethnicity, 11, 15, 40–42, 51–64; and culture, 62–64; defined, 52–53; and familism, 11, 40, 51–64, 175–176; and immigration, 53; and social structure, 53, 62–64. See also Assimilation; Race
Exit rates, 102–103, 112
Expectations: and behavior, 9, 46, 113–115, 172–174; determinants of, 9, 48; and life course, 9; as norms, 8–9, 29–30; of parents, 9, 20–22, 154–168, 170–172; as plans, 8–9, 113–127; as predictions, 8–9, 25–30, 49, 218 n8; and preferences, 9; and the unexpected, 113–127

Families: child-innovative, 160–168; parent-innovative, 160–168. See also Family: structure; Mother-only families; Stepfamilies
Familism, 11–12, 15, 40–42, 49, 80–95; and adulthood, 81–82; and Asian-Americans, 84–86; and black-Americans, 84–85; and Catholics, 84; dimensions of, 80–81; and ethnicity, 11, 40, 51–64, 175–176; and Hispanic-Americans, 84–86; and Jews, 84; and male-female relationships, 11, 82–83; and parent-child relationships, 11, 81–82; and Protestants, 84; and race, 51; and religion, 78–79; as tastes, 40, 143
Family: black, 51, 55, 221 n2; centrality, 34–35, 52; changes, 34–35, 80–81; economy, 13–14, 36–38; extension, 30–33, 52, 71, 221 n1; as insurance, 34–35; structure, 38, 128–140, 151–152, 225 n1
Family closeness, 83–86, 152
Family values, 101. See also Ethnicity; Familism; Gender; Parent-child: relationships; Religion
Felson, M., 25
Fertility, 15, 155
Financial flows, 14, 39, 40, 147–153; and Catholics, 151; direction of, 149–153; and education, 152–153; and family closeness, 152; and family income, 148; and family structure, 151–152; and gender, 150–151; and Hispanics, 151; measurement of, 148, 226 n6, 226 n7
Fine, M., 129
Freedman, R., 218

INDEX

Socioeconomic status (*continued*)
expectations, 156–157; and planning,
116–117. *See also* Education; Income;
Resources
South, 43, 47, 62, 63, 108, 138, 219*n5*
Southern Europe, 70, 76, 109
Spain, 70
Speare, A., 25, 42, 100, 191
Stack, C., 221
Stepfamilies, 14, 128–140; and Asians, 137,
139; and blacks, 137–139; changes in,
128–129; definition of, 130–131; and
ethnicity, 130; and family closeness,
131–132; and gender, 135–136; and His-
panics, 137, 139; and marriage timing,
132–135; and race, 130, 136–137; and
religion, 130
Sun, T., 218
Survey data, 8. *See also* High School and
Beyond survey (HSB)
Sweet, J., 135, 137
Swicegood, G., 5

Taiwan, 218*n1*
Tastes. *See* Familism
Thomson, E., 25
Thornton, A., 4, 32, 34, 65, 67, 82, 83, 97,
100, 132, 134, 223
Tienda, M., 52, 56

Timing: marriage, 27, 96–112; and parental
education, 146–147; and "poor planners," 115–119; residential behavior,
23–25, 27–28; residential expectations,
19–22
Transfers: intergenerational. *See* Financial
flows.

United States, 34, 40, 42, 44, 60, 61, 63,
96, 103–104, 113
U.S. Bureau of the Census, 6
U.S. News and World Report, 5

Waite, L., 6, 7, 42, 44, 52, 67, 68, 82, 98,
100, 126, 132, 167, 170, 222, 223
Waldinger, R., 178
Ward, R., 178
Welfare, 138
West African, 138
Western societies, 34
Westoff, C., 101, 182
White, L., 82, 129
Witsberger, C., 7, 52, 223
Wilson, W., 138
Wister, A., 129
World War II, 4

Yancey, W., 54
Young, C., 5

242

Life Course Studies

David L. Featherman
David I. Kertzer
General Editors

Nancy W. Denney
Thomas J. Espenshade
Dennis P. Hogan
Jennie Keith
Maris A. Vinovskis
Associate General Editors